The People's Health

There is the need, so to speak, of a
hospital without walls that would help
physicians to become aware of the whole
range of community problems and
broaden the scope of medical help.

—René Dubos

THE
PEOPLE'S

REVISED AND EXPANDED EDITION

With an additional chapter by
Clifford R. Barnett
in collaboration with
David L. Rabin, M.D., M.P.H.
> Professor, Department of Community
> and Family Medicine
> Georgetown University School of
> Medicine, Washington, D.C.

Photographs by
John Collier, Jr.
> Professor of Anthropology, Emeritus
> San Francisco State University
> and Senior Instructor of Photography
> San Francisco Art Institute

Milton Snow, retired
> Photographer, Navajo Service
> Bureau of Indian Affairs
> Window Rock, Arizona

HEALTH

MEDICINE
AND ANTHROPOLOGY
IN A NAVAJO COMMUNITY

John Adair, Ph.D.
Professor of Anthropology,
Emeritus
San Francisco State University

Kurt W. Deuschle, M.D.
Ethel H. Wise Professor of
Community Medicine
and Chairman of the Department,
Mount Sinai School of Medicine
of the City University of New York

Clifford R. Barnett, Ph.D.
Professor of Anthropology
Stanford University

University of New Mexico Press: *Albuquerque*

Chapter 10 © 1972 by the American
Association for the Advancement of Science

Library of Congress
Cataloging-in-Publication Data

Adair, John, 1913–
   The people's health: medicine and
anthropology in a Navajo community / John
Adair, Kurt W. Deuschle, Clifford R. Barnett;
with an additional chapter by Clifford R.
Barnett in collaboration with David L. Rabin;
photographs by John Collier, Jr., Milton
Snow.—Rev. and expanded ed.
        p.   cm.
   Bibliography: p.
   Includes index.
   ISBN 0-8263-1027-3
   1. Indians of North America—Health and
hygiene.
2. Navajo Indians.
I. Deuschle, Kurt W.
II. Barnett, Clifford R., 1929–
III. Rabin, David.
IV. Title.
RA801.A3   1988
362.1'042'097913—dc19   88-17253

Credits:
The John Collier, Jr. photographs were taken
for Roy Stryker of the Standard Oil
Company.

This second edition is dedicated to the
memory of Walsh McDermott, M.D.,
a caring clinician, dedicated researcher,
and imaginative statesman.

Contents

A Note About Changes in the Second
    Edition   ix
Foreword by Robert Young   xi
Acknowledgments   xvii
Introduction to the First Edition   xxi
Introduction to the Second Edition by
    Doris Schwartz   xxv

1   Health and Disease: Navajo View   3
2   Health and Disease: Physicians' View   15
3   Convergence of the Two Views   29
4   Introduction to the Community   47
5   Training the Navajo Health Workers   85
6   Developing a Cross-Cultural Approach
       to Medical Files   109
7   Bridging the Gap of Language and
       Culture: Conceptual Transfer   123
8   Community Response to the Clinic   143
9   The Indigenous Curing System and
       Modern Medicine   161

10 Health Care Experiment at Many
      Farms   179
11 Collaborative Study by Physicians
      and Anthropologists: Congenital
      Hip Disease   201
12 The Culture of the Innovator   213

Conclusion   237
Afterword   241
Notes   243
Appendix I   Navajo Culture and
   Environment   249
Appendix II   Health Visitor Medical
   Form   ·   259
Appendix III   Useful Medical Phrases for
   Doctors and Nurses   261
Appendix IV   Publications Emanating
   from the Project   263
References Cited   267
Index   274

A Note About Changes in the Second Edition

The first edition of *The People's Health* in 1970 was written with a focus on how a cross-cultural health delivery system was organized and implemented as a collaborative effort involving the United States Public Health Service, Cornell University Medical School, the Navajo Tribe and the local community at Many Farms, Arizona. At the time the book was written, final data on the impact of the program on morbidity and mortality in the community as well as the effect of the program on the Navajo curing system were not available. This edition fills in those significant gaps.

The first seven chapters of this edition, as well as chapters 11 and 12 are taken directly from the original edition. Chapters 8 and 9 which detail, respectively, clinic usage and the relationship between the clinic and the indigenous curing system, are completely new. Chapter 10, which presents demographic, morbidity and mortality data and evaluates the clinical impact of the project also is new to this edition. Chapter 10 appeared originally in *Science* in 1972. Also new to this edition (Appendix IV) is a bibliography of the publications which have emanated from the Navajo–Cornell Field Health Project. The new edition has been enriched with additional photographs taken by John Collier, Jr.

Foreword

The Many Farms Clinic stands out as almost unique in the long history of Indian relations, for the simple reason that it was one of the few cross-cultural undertakings that was planned and executed in just the right way, from its inception in 1955 to the day of its termination in 1960.

Establishment of the Clinic was the fortuitous result of an event that took place in 1952, involving the outbreak of an epidemic of infectious hepatitis in the Bureau of Indian Affairs Boarding School at Tuba City, on the western fringe of the Navajo Reservation. Medical expertise at Cornell University College of Medicine, where intensive research had been carried out on the control and treatment of hepatitis, was brought to Tuba City in a consultant capacity. The Cornell team carried out its mission under the direction of Dr. Walsh McDermott, Chairman of the Department of Public Health and Preventive Medicine at the University.

The epidemic was curbed, and the involvement of Cornell might have ended at that point were it not that the Cornell team found in the Navajo Reservation an environment that, in microcosm, was a near counterpart of that found in many third world countries: underdeveloped, with a depressed economy; a culturally and linguistically distinct population; an enclave characterized by the full range of diseases generally associated with poverty and low sanitation.

The Department of Public Health and Preventive Medicine at Cornell was actively involved in the World Health Program at that period; and scientists at Cornell, in collaboration with colleagues at the Rockefeller Research Center, had developed the drug, isoniazid, which appeared promising as the long sought chemotherapeutic medium for the treatment of tuberculosis.

The twin scourges, tuberculosis and dysentery, were rampant within the Navajo population of a generation past, ranking high among the ten leading causes of death. Dysentery was reflected in an infant mortality rate nearly four times greater than that of the general population; and tuberculosis, in 1952, was more than ten times as prevalent in the Navajo population than in the population at large.

The Cornell team realized that the Navajo Reservation offered a natural, readily accessible laboratory within which to develop procedures and techniques applicable to the conduct of preventive and therapeutic medical programs in India, Africa and other parts of the world where comparable environmental conditions prevailed, and where application of modern scientific technology required the bridging of a wide cultural gap; while at the same time an attack on Reservation health problems offered an opportunity to perform a valuable service at home.

In 1952 the Bureau of Indian Affairs, Division of Indian Health conducted a case finding survey involving the X-raying of 20,000 adult Navajos. This study disclosed the immediate need for 500 beds to accommodate tubercular patients—a need that could not be met by existing hospital and sanatorium facilities on the Reservation. As a result the Health Service embarked on a program involving contracting for space with sanatoria located in California, Colorado, Arizona and New Mexico—between 1952 and 1956 ten such institutions participated in the Navajo Tuberculosis Control Program.

At this point the Navajo Tribal Government itself became an active participant in the effort to wipe out tuberculosis. The reluctance of patients to undergo a long period of treatment, isolated from their homes and families, posed an obstacle in the way of success. Isolation, coupled with a radically different Navajo concept of the cause and treatment of disease, led many patients to refuse hospitalization, or to leave before the course of treatment could be completed. Dr. Annie Wauneka, daughter of Chee Dodge and a member of the Tribal Council, was Chairman of the Council Health Committee. She traveled personally to the off-reservation sanatoria to encourage the patients; she acted in a liaison capacity between them and their families; she conducted local meetings on the Reservation, and she cooperated closely with medical personnel.

The partnership that developed between Cornell University College of Medicine and the Navajo Tribal Government had its beginning at this period, in 1952, with the launching of a jointly sponsored program involving the development and use of newly discovered drugs for the treatment of tuberculosis. The undertaking was operated initially within the Reservation hospitals, under the immediate direction of Dr. Kurt Deuschle, who was serving on the Reservation in the Doctor-Dentist Draft. It proved highly successful, not only in the development of drug therapy, but in identifying and coping with the complex of problems involved in working cross-culturally in the field of health. Dr. Deuschle provided training sessions at which Council members and Navajo medicine men were provided an opportunity to look at tubercle bacilli through a microscope and to learn how the disease is spread. The cooperation of the medicine men was invited and readily given, with the result that they too came to play an active role in the successful conduct of the tuberculosis control program.

In July 1955 the Indian Health Program passed from the Bureau of Indian Affairs to the United States Public Health Service, and the Public Health Service immediately set about the task of instituting a greatly expanded and diversified operation aimed at the prevention as well as the treatment of disease. Those charged with the planning and execution of the undertaking were well aware of the many problems attendant upon the introduction of new health practices, and they were in full agreement with the Cornell medical team on the necessity of establishing a small scale pilot program to permit the testing and modification of innovative health practices prior to their application areawide.

Cornell University–New York Hospital was chosen as the agent to conduct the pilot project, in the form of a clinic. Accordingly, the Cornell team was expanded to include field technicians, trained nurses, interpreters and behavioral scientists. Under the overall direction of Dr. McDermott, they proceeded to establish the facility. They acted expeditiously, but with caution, in the choice of the geographic area to be served by the clinic, seeking the recommendations of the Health Committee of the Tribal Council as a first step. After careful review of a number of alternative locations, and with the full cooperation of Tribal officials, the Public Health Service, the Bureau of Indian Affairs, local leaders and the local people themselves, the Many Farms–Rough Rock area was selected. All joined as active participants in the project, not only in site selection, but in shaping the clinic program, as well.

In a series of meetings with the people to be served by the clinic the Cornell team was entirely candid in explaining the purpose, scope and nature of the pilot undertaking. It was clearly explained to the people that, in exchange for high quality health services, they would constitute, in effect, the instructional medium through which the Cornell team and the Public Health Service would perfect the special techniques and procedures required for the conduct of an effective health program under Reservation conditions. The people listened, asked many questions, and gave their welcome to the clinic project despite the knowledge that it was designed to operate only for a five year period, and despite the fact that it would serve only a circumscribed area population.

The Many Farms Clinic operated harmoniously and productively throughout the term of its existence. It had the unwavering support of the Tribal Government and the local people, and the results of the several research projects carried out by behavioral and medical scientists attached to the Clinic team were translated into techniques and procedures that continue to play an active part in the Reservation health program.

Infant mortality from all causes has declined from an average rate of 85/1000 live births, as reported for the 3-year period 1954–1956, to 13.3/1000 in 1980, comparing favorably with the 12.6 rate for all races in the general population in 1980; and the tuberculosis rate has dropped from 896.1/100,000 for the 3-year period 1953–1955 to 10.3 in 1985. Cornell University College of Medicine and the Many Farms Clinic made a very substantial contribution to improvement of the health of the Navajo people, as reflected by the statistics quoted above, beginning with the introduction of drug therapy in the treatment of tuberculosis, and including the effective field health programs developed and tested by the Clinic during the period of its operation.

Of equal importance, the Many Farms experience clearly points to the fact that, although many obstacles lie in the way of successful cross-cultural programming, they are by no means insurmountable.

Personally, I shall always take great pride in the fact that I was privileged to play a part, albeit a very minor one, in the planning of the Clinic and in its relationship with the Navajo Tribal Government.

Robert W. Young
Professor Emeritus
Linguistics
University of New Mexico

Acknowledgments

The Navajo–Cornell Field Health Research Project was organized jointly by the Navajo Tribe, Cornell University Medical College, and the U.S. Public Health Service in 1955 when the responsibility for the health of the U.S. Indian was transferred from the Department of the Interior to the Department of Health, Education and Welfare. The stated purposes were: to develop effective methods for the delivery of modern medical services to the Navajo people; to see to what extent the knowledge so acquired would have generally for people in similar socioeconomic circumstances elsewhere; to study discrete disease entities with particular reference to their possible shaping by Navajo culture; and to explore whether the sudden apposition of modern biomedical science and technology and the disease pattern of a "nontechnologic" society could provide knowledge of value in the attack on contemporary U.S. medical problems. A wide range of individual studies addressed to these questions have been published elsewhere or will soon appear. Despite the diverse nature of these studies, however, there was one research question common to them all, namely, how can social scientists and members of the health sciences and professions work

productively as full partners *from the beginning* of such an enterprise. This is the question to which the present volume is addressed.

The project was conducted by members of the Department of
Public Health of Cornell University Medical College and of the
Cornell–New York Hospital School of Nursing of the New York
Hospital–Cornell Medical Center in New York City.

The authors are indebted to many different people and institutions who assisted us in a variety of ways. First we wish to thank
the Russell Sage Foundation of New York City, which gave generous financial support to the anthropologists. We should like to
mention Dr. Donald Young, Director of the Foundation, and Dr.
Leonard Cottrell, and thank them for their support and personal
interest in this project. Dr. Esther Lucille Brown visited the field
site at Many Farms, Arizona, and gave us valuable assistance in
the clarification of our objectives.

Additional financial support was obtained from the Navajo Tribe,
acting through its Tribal Council; by contract with the Division
of Indian Health and by a research grant (RG 5209) from the
Division of General Medical Sciences, National Institutes of Health,
agencies of the Department of Health, Education and Welfare; and
the Max C. Fleischmann Foundation. In addition, generous gifts
of valuable commodities or equipment were made by the Hyland
Laboratories (Los Angeles), Charles Pfizer and Company (New
York), the E. R. Squibb Division of Olin Mathieson (New York),
and the Santa Fe Railroad.

Much of the work accomplished by the anthropologists was that
of those who were in residence at Many Farms for two-year terms.
The late Donald Rieder, Dr. Cara Richards Dobyns, Dr. William
Nydegger, and Dr. Clifford Barnett each carried on collaborative
research with the physicians and nurses. We are also much indebted
to the wives of three of these anthropologists who lived on the
project, assisted in the research, and did much for the community
life of the whole team. Dr. Tom Sasaki, sociologist, was with the
research team and conducted surveys on economics during several
summers; the linguist, Dr. Herbert Landar, gave valuable guidance
in training the health visitors in medical interpretation.

None of the work in anthropology, sociology, or linguistics could
have been done without the invaluable assistance of our interpreters: William Morgan, who was with us for most of the life of
the project, and the late Albert Sandoval, who assisted Clifford

Barnett during the last two years. They not only acted in the capacity of interpreters, but conducted field surveys and were invaluable in maintaining good community relations.

The entire team is most grateful to Robert Young, linguist and administrator for the Bureau of Indian Affairs. Cornell University Medical College could never have carried out this program had it not been for his counsel with respect to political realities as well as the guidance he gave us in medical interpretation.

John Adair remembers the guidance the late Dr. Edward Spicer gave to the anthropologists during the first year at Many Farms. Thanks are due to both Dr. George Foster and Dr. Walter Goldschmidt for the careful reading each gave to the manuscript.

We are especially grateful to the late Dr. Walsh McDermott, who conceived of the need for the field health research project and gave leadership, inspiration, encouragement, and wise counsel to the authors throughout the conduct of the study. There were many doctors and nurses who participated in the field studies and health care services provided by the Many Farms Clinic. The authors are indebted to those physicians who lived and worked at Many Farms in the Cornell–Navajo project: Dr. Hugh Fulmer, Doctors Eugene and Linda Farley, Dr. Thomas Moulding, Dr. Fred Burkhardt, Dr. David Rabin, Dr. Abdul Omran, Dr. James Hitzrot, and a whole series of bright young Cornell medical students.

The public health nurses who participated in this project were a special breed of dedicated and outstanding professionals, who contributed so much to the outcome of the field health program. The late Bernice Loughlin deserves special thanks for her outstanding contributions and leadership.

Each of us feels deep gratitude toward Doris Schwartz, Cornell University–New York Hospital School of Nursing. From the very start she took a keen interest in our health visitor program and gave wise counsel to all of us at Many Farms. Miss Schwartz was a major recruiter of nursing talent, including short-term consultants as well as nurses who remained with the Many Farms program for several months to several years. We express our thanks to Miss Frances McVey, Dr. Jean French, Dr. Ellen Mansell, Miss Gyla Brooks, Mrs. Marjorie Overholtzer, and Miss Hendrika Rynbergen.

Miss Martha Ann King, Administrative Assistant to the Many Farms Clinic, was one of the key supporting members of the staff.

Special thanks are due Mrs. Eileen Green and Dr. Marjorie Grant Whiting for their important work in nutrition and to Miss Mary Rockefeller for her contributions to the project.

Albert Sway prepared the drawings for the Syllabus, and Milton Snow took the photographs for the plates 1, 3, 4, 5, and 6.

Introduction to the First Edition

In recent years there has been a growing realization of the need for incorporating the concepts and knowledge of anthropology into the practice of public health, especially in those areas where the health professions are extending services from the economically advanced countries in America and Europe to those countries with a less advanced technology in Africa, Latin America, and Asia.

The administrators of technical aid programs, including those in public health, have come to recognize the relevance of the concept of culture—central to anthropology—to the analysis of their programs. Such administrators have turned to anthropologists for help when they have encountered resistance. For example, in a nutritional program designed to combat deficiency diseases, *ex post facto* analysis revealed that the administrators had built organizations that were effective in working with the male population, but had ignored the women responsible for food preparation and child bearing. In another area a program in tuberculosis control had failed because of a lack of appreciation for religious sanctions, which had not been perceived as relevant by the Western-trained physician. The anthropologist was able to point out to the practitioner of public health all-important linkages between the various aspects of culture. But the skills of the anthropologist and the utility of cultural analysis were severely limited when confined to such after-the-fact consultation. The questions then arise: Can the anthropologist be effective in the planning process? Can his knowledge of the native peoples' language, social organization, value system, and religion be used in the design and carrying out of programs so that such pitfalls might be avoided?

The anthropologist was offered such an opportunity by Cornell University Medical College in the summer of 1955 when Dr. Walsh McDermott, Livingston Farrand Professor of Public Health, asked the physician, Dr. Kurt W. Deuschle, and the anthropologist, Dr. John Adair, if they would help him design and administer a program in field health research in a remote area on the Navajo Indian Reservation. Dr. Deuschle had had experience as Medical Officer in Charge at the Fort Defiance Tuberculosis Sanatorium when the late Dr. McDermott and the late Dr. Carl Muschenheim carried out studies of the effect of isoniazid on hospitalized tuberculosis patients. This drug, in combination with others, proved most effective, and soon after the completion of the tests became widely used in many parts of the world, including use in off-Reservation sanatoria where Navajo Indians were hospitalized.

After this technologic breakthrough, Dr. McDermott turned his attention to intervention in the disease process in a typical community, distant from Fort Defiance with its full set of hospital services. Disease would have to be diagnosed early, and not left to treatment on advanced cases in the hospital. Effective programs of prevention would need to be designed. To accomplish these goals, the patterns of health and disease should be seen in relation to the pattern of community life; it was recognized that effective intervention in the biologic process would necessitate innovation in the social process.

It was at this point that the experience of those anthropologists who had analyzed success and failure of intervention and innovation in technologic aid programs overseas became relevant to our needs in designing this program in social medicine. In part, what they had learned may be stated in the following broad propositions:

1. Those members of the donor society concerned with planned change must have a comprehensive knowledge of the culture of those for whom the innovations are designed.

2. In addition, there must be constant awareness on the part of those planning change of their own culture (or subculture), its values, structure, predelections, and biases.

3. The innovations must meet a felt need of the recipient society which must share in making decisions which will affect the community.

4. Further, the cultures of both the donor and the recipient society must be conceived as undergoing constant change. Plans based on a conception of culture as static are bound to fail.

5. In large measure, change is due to the interchange that takes place when any two societies are in contact. There must be knowledge of the attitudes and beliefs that have shaped the behavior of the one society towards the other. What has the one society accepted from the other? Or rejected?

6. There must be an understanding of the role that the acculturated individual plays in transmitting new ideas, techniques, beliefs, and so forth to the more conservative members of the society.

7. The political structure (as well as prestige structure) must be understood and its leadership identified and worked through.

8. Communication between the two cultures must be facilitated, as well as communication between components of both the donor and recipient societies.

Couldn't a modern urban-based medical college follow these propositions and adapt its skills and technology to meet the needs of such a tribal society? Wouldn't such training be invaluable for a new generation of physicians faced with an expanding cross-cultural frontier in public health? The less-developed worlds of Latin America, Asia, and Africa, as well as our own American Indian reservations offer the medical educator as well as the applied anthropologist such a challenge.

The problem which faces the medical educator in this new era of public health is how to work effectively with modern medical technology in developing programs designed for peoples from the non-Western rural world whose communities are rapidly coming into the twentieth century. It is in this context that the Navajo Indians living in a remote, high plateau, desert environment offer many parallels to those countries overseas—functional illiteracy in the middle and older age groups; a tribally organized society which resembles many of those in the less-developed areas of the world; a language totally different from those of Europe and America; and an infrastructure that offers little in the way of roads, transportation, communication services, food distribution, and other appurtenances essential to the developed economy of our urban civilization. In short, the Navajo people presented an ideal area for joint exploration by the physician-educator and his anthropologist colleagues into just what type of medical service should be provided.

This program, financed by the United States Government and private foundations, was a pilot study for better health services to the Navajo Tribe, but additionally was of direct value for gaining scientific knowledge and administrative experience that might be applied to the rural health needs of people overseas.

This book endeavors to answer the question posed by Donald Young, Director of the Russell Sage Foundation: How did anthropology and medicine work together in the design and administration of this program? This question is answered by an analysis of this experiment in the context of the propositions listed above. The physicians, nurses, and other members of the medical team as well as the anthropologists were in the role of innovators. To what extent did they follow these propositions concerned with the innovative process? When they were ignored, what was the result?

Introduction
to the Second Edition

by Doris Schwartz, R.N., F.A.A.N.
Formerly Associate Professor of Nursing (Public Health)
Cornell University—New York Hospital School of Nursing

It was my privilege to be a public health nursing consultant and an occasional on-the-spot staff member at the Cornell–Navajo Field Health Research Program at Many Farms, Arizona. No professional assignment in forty-five years of nursing has been a more rewarding experience.

The melding of the hardworking (and at that time almost entirely Anglo) public health nurses on the Reservation with the efforts of a new type of Navajo health worker trained at the clinic functioned in tandem with the clinic-based physicians to bring about the delivery of home care services. This design seemed to us, at the start, a potential model for third world countries with too few health workers.

Over the next several years, our department of Public Health Nursing at the Cornell University–New York Hospital School of Nursing contributed to the project at Many Farms in various ways: by rotating senior nurse faculty to the project to assist with the health visitors' curriculum and training; by participating later in the evaluation of their skills throughout the entire time of the project; and by continuing an outreach of support and practical assistance to the on-site public health nurse who was responsible for the health visitors' training. At times, there were sizable periods when direct services were given.

One service, unique at the time, was begun early when the on-site public health nurse who was with the project from start to finish was without another on-site nurse colleague. To our knowledge this type of backup help had not been used before by any school of nursing faculty. Collaborating with an isolated colleague in a remote service setting was an innovation.

The Many Farms home care program and our own Medical Center's program in New York seemed a short distance apart in those days and the patients of both were of equal concern.

This interaction was not a one-way street. At about this time a number of our School of Nursing graduates were entering the Peace Corps and other international service programs. Tapes of long-distance consultations with Many Farms spread to nurses in Afghanistan, Haiti, Chile and other distant spots.

Two of us later taught in programs preparing Nurse Practitioners, four taught at schools of public health where numerous students came from other countries and one, for a period of many years, provided summer relief back on the Navajo Reservation and later in Alaskan Eskimo villages. Throughout this time Anglo students attending traditional university nursing schools profited as much from the taped Navajo experiences sent to New York from Many Farms as the Navajo health visitors and their supervisor, Bernie Loughlin, profited from the tapes prepared in New York to go back to Many Farms. Thus, the Navajo patients and their families reached out to help citizens of other nations and began to change the public health nursing approaches in our own inner cities.

Minimally trained indigenous workers are far better prepared today than was true when the Cornell–Navajo Field Health Project was begun, or when *The People's Health* was written. Nurse Practitioners are now generally prepared in university graduate programs with cross-cultural clinical experience taken for granted as a "must" after exposure to well planned social science courses.

Primary care is increasingly available to people, however remote. Health providers are more varied in their preparation than heretofore and the preparation is better planned. They are likely to be working more collaboratively with trained interdisciplinary professionals. A whole new literature of health care has come into existence since the Many Farms project started. The World Health Organization's widely proclaimed goal of "Health Care for All by the Year 2000" makes the reissue of *The People's Health* especially useful.

No one looks to the new edition as a text. The ideal content for tomorrow's health workers puzzles educators in all the health professions, so fast does new knowledge come. But the *concepts* contained in this volume, the account of recognizing and assessing the problems of delivering care when recipients and providers have different basic beliefs, and the need to open oneself to unfamiliar thinking is of the essence. New patterns of collaboration must be set up. The need has never been more important. Providers and consumers of health services have so much to learn from each other; this is the basic reason for today's study of *The People's Health*.

The
People's
Health

Location of service area of Navajo–Cornell Field Health
Research Project at Many Farms–Rough Rock.

1.

Health and Disease:
Navajo View

Two Ways of Medicine

A 4-month-old baby boy (Tracy Begay) was brought to the clinic by his mother. She reported that he had had diarrhea for about a month. On examination the child showed no signs of dehydration. The physician of the clinic staff made two calls at the hogan urging the family to bring the child in for another checkup. Lack of transportation prevented this.

When the baby was 6 months old he came down with diarrhea once more. On that occasion the grandmother (Bah Begay), who had been away at a fire dance in Lukachukai, was asked, upon her return, to hand tremble over the child. She recommended that they take the child to the clinic on the next morning. They were able to obtain transportation to the government clinic at Chinle, so they took the baby there.

Stringy, bloody stools were noted by the physician there who prescribed an antibiotic. Upon return home the baby seemed worse. Lack of transportation prevented a return to the clinic so a second hand trembler, Nakai Tso, a resident in a neighboring camp, was called in. This man said that a broken taboo was the cause of the illness and determined that one of the parents had seen a dead dog or cat during the mother's pregnancy. He told the parents, "that is the main cause. It's up to you whether to call the medicine man or go to the clinic first." They decided to put off having a sing and were able to ride to the Many Farms Clinic with one of the staff who happened to be in their camp on another matter.

Examination at the clinic revealed that the child was acutely ill with diarrhea and pneumonia. The mother was told to take the child to Ganado Hospital for treatment there.

Nine days later, a phone call from the Many Farms Clinic to Ganado ascertained that the child had responded favorably to treatment and soon would be released. The family of the child planned to have a sing for him upon discharge.[1]

This account, based on medical charts and interviews with the mother of Tracy Begay, would raise many questions in the mind of the public health practitioner or government administrator who is a new arrival on the Navajo Reservation.

Why did the mother wait for a whole month before she brought the child to the clinic? What was the sanitary condition of the home environment? Why didn't the family obtain transportation for a checkup as the clinic worker suggested? What is hand trembling, and what does that have to do with illness? Why was the grandmother asked to perform the act? Why didn't they go to the clinic where the baby was first seen rather than to another one? If the grandmother was effective in hand trembling, why was another one called in when the child became worse? What do taboos have to do with illness? Why didn't the hand trembler tell the mother what to do? Why should he suggest a medicine man if the family was accustomed to modern medicine? What is a "sing"? Finally, why did the family have such a sing performed after the baby was cured at the hospital?

The answers to these questions take us far afield from what the practitioner of Western medicine is likely to construe as facts of medical relevance. *But what is medically relevant is culturally determined.* In modern western thought, relevance is largely determined by the germ theory which is basic to the belief system of the doctor and his patient. Infectious disease is caused primarily by microorganisms, or by other biologic events. However, for the Navajo medicine man and his patient disease is caused by the infraction of rules of human conduct backed up by religious sanctions which are basic to their belief system. For the old-fashioned

Navajo, the washing of hands before handling food, for example, is quite as irrelevant to health as moral conduct would be to the conservative physician.

However, in order to answer these questions and thereby better understand the behavior of the cultural whole, the mother's medical behavior must be understood not only in terms of the belief system but in terms of her relations to other members of her family and community. For example, the mother of the sick baby plays a very different role in her relationship to the grandmother than would be the case in modern urban society. Also, her behavior is affected by Navajo economics and technology. The availability of a ride in this remote desert area is more important from the mother's point of view than seeing the same doctor. Thus, a meaningful and useful understanding of this woman's behavior necessarily involves a comprehensive view of her culture. Once the concept of the cultural whole is thought of as relevant to medical behavior, it is of equal importance to gain an understanding of the dynamics of the culture—of the fact that it is always in the process of change. Thus, in the case of Tracy Begay we learn that the child was treated in the clinic for an intestinal complaint. Twenty years ago, the mother would not have brought the baby into a clinic at all. She would have relied solely on the medicine man and the correct sing (curing ceremony) would have been prescribed—in terms of the broken taboo revealed by the hand trembler. The acceptance of Western medicine as a means to cure such an ailment is an indication that the original belief system has been modified by contacts with the non-Navajo world. However, bringing the baby to the clinic does not mean that the mother has abandoned her belief system and her religion; ritual observation is still essential, from her point of view, for restoring complete health.

Some of these cultural dynamics, particularly in relation to the health and religious beliefs and practices of the Navajo, are essential to gaining an understanding of the kinds of questions raised by the case of Tracy Begay.[2]

Religion, Health, and Medicine

Most Navajo men and women still believe in their own religion and participate in its rituals. A person may well have lost the knowledge of the legends that go with the ceremonies, he may not know the prescriptions and procedures as his elders do, but he still attends sings performed in his region of the reservation and turns to the healing ceremonies of his own people when he is faced with a crisis. Recently, a Navajo professional nurse with diagnosed cancer, who had been converted to the Protestant faith many years ago, had many sings as well as modern medical treatment before her death. Only a small minority of the people have been Christianized to the point that they abstain from participation in the religious life of their people. The religion provides those Navajo who live in California, or anywhere off the reservation, with a constant bond with the homeland traditionally designated as that area between the four sacred mountains, for only there will the sings be effective.

In contrast to Christians, the Navajo is not concerned with life in the hereafter. Life after death is a hazy concept—there is certainly no thought of reward for good conduct, or punishment for bad—just a dim sort of existence that is ill defined.

Religion is concerned with the here and now. It has as its focus the maintenance of balance between the individual and his total physical and social environment, as well as the maintenance of balance between the supernatural and man. When these forces are in a state of balance, good health is the result; an upset in this equilibrium causes disease. This concept in which there is no significant distinction between mind and body is the basis for Navajo beliefs about disease.

The Navajo world is inhabited by various kinds of beings which can be differentiated by the amount of power they possess and by their tendency to act favorably towards human beings. "The more power they possess, for good or evil, the more careful one must be in one's behavior towards them." These beings may be divided into *Holy People,* the divinities, and *Earth Surface People,* ordinary human beings. "The Navajo word translated by *holy* defines 'power which exceeds human effort' . . . natural forces are conceived of as quasi-human beings and belong properly among the Holy People." Thunder, lightning, and whirlwinds are some of those which are especially dangerous. On the other hand, rains, mountains, and corn are favorably disposed towards man. *Animals* have a divine as well as human aspect. *Ghosts* are the malignant parts of dead people and are greatly feared. *Witches* are human beings with supernatural power who are also greatly feared and a major source of evil.

Man is surrounded by dangers on all sides; all of these beings are potentially harmful and every child is brought up to observe a large number of restrictions to his behavior. Loosely speaking, these may be called taboos; in the Navajo language the term *bahadzid* is used, which may be translated as "dangerous to do." Thus there are taboos concerned with antagonizing ghosts, deserted hogans should be avoided, corpses buried according to certain rules. Fingernail parings, hair, and feces must be disposed of with care for fear they will fall into the hands of witches. Birds, snakes, bears, and reptiles should not be killed except under unusual circumstances. Anything that lightning has struck becomes dangerous. In addition, there are a host of taboos concerning native technology, pregnancy, and conduct at ceremonials.[3]

It is the function of the medicine man, or *singer* as he is called in Navajo, to bring the dangerous under control, to drive out evil and attract the good and beautiful. That is, restore new harmony between the individual and his total environment. But such therapy which affects the total individual—they do not make the distinction between mental and physical illness that we do—cannot be performed until the therapist is told what is the cause of the illness. Thus, when a Navajo falls ill, when he feels pain or fever or has a disturbing dream, he tells his family of his illness and they seek out a diagnostician who will, through a prescribed ritual, detect the cause of the illness. The cause of most illnesses is the infraction of a taboo. So we find that when Tracy Begay had an advanced case of diarrhea, the family called in the grandmother who had this power of divination.

The ritual act of diagnosis is performed by a number of means: gazing at the stars, listening to noises in the night, or most commonly by hand trembling. In such cases the diagnostician is in a self-induced trance state. When the latter method is used, an involuntary motion spreads from the fingertips, through the hand to the arm which flails about in a convulsive manner. During this session the transgression which has caused the illness is revealed: the patient may have used wood from a lightning-struck tree, or crossed a trail left by a snake, or violated any one of a great number of such religious sanctions. The correct ceremony which will counteract the misdeed will be prescribed. The patient goes back to his family and a decision is made as to which of the singers who perform that ceremony should be called in. It should be noted that this ability to diagnose is a power which comes suddenly to the individual during the course of his life, in a manner comparable to the way a shaman acquires his power among other Indian tribes. The power of the medicine man, however, comes from many years of learning long and exact rituals, and historically it is related to priestcraft which was derived from the neighboring Pueblo peoples.

One type of ceremonial, Blessing Way, protects the individual from future harm. According to Leland Wyman, there are extant some 17 different ceremonials, some of which have numerous variations (Wyman, 1950). A ceremonial is a complex interweaving of praying, chanting, sandpainting, medication with herbal infusions, and other procedures which are carried out precisely. The old-time Navajo distinguish hundreds of different plants that are used for such medicines, and the correct curing properties of each, in terms again of their own homeopathic beliefs. Sandpaintings are made depicting the *Yei* (the gods) and animal spirits. The power and beneficence of the figures depicted in such sandpaintings are brought in contact with the ailing body parts, starting with the ankles and working up the body at the joints. Evil is driven out and then blessing and good health restored. These ceremonies, lasting from a few hours to as long as nine days and nights, must be carried out in a hogan. There the medicine man and his patient are surrounded by the immediate family, relatives, and friends of the ailing person. They join in the chanting, often accompanied by a rattle, and a few act as helpers to the singer in the making of the sandpaintings. The most elaborate of the ceremonies, those lasting nine days, attract Navajo from hundreds of miles away. At such times there is also ritualized singing and dancing held outside of the hogan and the relatives of the patient are responsible for feeding all visiting friends and fellow clansmen. "They are performing the very songs and rituals that the gods used to bring about creation. It is more than reenactment, it is the real thing, it is the laying of their hands on the machinery of the infinite and straightening it out." (Leighton and Leighton, mimeo). Through such means the medicine man does not beseech the gods, he compels the gods. Knowledge is power; if correctly used, it will bring about the desired results automatically, that is, the curing of the patient. The Navajo are mechanists par excellence. Failures are explained by human error; the singer lacked proper control of his knowledge. If the singer makes even a small mistake the cure will fail; and likewise, if the patient does not get well, the family criticizes the singer for some slip-up in the ritual. It is a case of after the fact, therefore because of the fact, but causal relations are not put to the test.

The singer has a high status in his own society, especially if he is an accomplished one, that is, if he knows many of the major sings and earns his living from his medicine activities. The world of religion and the world of health are not distinguished, nor are the provinces of the body and the mind viewed as separate entities.

The Navajo usually starts learning sings as a young man, often in adolescence. The older men pick out relatives who seem to be bright, interested, and above all, have a good memory. This is essential as hundreds of hours of singing, legends, and ritual procedure as well as knowledge of the plants and the complex design of the sandpaintings must be memorized and correctly coordinated in the actual performance of the ritual. In the old days, and to a degree even now, the medicine men were the intellectuals of Navajo society, and were men of great power who swayed public opinion, often from behind the scenes.

The religious life of the Navajo people was a major focus of their day-to-day living. Clyde Kluckhohn calculated in Ramah in 1940 that the average male spent one-third of his waking hours in religious pursuit; in attending sings, in gathering plants for them, in helping with the sandpaintings, or as a singer himself. The women spent only slightly less time doing the same. The amount and complexity of esoteric lore is truly amazing.

Here among the Navajo we find medical folkways that are still firmly embedded in religious sanctions; medical needs are met through ritual acts. Religion and medicine are completely intertwined. The healer is still the singer; medical acts have not been secularized, and, as Alexander and Dorothea Leighton (1944) have pointed out in *The Navaho Door,* such rituals have considerable psychotherapeutic value. The powerful appeal to the emotions, the close identification with the singer, and through him with the Holy People, have a strong therapeutic effect. Furthermore, the presence of the whole family, clansmen, friends, and neighbors, all of whom gather to help the patient get well, gives great support.

The Change in Navajo Medical Behavior

The foregoing description of Navajo religion and related medical behavior is written as if the Navajo were living in a vacuum, cut off from all outside influences which, of course, is not the case. But the physician, teacher, or government worker who is new to the Reservation is apt to have just such a flat and static picture, lacking time perspective. He sees the primitive houses, the women in old-fashioned dress carrying babies strapped to cradle boards; he hears an exotic language and may witness a heathen ritual. At his clinic, in his classroom or office he becomes acquainted with what seem to be an unchanging people, and he is often quick to make a judgment about their stubbornness in clinging to ancient ways. For the newcomer, the elements of culture which are resistant to change loom large: housing, which for the Navajo has deep religious significance; the old-fashioned dress of the women, indicative of their modesty; the child-rearing practices and religious and linguistic behavior, slow to change in any culture. These dramatic differences from our way of life blind the newcomer to changes that are taking place. But quite to the contrary, historic and archaeologic records reveal that the Navajo have gone through a rapid transition from a primitive, hunting, food-gathering economy through an era when the basis of subsistence was horticulture and stock-raising, and into the present period of wage work in our national industrial economy.

It is only when compared to our own way of life, especially to our recent rapid technologic change, that the ways of other peoples in China, India, Africa, and in the Navajo country seem to be changing hardly at all. For this reason the newcomer to the Navajo Reservation fails to realize that the culture of these people too is constantly in flux. Starting as far back as 1880, there have been physicians in the area practicing Western medicine. They have had a great effect on the Navajo who have considerably modified their behavior as a result of this contact with the white man, just as they have been influenced in so many other aspects of their culture. Interaction with the white man enormously accelerated with the advent of World War II, when many thousands of Navajo men served with the armed services, cut off from their own curing practices and exposed to the advantages of modern medicine as administered by military doctors. Additionally, thousands of Navajo left the Reservation to work in war industries all over the western states, and they too were exposed to Western medicine as never before.

To return to the case of Tracy Begay, the behavior of the mother illustrates a generalization made by Ralph Linton (1936) many years ago:

> When a new element is offered to any society, full acceptance is always preceded by a period of trial. During this period both the new trait and the old trait or traits with which it is competing become alternatives within the total culture complex. They are presented to individuals as different means to the same end. (p. 280).

The Navajo attitude toward Western medicine is not unlike their response to all the other new ideas and techniques with which they have come in contact. Thus, in his curing behavior, if one sing is unsuccessful he will keep on trying others until he hits upon one that works. Scientific medicine is but one of a long series of alternate *means of curing* that have been borrowed from other peoples.

From the neighboring Pueblo Indians he has taken masks, paintings, fetishes, and many other ritual techniques. But he has made them his own and fashioned them to serve his own ends; he has adapted them from a religion in which they were used primarily for their power to bring rain and fertility. By experimentation he has changed these techniques into a means of serving the health needs of his people. Evon Vogt (1961) has characterized this as an *incorporative* model of culture change, and has pointed out how the technology and institutions of others have been made to serve the Navajo in all aspects of their culture. In a similar fashion, hand trembling and the elements of one of the Wind Way ceremonials were borrowed from the Apache. But it cannot be said that Western medicine is the last of such a long series. Peyote ritual as an alternate means of curing has come in during only the last 30 years, but it has been accepted as a total religious complex (Native American Church) with curing as only one of its objectives.

All of these primitive techniques have a limited usage in affecting the biologic processes, but they have proved to be of merit in coping with man's psychologic needs, and have real psychotherapeutic value. The Navajo, through his own prescientific experimental behavior, has accepted chemotherapy and surgery as the proper ways of curing tuberculosis. Thus these methods have become virtually the universal means of treating the physical aspects of that disease. But only 20 years ago, when bed rest and custodial treatment were all scientific medicine had to offer, this method was held as an alternate to native curing practice, which in turn during an earlier era had been the universal method of cure. Here we find a perfect example of the cycle of change, pointed out by Linton (1936), whereby one universal mode of behavior replaces another, but only after a period when "the alternatives serve as a proving ground for innovations."

Medical technology for diarrhea has not advanced as far as it recently has for the treatment of tuberculosis, and the traditional cures are still practiced as alternatives, as we saw in the case of Tracy Begay. With the advent of more effective Western medicine, the treatment of that disease by the physician may also become universally accepted.

"The Navajo Individual is the reason for the coordination of universal phenomena; he therefore directs his ritual from the individual outward." (Vogt, 1961). However, as the individual man is the focal point of this religion and his welfare the central concern, modern clinical medicine has become incorporated into the total means of maintaining equilibrium, because the Navajo sees it too as beneficial to the individual patient. Sam Yazzie, an old Navajo singer at Pine Springs, expressed this feeling when he said, "After all, the medicine man and your doctors are working towards the same goal. They are both trying to cure the patient, so why should there be any feeling of rivalry between them?" The attitude and behavior of most medicine men confronted by this alternate curing system were further elucidated as Sam Yazzie went on to say:[4]

> I have great respect for white doctors; there are things they can do that we cannot. For example, they can remove an appendix, they can take out a gall bladder, or treat a urinary tract infection. They also can take out a section of the intestines and sew the patient's stomach up again so that he will recover.

> There are certain sicknesses that a doctor can never cure that we can—lizard illness, for example—or an illness that comes from one of those small green worms you sometimes find on an ear of corn. Sickness might last over a long time and it might be a lingering illness. No white doctor can cure an illness of that type, only a medicine man can cure such patients. . . . In any situation when a

patient isn't getting better then I, or any other medicine man who knows his business, should allow the patient to go to the hospital and have his x-rays and other treatment there. Then he can come back and have the rest of the sing in the hogan. This has happened many times even right here at Pine Springs to our own children. They have started a sing here, the children don't seem to be getting any better, we then let them go to the hospital, and then, after they come back, we finish the ceremony. Even after a period of more than 3 months we will complete the ceremony if it was left unfinished. That is most important, especially with the *Beauty Way* ceremonies; they must always be completed.

In the anthropologic literature, the hand trembler has been described as one who revealed the cause of illness only as that illness was thought to be brought about by the infraction of a religious sanction, and also as one who prescribed the appropriate curing ceremony. However, change has also taken place in the behavior and attitudes of these diagnosticians. On one occasion a sheepherder collapsed near a hogan and a hand trembler was called in immediately to diagnose his trouble. He said that the man should be taken to the clinic; his advice was followed and the man was given medicine and cured. On being questioned about this, the hand trembler stated, "Sometimes your hand will point where there is a hospital, so you will know that the patient needs to be taken there. This is just what happened when I did hand trembling for this man. That is why I told him to go to the clinic right away."

Christianity as an Alternate Religion

The Christian religion has not gained converts to the degree that modern medicine has attracted patients. It has not become an alternate religion to the degree that modern medicine has become an alternate curing system. Why? It has met with resistance because it preaches against the very core of the religion—the worship of the Navajo gods from whom the medicine men derive their curative powers. Furthermore, the Christian concept of sin, belief in heaven and hell, and the salvation of the soul are all in sharp contradiction to Navajo ideology.

It may be argued that the germ theory is equally abstract and foreign to Navajo thought, but, as mentioned earlier, the Navajo are a very practical-minded people. The way in which results are obtained has less interest for the Navajo than the fact that certain means bring desired ends. They are willing to go along with the doctor and follow his advice as pain is relieved, anxiety allayed, and the patient recovers from his illness. Long ago the Navajo discovered that recovery from tuberculosis, to take but one disease, was possible even if the patient did not change his basic belief system as to what caused his illness. That is, he would recover even if he failed to comprehend, or disbelieved, what the doctor or nurse told him about germs or his bodily processes. Further, it was his experience that he felt even better if he participated in the sing sometimes, even going alternately to the doctor and the medicine man. His psychological and spiritual needs were being satisfied by his own religion, whereas they were not fulfilled by Western medicine.

On the other hand, what are the tangible benefits obtained from a foreign religion which demands that the belief system be changed and ceremonials which are so highly prized given up? The advantages of Christianity and its creed, that good conduct has its reward in heaven and bad conduct takes one to hell, has had a hollow ring for most Navajo even after over 100 years of listening to the words of the missionaries. Bad conduct has its revenge in illness now, good behavior brings with it health.

2.

Health and Disease:
Physicians' View

"Your government should start a Point-4 program here in the Navajo Reservation," was the appraisal of a visiting physician from one of the developing countries in the Middle East. Like many foreign visitors to the United States, he had the advantage of seeing the American Indian through fresh eyes, and was not subject to the emotional involvement and the stereotypes of the American Indian that often affect the American citizen when he visits the Indian country.

After World War II, the discrepancy between the level of health of the American Indian and the rest of the nation became even more evident. Various private agencies, including the American Medical Association, the National Tuberculosis Association, and the Association on American Indian Affairs, along with certain government agencies, advocated a transfer in responsibility for Indian health from the Bureau of Indian Affairs to the United States Public Health Service. In the 84th Congress, First Session, the Committee on Appropriations of the House of Representatives reported:

> Health services for Indians have been provided for over a hundred years; but in spite of this fact the American Indian is still the victim

of an appalling amount of sickness. The health facilities are either non-existent in some areas, or, for the most part, obsolescent and in need of repair; personnel housing is lacking or inadequate; and workloads have been such as to test the patience and endurance of professional staff. This all points to a gross lack of resources equal to the present load of sickness and accumulated neglect. . . .[1]

The Surgeon General reported to that same Committee:

Indians of the United States today have health problems resembling in many respects those of the general population of the Nation a generation ago. Diseases that are largely controlled among the general population still cause widespread illness and death among the Indians.[2]

In brief, the general conditions of Navajo health in 1955 exhibited the same characteristics as those found in less developed countries. These features are listed below:

1. The major disease problems are infectious illnesses or the consequences of infectious illnesses.
2. There may be one or more so-called "mass diseases" which are of epidemic proportions. Tuberculosis is an example of this disease problem in the Navajo.
3. There is rapid population growth which can be attributed to the continuing high birth rate in the face of a falling death rate.
4. The infant death rate—usually considered a sensitive index of health and living conditions in a community—is inordinately high compared to the general U.S. population.
5. The treatment, control, and prevention of the health problems are hampered by inadequate or even nonexistent health statistics, inaccurate population census, and by the considerable gap between the advanced knowledge of modern medicine and the application and acceptance of this technology in the community, which may depend upon the extent of adherence to native medical practices.

Frustration in dealing with the medical problems of the Navajo begins, as in any other less developed area, when one turns to the first tool of the qualified public health physician; vital and health statistics are needed to define the nature and scope of the problems. It is impossible to exaggerate the importance of full and accurate statistics. Failure to obtain accurate health information was sharply presented by an evaluation in the Meriam report on Indian problems in 1928; it applies to the situation in 1955 equally well:

> ... The Indian Service has for many years had rules and regulations requiring the collection and tabulation of some vital statistics, but they have achieved the form, and not the substance. Really accurate figures based on reasonably complete records are not yet secured. ...

In this same vein, J. Nixon Hadley, statistician with the Division of Indian Health, United States Public Health Service, summarized the problem of evaluating the health information in a publication in September 1955:

> Measurement of health conditions among the Navajo is hampered by lack of complete data either on the base population involved or on deaths and illnesses. Even with this lack of specificity, however, it is obvious that mortality and morbidity rates for most of the major diseases are far in excess of the rates for the total United States population.

A primary need for the development of valid health statistics is an accurate population census. There has never yet been an accurate or reliable count of the Navajo Reservation resident population. The Navajo population in 1955 was estimated at 77,300. This, of course, is not a pure guess, but is based on annual school census information which has been especially useful since 1950. Birth and death records are incomplete and sometimes inaccurate. Navajos are not a record-conscious people and see no pressing reason to make special efforts to notify a tribal or government office about the registration of a birth or death in the family. The death of an infant who may be only a few days old may not seem an event which should concern the distant government official. Such a family problem is regarded by the Navajo as his personal concern and, for reasons which are culturally determined, he may not wish to discuss this death with anyone. On the other hand, a birth in a Navajo family is regarded as a natural and commonplace event which would certainly not justify a difficult journey to a government outpost for the purpose of registration. The incompleteness of birth registration records was indicated from a study carried out by the United States Public Health Service, wherein only 60 percent of the births from a population sample were actually registered and 40 percent were not officially recorded. Thus, the all-important health statistics such as population growth, birth and death rates, disease, mortality, and morbidity rates lack completeness and precision. The magnitude of the differences between health conditions among the Navajo as contrasted with the national picture, however, does outline in broad strokes the type of health problems on the reservation.

When one turns from the available Navajo mortality statistics to morbidity statistics, the data in 1955 is also grossly inadequate as well as imprecise. Again the sheer weight of health problems seen in the hospitals and clinics, though admittedly a biased population, allow one to make certain assumptions about the pattern of disease. First, it follows from the mortality picture that infectious disease problems and their consequences were the most frequent source of health impairment among the Navajo. About 60 to 80 percent of all patients coming to the reservation medical facilities were in the pediatric age group (14 years of age and under) and most of these youngsters were suffering from infectious and communicable disease problems. Nontuberculosis respiratory infections complicated by middle ear infections that frequently perforate and scar the ear drum were commonplace. It was recognized that a significant number of these youngsters developed hearing loss.

Acute and chronic middle ear disease caused by infection is a common problem in children in general, but reaches a serious and widespread problem among Navajos, other American Indian, and Alaska Native populations. Conditions of poverty, overcrowding, poor housing, inadequate nutrition, sociocultural, economic, and educational circumstances may well contribute to the high degree of susceptibility which these groups have to middle ear disease. Unfortunately, the crippling effects of middle ear disease infection have serious consequences on growth and development as well as educational and vocational potential of these youngsters.

Conjunctivitis was common, and in many cases had the appearance of trachoma.[3] Isolated epidemics of trachoma had been observed in some Navajo camps, but more frequently in recent years in boarding schools where breaks in personal and environmental sanitation resulted in the spread of this infection from an active case to the classmates. Trachoma infection had been one of the leading causes of health impairment among the Navajo at the time of the Meriam report in 1928. However, since the advent of sulfa therapy and other antibiotics, the disease has fallen off considerably. It is always difficult to obtain accurate statistics on this health problem because the diagnosis was based on clinical evaluation and the laboratory has provided little practical help prior to 1957. Despite the overall decline in the prevalence of trachoma, there are still endemic foci of this disease throughout the reservation. Inasmuch as trachoma causes acute, distressing, painful conjunctivitis and also can produce chronic eye troubles, sometimes leading to partial or complete blindness, this disease is still an important public health problem among the Navajo. It is well known that the transmission of trachoma appears to be related to poor personal hygiene and sanitary practices. Trachoma is also a considerable problem in many of the underdeveloped areas of the world where similar living conditions prevail.

Impetigo, a superficial infection of the skin, is another common health problem among Navajo infants and young children. This is unquestionably related to hygiene and sanitary practices in the household. Public health workers agree that in virtually every Navajo family living under traditional reservation conditions, impetigo afflicts the youngsters repeatedly even though the cure for this can be demonstrated by simple rules of cleanliness. Unfortunately, when water and sanitary facilities are difficult to secure, knowledge about cleanliness becomes academic.

Tuberculosis has been a major cause of death and suffering on the Navajo Reservation for many years. Until adequate hospitalization facilities and modern antituberculous chemotherapy became available in 1952, the Navajo were in the throes of a tuberculosis epidemic. It was estimated that in the period following World War II, tuberculosis in some form affected one of every 10 Navajo. Mobile case finding, roentgenographic surveys had been abandoned because the few sanatorium facilities that were available on the reservation were already overcrowded. Active pulmonary tuberculosis occurred in at least 3 percent of the population. Acute miliary and meningeal forms of tuberculosis (fatal before modern chemotherapy) were common and almost every family on the Reservation had firsthand experience of one or more in their group afflicted by tuberculous disease. It was not uncommon to find 50 to 60 percent of the school children in the 6 to 10 year age group infected with tubercle bacilli, as evidenced by a positive tuberculin skin test. This was the infection rate in the period prior to 1952, which exceeded the national rates by 10 to 60 times. This marked the Navajo community as a high incidence tuberculosis area comparable to populations in the areas of Asia and Africa which were receiving technical assistance in health for mass disease problems, notably tuberculosis (in some areas malaria). Here there was a mass-type disease problem of the Navajo. This is not surprising either, for tuberculosis, like impetigo, trachoma, and other infectious disease problems, is, in part at least, an expression of the socioeconomic and cultural situation of a community. Tuberculosis has been described by Dubos and Dubos (1952) as a disease of gross social mismanagement both on the individual and the community level.

Other serious health problems among the Navajo included pneumonia and infant diarrhea. The latter problem is an example of an infectious disease related to personal and environmental sanitation. Modern toilet facilities are, of course, out of the question in an area where drinking water must be hauled many miles to a primitive one-room dwelling. Moreover, privies, which are found only rarely in the more densely populated sections near a government outpost, are usually in neglected condition. Disposal of garbage, and other sanitary problems related to such environmental factors as sheep corrals, horses, and chickens and a variety of other animals near the dwellings, attract flies. Water at the source (wells, springs, pumps) has not been responsible for infection and appears unrelated to the diarrhea problems at the supply level. It is not known whether water and food became contaminated by an infectious agent carried by the family or just what the real etiologic agent might be. Studies prior to 1955 revealed that bacterial pathogens (shigella predominantly) might account for about 10 to 20 percent of the diarrheal illnesses. What the spectrum of etiologic agents might be (bacterial, viral, or nonspecific agent) was not known. But it is clearly apparent that if the Navajo infant could be seen early before he became dehydrated and weak, he could be treated by simple administration of fluids and close control of the food intake. Navajo have a diarrhea season which, on the basis of clinic and hospital observation, occurs in the summer and fall months, not unlike the so-called summer complaint in the United States general population at the turn of the century. Diarrheal disorders of a similar clinical type are found in the underdeveloped area populations, confined as a serious health problem to infants.

As with the Navajo, diarrheal problems can easily be treated if the infants are seen early in the course of the illness before severe dehydration occurs. Preventive measures to control this health problem might necessitate changing the pattern of living from primitive to modern since it may be that diarrheal diseases are environmentally born.

Two other health problems may be mentioned here that are of a noninfectious nature, but which are extraordinarily common among Navajo Indians for reasons which are as yet unclear. These are congenital hip disease and gall bladder disease.

In recent years, the newspapers and magazines have run occasional articles concerning the immunity of the Navajo Indians to such modern health problems as hypertension, diabetes, cancer, and coronary heart disease. Diseases of an allergic or metabolic type and mental illness have also been infrequently reported among this tribe. Despite the low incidence of these diseases in the vital and health statistic records, it is not settled as to whether they actually do not occur frequently or are simply not seen, diagnosed, or reported. Moreover, it has been pointed out that the Navajo are a young population so that they would not be as susceptible to the neoplastic and degenerative diseases which are seen more frequently in the older age groups. Clearly, what was needed was a more detailed and precise study of the pattern of health and disease in the Navajo community which would answer some of these questions.

In short, then, the pattern of health and disease which was reflected in the clinic and hospital admission information was essentially what one would expect from the circumstances known of the Navajo community and tribal life. Infectious diseases, respiratory (nontuberculous), diarrheal disorders, impetigo, conjunctivitis, trachoma, tuberculosis, chronic ear infections with deafness, were the basic health problems. Congenital hip disease and gall bladder disease were examples of noninfectious diseases seen commonly among the Navajo.

At the risk of oversimplification, it can be said that there are at least three major reasons why the Navajo have had a persistently substandard health picture despite the considerable strides made in the health field on the national level:

1. The federal responsibility was vested in the Department of Interior, which is not primarily concerned with health matters.

This meant that the Branch of Health had to compete with the other aspects of Indian affairs (and with other bureaus in the Department) for adequate financing and personnel. It was this problem in administration which, in part at least, made the transfer to the Division of Indian Health, United States Public Health Service, Department of Health, Education, and Welfare so attractive and desirable.

2. Prior to the antibiotics period in medicine, there was often little choice between the modern physician and the Navajo medicine man. Hospitals were frequently regarded as death houses and so were avoided unless one were ready to be admitted for a terminal illness. In short, if the Navajo did not always accept modern medicine, this could be understood in the light of their traditional beliefs. As a result, there was very little serious agitation to remedy the lack of medical facilities or personnel by way of petitions to the Federal Government. It was only since the early 1950s that the Navajo themselves became insistent that something be done to correct the miserable health situation on their reservation.

3. It was not a simple matter to introduce modern medical care to the Navajo where geographic, socioeconomic, language, and cultural barriers existed. In effect the Navajo Indians offered the same challenge to the medical team that was present in an overseas program. Moreover, because of previous broken promises and government failure to consult Tribal leaders, the Navajo viewed any innovation by federal agents with great suspicion. At best, one could only hope for slow acceptance of new ideas and methods if they proved to have value.

In order to gain a perspective on the nature of its responsibility for Indian health, it should be made clear that the Bureau of Indian Affairs, under the overall jurisdiction of the Department of the Interior, has had the total responsibility of administering Indian affairs since 1849, when they took over from the War Department. During that century, acting as trustee for the Indians (these lands were held in trust by the United States Government), the Bureau of Indian Affairs was involved in administering not only an educational and health program, but also in developing Reservation resources and law enforcement. In short, the Bureau, as a monolithic organization, dealt with individuals and communities of Indians in the same way that local, county, and state governments have jurisdiction in the usual American communities. From the

Indian point of view, the Bureau was not only all-powerful but all-providing—the Great White Father.

Perhaps the greatest problem of all was within the framework of the Bureau itself: that of developing, on the one hand, leadership and effective local government whereby the various Indian communities would assume responsibility for administering their own affairs and, on the other hand, satisfying Federal laws and regulations which imposed uniformity.

During the reform administration of John Collier (1933 to 1945), much was done to right these wrongs. Tribal government and fiscal responsibility were encouraged and a cultural point of view on the part of officials was incorporated in the administration. But with the end of the New Deal and the diverting of much needed funds from the Bureau during World War II, many of the gains made by the Collier administration were lost because of these local and national political pressures.

Harold E. Fey and D'Arcy McNickle (1959) have written:

> Increasingly in recent years the staff employed by the Bureau of Indian Affairs has been professionalized within the Civil Service, until today most positions in administrative management, professional services, and legal branches require college training and even graduate training. But a professional staff is effective to the extent that it is trained for a given task, and almost without exception the individuals who have gone to work in the Bureau have not been trained to work in a culture other than their own. (p. 195).

The principal advantage of a transfer of health services from the Bureau of Indian Affairs to the United States Public Health Service was that the latter had wide political support. Senator Watkins stated in a Committee hearing:

> You have a few Indians in the United States compared to the 161 million people in the United States that are white. But the general public is interested in the Public Health Service. . . . It affects the States and so many citizens that it is always in a much preferred position to the Indian Service.[4]

Health Facilities Available in 1955

No matter how well-meaning and capable the United States Public Health Service administrator might have been, in July 1955 the Service had to start its program with the health facilities and personnel that it took over from the Branch of Health, Bureau of Indian Affairs. Essentially this is what was available at that time.

The main hospital facility existed at Fort Defiance, Arizona (see Map 1) at the south-central border of the Navajo Reservation. At that time this 115-bed general hospital and the 100-bed tuberculosis sanatorium constituted the "Navajo Medical Center" and served as the central diagnostic and treatment facility for the entire reservation. Patients who required more specialized medical care were transferred to urban hospitals located in Albuquerque or Phoenix. Small hospitals were located at strategic points on the reservation—a modern, newly completed 75-bed hospital at Tuba City, Arizona, an excellently constructed and equipped 56-bed hospital at Crown Point, New Mexico, a 41-bed obsolete hospital in Shiprock, New Mexico, and another excellent hospital with 57 beds at Winslow, Arizona. At Keams Canyon on the Hopi Indian Reservation, which is located within the boundaries of the Navajo Reservation, there was a 35-bed hospital that actually served both Tribes. There were two mission hospitals which serve the Navajo people; an 88-bed hospital, the Sage Memorial Presbyterian Hospital, in Ganado, Arizona, only 30 miles west of Fort Defiance, and the Rehoboth Reform Church Hospital with 30 beds located on the edge of the town of Gallup, New Mexico.

In addition to the reservation hospital facilities, the Government had provided off-reservation hospital facilities for Navajo tuberculosis patients in 10 state and private sanatoria in Arizona, Colorado, California, and New Mexico. There were as many as 500 Navajo hospitalized at one time in these sanatoria for treatment of tuberculosis.

In addition to the hospital facilities, the United States Public Health Service became heir to two field health centers, one at Tohatchi, New Mexico, and the other at Chinle, Arizona.

Although it was recognized that the hospital and clinic facilities were less than optimal for the medical care needs on the Navajo Reservation, plans and money were at hand to expand and construct hospitals and field clinics. Just as important was the need for proper housing so that the doctors, nurses, and ancillary health workers would have adequate living quarters. The shortage of proper housing had been one of the major problems that plagued the Bureau.

What of the health staff on the Navajo Reservation that manned the hospitals and field clinics for the government? The number of doctors and nurses needed to operate a full-scale health program was far more than were on hand. To make matters worse, even some of the professional health workers who were available did not perform a wholehearted job. While some of these people worked tirelessly in a completely dedicated and devoted manner, others spent much of their time complaining and finding fault with everything from housing to the way the drugs were ordered in the hospital. Many of the physicians were young and inexperienced, having only recently completed their internship. Since most of these men were on 2-year assignments to the Indian Reservation as fulfillment for the "doctor draft" obligation, they were not interested in a career in this type of work. In fact, they were primarily trained in clinical medicine and had no background and often little interest in public health or the administration of a hospital. To these doctors, facing the health problems on the Navajo Reservation, many difficulties were presented for the first time: learning to work effectively in a government organization; living and working within a relatively isolated social and medical community; comprehending the importance of cultural differences and language barriers as they are related to the medical program; and recognizing the pattern of disease and the nature of the clinical work on the reservation.

Once a physician joined the Bureau of Indian Affairs and accepted an assignment on the reservation, he found himself cut off from professional contacts. Lack of other professionals with whom he could review his cases and lack of journals essential to keeping up on changing medical technology had a demoralizing effect. The physicians and nurses after a few years became marginal to their own profession and over a period of years it became difficult, if not impossible, to maintain the standards of clinical practice which they had been taught to respect. Coupled with all of the problems that arise from professional isolation, it became difficult for the physicians to face the overwhelming work load caused by a backlog of morbidity, much of which resulted from lack of sufficient clinical facilities and personnel and almost total lack of a preventive program essential if morbidity was ever to be significantly reduced. It was not at all uncommon, and in some clinics customary, to treat 75 to 100 patients a day. The frustration of the well-trained physicians and nurses mounted and after a few years they left the service (for further details see Adair and Deuschle, 1957). For example, at Crown Point, on the Navajo Reservation, there was a series of 30 doctors between 1946 and 1955. Those who remained behind became even more demoralized, if not apathetic. Others retained only their spirit of the medical missionary which was essential to the task.

In the case of the physicians recruited on the doctor-draft basis, even the conscientious and perceptive ones would be just beginning to function effectively in terms of the total situation when their 2-year tour of duty ended. Thus, in terms of the long view of Navajo health, this rapid turnover of field and hospital physicians was a great disadvantage. Moreover, the field health service was almost nonexistent on the Navajo Reservation before 1955. If every one of the 24 public health nurses had worked day and night, it would have been impossible to provide even token public health services to the 77,300 Navajo living on 25,000 square miles of mountain and desert country.

This, then, was the health picture on the Navajo Reservation which confronted the Public Health Service in 1955.

This account would be incomplete without pointing out that the traditional attitude of the older physicians towards the medicine men, which was one of disrespect if not outright contempt, had not changed perceptibly since Father Anselm Weber (who established the first permanent Catholic mission among the Navajo at St. Michaels, Arizona) claimed that the "government doctors had failed to a large extent because up to that time (1903) most Indian Service medics had only ridiculed and antagonized the medicine men and the people" (Wilken, 1955, p. 211). They were oblivious of the religious function of the curing rites and did not appreciate the psychotherapeutic benefits the Navajo received from these religious practices. One of these older physicians, in a discussion of Navajo religion with another doctor (1956) remarked, "The fact that Navajo medicine men came to me for treatment proves that they are fakers and do not have confidence in their own methods."

Lack of interest in Navajo belief and custom resulted in alienating the people whom they were attempting to attract. On one occasion around 1941, the Director of Navajo Health arranged for an exhibit on tuberculosis and its prevention. This exhibit, at the Navajo Fair, would catch the attention of many men and women. Unfortunately, ignoring the Navajo feeling about a dead person, a skeleton was put on display to illustrate tuberculosis of the bone, and once this was known not a single Navajo would enter the building.

The physicians often discouraged their Navajo patients from attending their own ceremonies, pointing out that disease was transmitted when the dish containing medication was passed from the patient to all the others in the hogan and by other unsanitary practices.

This antagonistic attitude, of course, had its effect on the medicine men. One prominent singer, Manuelito Begay, who was the delegate to the Tribal Council from Crown Point, put it this way:

> I want to refer to what has gone on in the past relative to treatment of our people when they were ill—when the doctors and hospitals were first established among us, the doctors thought they were the only ones who knew how to apply medicine to the patients. The Navajo people were not recognized at all and, in that connection, we thought the same way, we could not agree as to whose treatment should be recognized. The doctors thought they were the ones, and we thought we were the ones. When we brought a sick child to the hospital and the child became worse in one week or two weeks, they would not return the child to us to treat, and even though they had the child long enough and had not improved it with their medicine, and they would only return the child if we signed a paper which said that *the child would not be eligible to go back to any hospital from now on,* and that is the way we signed the paper.

Sam Yazzie, the medicine man interviewed at Pine Springs (Chap. 1), when asked about his opinion of the white man's medicine, had many words of praise, but with this qualification:

> I have great respect for the doctors. I would not have done to them as they have done to us and try to shame many of us from practicing our own medicine. At one time the American physicians would have all of us medicine men put out of business. I have never felt that way towards the white doctors.

3.

Convergence of the
Two Views

We have presented the picture of health on the Navajo Reservation from the point of view of modern medicine—the actual state of health of the people, the historical situation with regard to health administration, and the earlier attitudes of the physicians and staff who were sent out by the Bureau to work in its Health Division.

In this chapter, there will be an assessment of the changing attitudes of the medical staffs and the improvements made by the United States Public Health Service when it took over responsibility for Navajo health in 1955.

As we have seen, the behavior, beliefs, and attitudes of the Navajo towards disease have changed as a result of contacts with the white man and his more effective medical technology. Likewise, a change had taken place in the culture of the physician. Both the Navajo and the white man who was in contact with him were responding to three important factors:

1. The participation of the Navajo in World War II and in war industries;
2. The introduction of antibiotic drugs;
3. The doctor-dentist draft.

The total *gestalt* was very different in 1950 from what it had been in 1940, when the doctor draft became effective.

The Navajo on the reservation—always receptive to innovations that were useful to them—were impressed by the efficacy of the new drugs, which in a period of a few days cured them of infectious disease. Without a doubt this medical breakthrough affected the attitude of the physician, as he in turn responded to patients who were now much more willing to follow his orders. The hospitals, which as recently as 1940 had been thought of as only a place to bring people to die, now were in great demand, and new facilities were built to meet this need.

Further, it is quite likely that this new relationship of trust and faith between the doctor and his patient minimized the rivalry between the doctor and the medicine man. The doctor could now have confidence that the patient would return for his treatment in the hospital if he was allowed to go home for a sing. By the same token the medicine man was confident that his patient whose pneumonia did not respond to his treatment would come back to him for completion of the ritual.

With regard to the third point, young physicians who came in contact with Navajo patients as a result of the doctor draft were all the products of a different era in medical education. They were exposed to psychiatric thinking, less known to the doctors of the earlier era, and were aware of the social sciences. These young men and women had a positive response to their Navajo patients. They brought with them the enthusiasm of their youth and a fresh point of view. Although they had difficulty in adjusting to government service, they had a positive response to their patients which was lacking on the part of most of the older men who had experienced many years of frustration and isolation from their profession.

Up to now, these younger doctors had had their internships in urban centers; they commented on the model behavior of the patients, who were very uncomplaining, as contrasted to patients they had known before. All of this was in sharp contrast to the prewar situation.

This new attitude was well expressed in the following letter:

I think it is fair to say that . . . we have a deep sense of the fact that concepts of illness are more closely integrated with spiritual concepts among the Navajo than is the case in our own culture. Moreover, when one considers the more modern notions enjoying examination in our own culture with respect to environmental and emotional influences on what happens to the tuberculous patient, the concepts of the Navajo singers and of our own people are really not too far apart. By this I mean that, for example, Doctor Dubos has defined in *The White Plague* ... the problem, by saying that tuberculosis is a disease of gross social mismanagement, both on the part of society and on the part of the individual. This is not an exact quote, but is what he said in substance ... certainly that point of view which all of us so heartily embrace is really not too far away from this idea of "disharmony." Obviously such a comparison can be labored to the ridiculous. ... I am simply trying to make the point that we have sympathy and respect for the Navajo point of view, as I gather they have for ours.[1]

A plea for the value of a comprehensive view of the total situation embracing both modern medicine and traditional belief had been set forth in *The Navaho Door* (Leighton and Leighton, 1944). Drs. Alexander and Dorothea Leighton, psychiatrists with training in anthropology, had spent some months living with Navajo in the Ramah area. They were able to gain an understanding of Navajo life as related to sickness and health.

It does not seem that Navajo theory of disease and treatment presents insurmountable obstacles to the use of white man's medical understanding and treatment, but the Navajos will have to be educated, intelligently and painstakingly, along lines of health and hygiene. It will not be necessary, nor desirable, to try to do away with Navajo religion in so doing, but the people and the practitioners will have to come to recognize the difference between the sort of illnesses that need hospital care at once and those they can care for at home, and to learn how to use their resources to produce better health. This education will probably be most effective if it is built upon the already existent beliefs and practices, rather than introduced as a totally new and different factor which has nothing to do with "old ways" of the people (p. 37).

While the direct effect of this book has not been ascertained, it can be said that these young physicians under the doctor draft were more receptive to its content than those of the previous decade.

Thus, one of the Cornell investigators, who was also the director of the Fort Defiance Sanatorium in 1952 to 1953, found that a sympathetic attitude towards the patients' customary ways was essential to the medical care of the individual and his family. He talked with the families of the patients about to be hospitalized and learned that it was not just the spouse of the patient, but his (or her) parents whose advice was sought according to the Navajo custom. He also learned that if the patient had a *Blessing Way* ceremony before entering the sanatorium, he would be less inclined to ask for such a ceremony during hospitalization, and that when it was ill advised to permit medical leave for a sing, the patient and his family would often be content to hold a ceremony over his clothes. Such in absentia treatment resting on Navajo belief that "the part stands for the whole" was routinely used by the Navajo during the war, when such *Blessing Way* sings were sung over the clothes of young men serving with the armed forces overseas (Vogt and Kluckhohn, 1951).

This was, generally, the growing attitude of other young physicians as well. They and their administrative officers were taking an interest in Navajo culture as it was relevant to the treatment of their patients in the hospital. The Acting Head of Public Health cooperated in the making of a television film which depicted the old and new ways of medicine.[2] Doctors at all of the contract sanatoria where Navajo were being treated with the newly discovered drugs asked advice of the Navajo Tribal Health Committee. Its Chairman, Annie Wauneka, counseled with them about their administrative problems in treating patients confined to hospitals many miles from home. Additionally, she and her committee performed invaluable service by visiting restive patients and persuading them to remain in the hospital until they were discharged by the physicians.

On one occasion, a medicine man was called to a sanatorium in southern Arizona after two patients had fled and others remained terrorized by lightning striking a tree on the hospital grounds. A public address system carried his chants into every room in the hospital. This incident was reported in an article written some years later by Dr. James R. Shaw, Chief, Division of Indian Health, United States Public Health Service, an indication of Washington's approval. He wrote, "The white man's medicine had been reinforced by Indian religious concepts" (Shaw, 1957a).

On another occasion in the fall of 1955, the government physicians meeting with doctors from Ganado and other medical missions on the Reservation asked Scott Preston, Vice Chairman of

the Navajo Tribal Council, and a medicine man himself, to talk
to them about Navajo health beliefs, religion, and curing practices.
At this meeting, a pediatrician asked if it would be appropriate
for a hogan to be built near the Tuba City Hospital where sings
could be held over babies under treatment without subjecting them
to hazards of a long journey away from the hospital. Mr. Preston
replied that such a decision was the responsibility of the medicine
men in the community and that it would be well to ask them.

They were attentive to his words when he said:

> As I see it, all the diseases which hurt the Navajo people may be
> divided into three kinds. There are those diseases that we medicine
> men have given up on. We know that you white doctors have better
> cures than we do. One of the diseases of that sort is tuberculosis.
> Then there is sickness which comes from getting too close to where
> lightning has struck. Right now there are probably some patients
> in this hospital who are sick from that illness and you doctors have
> no way of even finding out what is wrong with them—but we
> medicine men can, and we are able to cure such cases. A third type
> of illness is snake bite. You can cure that, and we Navajo also have
> our own medicines for that.

Professional health educators played an important part in furthering this understanding. One such health educator, working on
a community development project at Crown Point,[3] on the eastern
edge of the reservation, arranged for the Cornell doctors to come
over from Fort Defiance to talk to the people assembled at a
community meeting on the subject of tuberculosis. There at the
Crown Point hospital they demonstrated x-ray procedures and
showed the community, including several medicine men, slides of
tubercle bacilli and cultures as well as pictures of diseased lungs.

On another occasion during the fall of 1953, arrangements were
made for members of the community, and others who were interested, to visit the Medical Center at Fort Defiance.[4] Again the
doctors at the hospital and sanatorium explained to them modern
methods of treating tuberculosis. Annie Wauneka and Paul Jones
(Chairman, Navajo Tribal Council, 1959 to 1962) were in attendance at this educational session. The latter had had considerable
experience in medical interpreting and assumed that role on this
occasion and subsequently at the Tribal Council.

Paul Jones showed his broad understanding when on this same
occasion one of the medicine men in the group demonstrated for

the doctors how he used a variety of native plants in his own curing practice. This was a subject of embarrassment to the young English speakers in the group, but was handled with skill by Mr. Jones, who recognized the importance to the physicians of what this man had to say.

At another community meeting one of the staff physicians, a young man recruited through the doctor draft mechanism at the Crown Point Hospital, spoke as follows:

> I want to thank Mr. Perry for giving me this opportunity of talking to you. I am here to keep you well or to help you get well when you are sick. The medicine men, I recognize, have this same purpose. Neither the doctor nor the medicine man does this work just for the money he can make out of it. I have at times examined a patient, taken x-rays, and done all the things I know how, and still felt that I could not make the patient well. At times I have advised the patient to try the medicine man to see if he could bring about a cure. I understand that there are times when the medicine men feel that they cannot make a patient well, their sings do not work a cure. I hope the medicine men will get in the habit of sending such patients to me, let me see what I can do. Sometimes a patient gets in pretty bad shape, whether in the hospital or under a medicine man's care, before he is finally helped. I want to find out what kind of illness I can best cure, and which ones the medicine man is best at. I urge the medicine men to visit the hospital and learn how we do things, how we work on people, what facilities we have. I understand that more than 20 medicine men live in this area. This suggests that perhaps we might meet in small groups and become acquainted. I would like to invite a few at a time to come and have dinner with me. Then we can visit the hospital.[5]

Through such means better relations were brought about between the medicine men and the doctors not only at Crown Point but in Tuba City, Shiprock, and elsewhere on the reservation. Even though singers disagreed with the doctors as to the cause of tuberculosis, they recognized their superior technology in treating the disease. Thus, as we shall see later, medicine men who only a few years before had attempted to treat the disease by their traditional means now were able to recognize some of the crucial signs and symptoms of advanced illness and encouraged such patients to go to the hospital. The need for this type of cooperation had been pointed up by the Leightons (1944) in the previous decade.

It was in this favorable and constructive atmosphere that a

medical team from Cornell University Medical College first started its work on the Navajo Reservation. The attitude of doctors, and the realization on the part of the government that improvement in the health status of the Navajo entailed community education all made for a climate conducive to medical innovation: the introduction of the new medical technology for the cure of tuberculosis. Additionally, the Navajo leaders were particularly conscious of the pressing need to stop the further spread of this disease which was one of the prime causes of morbidity and mortality on the Reservation.

Just as the younger doctors working at the government medical centers were receptive to the cultural approach as indispensable to furthering mutual understanding with their patients and the community, the Cornell doctors, with the same awareness and with the application of political skill and sensitivity, were able to capitalize on this prevailing atmosphere of tolerance and cooperation.

The account of the way in which the Cornell team initiated contact with the Navajo, and how they were able to gain and keep the support of their political leaders is presented here in some detail. In the literature on innovation there are general reviews of what happened when new technology was introduced to a community, but there have not been sufficient accounts of the specifics of human behavior. Just what did the innovator say to the political leaders? In this case a stenographic recording of the proceedings of the Navajo Tribal Council meetings enables us to follow closely the words of the Cornell spokesman and those of the political leaders.

How did the Cornell group overcome the handicap of working across a language barrier? How did they work down through the power structure of the tribe in order to gain acceptance on the grass roots level in the community? These questions, which have a direct bearing on the propositions for successful innovation set forth in the preface, are answered by following this step by step from first contacts to the establishment of the clinic at Many Farms.

Because of the Cornell research in chemotherapy, the New York doctors, in January 1952, were called out to the Navajo Reservation as consultants on five cases of acute miliary tuberculosis that had been discovered at Tuba City among the 300 children confined to the hospital there with infectious hepatitis.

The following March, 3 months after the Cornell investigators

first began to work on the Reservation, a meeting was arranged
by the Superintendent of Navajo Service and his deputy for the
Cornell team to meet with the members of the Advisory Committee
of the Navajo Tribal Council. In this meeting, the first of a long
series which extended over the next 3 years, they explained to
those leaders of the Council just what they had been doing during
recent months at Tuba City, followed by work at Fort Defiance
and Winslow, Arizona.

On April 25, the Tribal Council as a whole passed a resolution
which stated:

> The Navajo Tribal Council hereby appropriates the sum of $10,000
> for donation to the Department of Medicine at Cornell University
> Medical College for its exclusive use in defraying the travel and
> other expenses of the New York Hospital–Cornell group in carrying
> on their work as consultants to reservation medical personnel in
> the use of isonicotinic acid hydrazide or other antituberculosis drugs
> on the Navajo reservation.

Additionally it was stated:

> The recipient of this donation shall report to the tribe regarding
> the use of which the tribal donation in reference was put.

Two months later, in July, the physician who subsequently directed
the Cornell field health project joined the Health Division of the
Bureau of Indian Affairs and reported to Fort Defiance, where he
was assigned as Chief Medical Officer at the sanatorium there.
Thus, on January 5, 1953, just a year after Cornell Medical College
had become involved in Navajo health matters, this group made
their first report to the Council of 74 members when they convened
at Window Rock from all over the Reservation. This initial presentation follows:

> Mr. Chairman, Members of the Council: I am very pleased to have
> this chance to come before you to report on what we have been
> doing on this joint enterprise between the New York Hospital and
> the group here on the Reservation. We are very grateful for the
> support which you have given us in this work and I wish to report
> at this time on what we have been doing and what it is that we
> hope to do in this enterprise which you have so very generously
> supported.
>
> As many of you know, the project started about a year ago as an

indirect result of an epidemic of another infection in Tuba City. Some of our young men were sent out on the epidemic of liver disease and, in the course of their work there in Tuba City, discovered that several young children were very ill with tuberculosis. At that very time we were working in New York with a new drug for the treatment of tuberculosis. We had just proved that this new drug was safe to administer to human beings. With that knowledge, we then went immediately to Tuba City and started the treatment of the young children who were in the hospital there very seriously ill with tuberculosis. These young children in Tuba City represented the first patients in the world with that type of tuberculosis who received the benefit of this new drug. From that small beginning, the project has greatly expanded to include other medical facilities on the Reservation. The results which have been obtained thus far in the treatment of the patients have been very gratifying indeed.

Tuberculosis has many forms. One form is an acute blood poisoning tuberculosis[6] and the other is the chronic tuberculosis of the lungs. The acute blood poisoning form kills without exception and usually within a very short period of several weeks, or, at the most, a few months. We have treated approximately thirty patients with that acute blood poisoning form of the disease. Of those thirty patients, only two have died, both within a few days of the start of the treatment. The remaining patients are either well or getting well, and a few children have already returned to school.

Much more important in terms of numbers . . . we have treated about seventy patients with various forms of tuberculosis of the lungs. All of these seventy patients were treated in the hospital and most of them, therefore, had a considerable amount of disease of the lungs. No patient has gotten worse since treatment was started. About one-half of the patients have obtained considerable improvement under treatment. About one-quarter have shown some improvement, but not a great deal, and the other quarter have shown no improvement but they have not gotten any worse. Those are the results in general.

Now, I would like to talk about the limitations of drug therapy. Tuberculosis of the lungs can be treated in three ways: by rest in bed, by drugs, or by surgical treatment. Some patients need all three types of treatment for the cure of their tuberculosis. Other patients may need only one of the three forms or one and another combined. Everybody who has ever had tuberculosis does not necessarily need drug treatment later. It is only when the type is active and the germs are being expectorated freely, that it is important that one or the other form of treatment is used.

Tuberculosis is more difficult to treat with drugs than most other infections. The reason for this is not that the drugs are less good than they are for other infections but, because with tuberculosis, a smaller or a larger amount of the lung is killed. If the amount of lung which is killed is small, it can be healed down with a scar like a cut on one's leg, but if the amount of lung which is killed is very big, even with a drug—one which leads to the death of most all of the germs—one still must get rid of the big area of dead tissue. So that some cases may be treated with the drug alone and, in others, one still has to remove the dead tissue.

The other reason why tuberculosis is difficult to treat with drugs is the fact that after weeks or months, the germs develop a resistance to the drug. A few germs are stronger than the others in their ability to resist the drug and they breed out while their weaker brothers are killed off by the drug. As a result, all of the germs in this particular patient can no longer be affected by drugs, and if he should infect a little baby, that baby's infection also would not be affected by the drug. It is for that reason that we must be careful not to give the drugs widely to everybody at one time, but to use them carefully under careful medical supervision. It is possible by the use of two drugs together, we may be able to control this problem of drug-resistant germs and we are doing that on the project here on the Reservation. I would now like to tell you what our purposes are and what we are doing at the moment.

When a new drug is developed in the laboratories or industry or any place in the country, it is brought to us. . . . We then make very careful studies at the New York Hospital as to whether this drug can be given to patients. We give it to patients there at the New York Hospital and we study its effect on the patient and its safety; whether it is safe to administer this drug to patients, and we do all that in the New York Hospital, and not here on the Reservation. Once its safety is proven, as was the case with the first drug we talked about and the second drug—and we have some more coming along—we then bring them to the Reservation for treatment of the proper types of tuberculosis. In that way, we have, here on the Reservation, units which were the very earliest safe treatment of tuberculosis—they were started the earliest of any place in the world. The results from this activity on the Reservation have been already very far flung. They have been appreciated far around the world. Last July, the Committee of the British Government appointed to study what they should do about the treatment of tuberculosis, requested and obtained a visit from one of our team with the very x-rays from Tuba City, Winslow, and Ganado with the case records, and they were presented to the Committee in London to allow them to make their decision. By having this activity here on the Reservation, you are not, and we are not, taking care of everybody with tuberculosis within a year, but what you are doing is insuring that when the patients are brought to the hospital, the patients with tuberculosis are in a position to get the most up-to-date treatment it is possible to give at any place because of the fact that you are sharing and contributing to make that treatment up-to-date. That ends my report, and I just wish to again take this opportunity to thank you on behalf of my associates and myself for this chance to report to you on this enterprise, this joint enterprise you have so generously supported.

In reading through the minutes of this meeting, one is struck with the theme of joint participation. The outsiders and the recipients of the new technology *together* are finding a new way of meeting the people's health needs. In their opening words, the Cornell doctors acknowledged the financial support the Tribe had given this project.

This donation gave the Navajo leaders a vested interest in the innovation from the very start. So when the speaker from the New York team reported back to them on this occasion, he was able to acknowledge not only that financial support but also to stress the theme of joint activity. The phrases, "you are doing," "you are sharing" and the repetition of the phrase "joint enterprise" gave this top leadership confidence and an identity with the work which was most important in its success.

In asking the Cornell investigators to render a report to the Tribe as to how the funds were spent, the leaders of the Navajo *were asking for much needed feedback of information.* Such information, of course, is vital if there is to be understanding and more than just token participation by the recipients of new technology.

It is important to note the way in which this information was fed back to the Tribal Council. Everything that was said was interpreted into Navajo, as more than half of the Council had little or no understanding of the English language. The spokesman for the Cornell group prepared himself for this task consulting a linguist, Mr. Robert Young, who was not only well versed in the Navajo language but who, as a government official, was responsible to the Bureau of Indian Affairs for following what was said in Navajo on the floor of the Tribal Council.[7] The speaker was advised to avoid figures of speech which might make sense in English but not come through in Navajo. Furthermore, he was cautioned to make statements with as simple a structure as possible and to be careful to give the interpreter only one thought at a time, thus minimizing distortion.

When he delivered his speech, carefully worked out in advance and checked with care by Mr. Young, he did not resort to technical medical language but spoke much as a well-trained doctor would in explaining the complexities of disease to a patient. He never "talked down," was never patronizing and was always warm and sympathetic in attitude.

A third theme, important in any political context, but especially important in an approach to people in an underdeveloped area, was appeal to the emerging "national" pride of the people. ". . . These young children in Tuba City represented the *first patients in the world*. . . ." That same note was touched upon several other times. Further evidence that such pride exists among the Navajo may be noted when the resolution to give $10,000 of tribal money was mentioned. The Councilman who made the motion said, "We are the first people to get this drug."

A final point: The experiment was explained so that the Navajo Tribe could understand why some were given drugs and others not, and why drugs were combined and some used with surgery. This gave the Council a basis for understanding what was being done, and even if what he said was not understood by all, he acknowledged the Navajos' intelligence in a way that the simpler statement, "This is a complex matter that demands medical judgment" would not. Additionally, he indicated the limitations of the drugs and pointed up the failures. This honesty, as will be shown later, was appreciated by the medicine men who developed a close empathy with the physicians.

This growth of understanding between the physicians and the medicine men was well expressed by Manuelito Begay, a Tribal Councilman and leading singer. The occasion was a year later, February 1954, when the Cornell team reported back again to the Tribal Council. On that occasion Mr. Begay was the first to speak and he said, in part:

> Last fall the doctors asked the medicine men how they treated the sick people and we came to meet with them and I was delegated to explain how we go about treating various illnesses of our people, as to tuberculosis treatment and all the various treatments, and we soon agreed and came to the point that we at least could understand one another and, since then, the doctors began to recognize the

medicine men among the Navajo people. . . . By understanding each other to help one another, we help the third party. . . .

One thing we do not agree on with the doctors and myself has been discussed and I do not fully agree with them on that, and that is the question of how tuberculosis is inflicted on a person. They tell me it is inflicted by a person coughing in your face—this is the way you get tuberculosis in your system. Right away I disagree with it. A person should not be that weak to susceptible to a man's cough. We have a definite point in mind and know of how a man gets to be afflicted with tuberculosis. One is the ceremony about the Wind Chant. If something goes wrong with that, it is tuberculosis and, if lightning strikes you, tuberculosis is the result. I just want to bring these things out so that we would agree on how tuberculosis afflicts the Navajo. Although we do not agree on this, we do recognize one another and that is at least a step forward.

The Cornell investigators replied. The speaker reviewed the 2 years of progress at Fort Defiance. Once more he went over the objectives of the project, and was careful to emphasize again that "every possible test of the safety of a new medicine is made in New York and in our hands before we introduce it to the area." He told of how successful the new drug (i.e., isoniazid) was in the treatment of miliary and meningeal tuberculosis: "As a result, no longer are the children dying from the acute forms of tuberculosis." He summed up the success of the program with, "We have been able to treat several hundreds of patients with tuberculosis of the lungs and in most cases have restored them to health."

He told of how in August the members of the Advisory Committee had "paid us a visit at the sanatorium." Then he went on to mention for the first time to the Council the direction for the future by saying that the goal was to perfect chemotherapy to the point that "the patients would spend only a short time in the hospital and then continue to take medicine at home." He told the Council of a field survey that had been made,[8] and again emphasized the importance of the Navajo contribution to the whole program.

. . . We have spent as much time as we can going around the area and seeing the people at their homes. We have obtained in that way advice and counsel from the people and various people have advised us as to how best to go about this problem of our mutual interest. For example: As I stand here before you, I can see Mr. Yellowman and Mr. John Lee Simpson, who gave us the privilege of having us in their homes on that trip. Many others are recognized whom we have consulted at one time or another and who have discussed these mutual problems with us. Once a method has been developed, as these methods have been, a method for treatment of tuberculosis, we do not keep that method a secret. Instead, we report the new method in the scientific journals and get it around to the doctors in the other hospitals off the Reservation in the off-reservation program, and indeed, all over the world. Thus, at the earliest possible moment, what we have established here, is communicated to others throughout the world so that their patients may benefit from it. When that is done in the scientific reports, it is clearly mentioned that these results, this new treatment, is developed from an enterprise jointly between the Navajo Tribe and Cornell University. It is mentioned at the same time that this enterprise is also generously supported by the Tribal funds. As a result, doctors all over the world have learned to look to this enterprise, among other sources, as one of the places where they will find the latest information on the treatment of tuberculosis.

Billie Bicenti, a leader from the eastern edge of the Reservation, who had attended some of the educational meetings on tuberculosis, rose to say:

You have heard from the two doctors who have been coming here for the last 2 years and I think you will agree that they have revealed to the eyes and minds of our people something that has been a miracle to us. We knew we were afflicted, but never knew to an extent what was ailing us and now these people have made it possible for us to see and realize that there is something that can be done about those things that have been harming us and killing us right along.

Educational conferences had been held not only for medicine men and members of various communities, but also a well planned symposium—the visit to which the Cornell speaker alluded in his speech—was conducted for the nine members of the Tribal Council's Advisory Committee. In August 1953, the medical investigators from the New York Hospital–Cornell Medical Center reviewed for the Committee a selected number of clinical cases. The men were introduced to the patients and a point was made of the infectious nature of the disease when gowns and masks were passed out to them before they entered the ward.

Those patients were pointed out who were practically well but who had been admitted to the hospital with extensive destructive lesions. They talked with a patient who was recovering from thoracoplasty.

Following that, the group assembled in the conference room and the x-ray films of various types of lesions from minimal to moderately advanced and far advanced were explained. These Navajo, viewing the film of the patient who had had surgery, saw that there was a regrowth of the periosteum—looking as though a rib had regrown in the area. This, as we shall see, made a deep impression on at least one of the Councilmen.

The doctors showed this group of leaders tubercle bacilli under the microscope and growing on culture, just as was the case with the citizens and leaders from Crown Point. Bottles of the drug isoniazid and pyrazinamide were shown in order to demonstrate the simplicity of this medication. Some of the Councilmen took notes on what the doctors said; all remained attentive throughout the long session. Mr. Robert Young played a most important mediating role as a bilingual between the doctors and the Councilmen and was in attendance in this session also.

The impact of that teaching session at Fort Defiance was vividly conveyed to the Council at large when Frank Bradley, a member of the Advisory Committee, spoke as follows:

> Mr. Chairman and Members of the Council: I want to make a brief remark on the report made by the two doctors from New York. It is true that the Advisory Committee did visit the Fort Defiance Sanatorium and we saw pictures of how the various treatments were given to our Navajo people. Not all of them receive the same treatment. Some received the new drugs, others have pieces of their lungs cut off and, when doing so, they have to get in there and remove the ribs of our Navajo people. When you realize the job here, it just makes you wonder how could a person be cut up like that with something taken out of their body and still live. Our lack of knowledge would indicate there is no other way to live. He surely has to die, but not so in this case, but how would a man live without ribs? That was a mystery to us until we saw with our eyes what was going on in the Sanatorium when these people were pointed out and they said: "So-and-so was operated on and so many ribs were taken out" and the patient admitted it was done and we were told at that time when you cut out a man's rib, you naturally leave the cartilage in there and it works on the same basis as a twig on a tree. You take it out and put it in a place with some moisture and even though the twig had no moisture, it would grow. Just so they leave the covering of the rib, it will grow back. In order for you to

believe what is being done by these doctors here, which is something hard to believe until you see it with your own eyes . . . I would urge you Councilmen to visit these hospitals. Seeing is believing and what you see with your own eyes you surely believe and that is what we saw over there and the people were very happy that they had gone through that in the way of getting their health back. They say: "Surely I was scarred up, but I am back as a man or woman and I am thankful I came here for treatment and will be home with my people shortly," and I want to express here that we are both appreciative and thankful that we were able to do a small part to make this possible for our Navajo people. I wonder if there is any money left that the work may continue and I want to say that we utilize that money that we talked about yesterday in regard to radio broadcasting, and utilize that $10,000 to do again our share in keeping the treatment and work of these doctors going. That is my Motion. I want to grant another $10,000 to these doctors so that they will continue this treatment to our people.

The spokesman for the Cornell group did not limit his educational endeavor to just what was going on at Fort Defiance but again, by using the device of informing a few, he was able to convey understanding of the broader aspects of the research to the Navajo Council—that is, the laboratory work at the New York Hospital, and the clinical investigations in which these same drugs were being used on patients from a 20th century urban environment. Mr. Coho, Tribal Councilman from Ramah, Mr. Maurice McCabe, Tribal Treasurer, and Mr. Sam Akeah, Chairman of the Tribe, were invited to visit the clinics, wards and laboratories of the New York Hospital. Mr. Akeah reported back to the Council about that visit.

When we went over to visit that city, we found they were working in a large building, real tall, 38 stories high or possibly more and we found out that all the work going on was not confined to tuberculosis but other diseases also treated and whatever was found to be useful, is open to various hospitals all over the country and we found out too, that doctors were being trained in this institution. The new drugs were tried on animals before being used on human beings—whether a dog, squirrel, or other animals there. One thing that was brought home to our understanding was the fact that the doctor said a dog was injected with the drug and the doctor did not know what effect it would have and possibly, before very long, it might kill the dog but, the next morning when you see that dog, he is one of the most friendly creatures you have ever seen. He is really friendly. That is the statement made to us over there.

One of the mysteries over there is whether the people did not know how to finish a building but they keep on putting stories on top of one another. They do not seem to quit. When we put one story on, we think we have accomplished a great deal. I do not know whether they are swallow people, because swallows always go for the high spots. The tall buildings are as tall as from here to Shiprock. There is no end to tall buildings in that area and it remains a mystery as to why people congregate to live in a place like that. You cannot see very far on account of the haze. There is plenty of water and plenty of boats in the harbor but what really took our eye is that there were so many tall buildings in New York City.

Since 1955, the United States Public Health Service has made tremendous progress in terms of hospital expansion and new construction, development of field clinics, construction of first-class housing for health personnel, the addition of physicians and nurses in the hospital and field program, and the assignment of experienced and seasoned hospital and field administrators. The farsighted planning of the top level Public Health Service people in conjunction with the Tribal leaders, particularly the Tribal Health Committee chaired by Mrs. Annie Wauneka, has also been gratifying.

Several universities were called upon to help develop field programs and the research essential to a broad program in preventive medicine. One of the greatest needs was in the area of health education. The Department of Public Health Education, School of Public Health of the University of North Carolina, on a contract basis, assumed responsibility for developing a multipurpose health education training program serving the Pueblo, Apache, and Southern Ute Reservations, including a few Navajo communities outside the main Reservation. A similar contract was written with the School of Public Health of the University of California for the development of a health education program on the Navajo Reservation.

It was at this time that Cornell University Medical College was engaged through contract with the government to carry out a pilot program. It was the implementing of this contract that resulted in the 7 years of work at Many Farms, Arizona.

4.

Introduction to the Community

The Many Farms–Rough Rock Community: Pilot Area for Health Development

At the time the contract between Cornell University Medical College and the United States Public Health Service was written, the Cornell medical team stated four objectives for the pilot program: (1) to define the proper concerns of a health program among a people such as the Navajo; (2) to find ways to adapt concepts of modern medicine for presentation in an acceptable form across formidable cultural and linguistic barriers without compromising essential medical standards in the process; (3) to study, insofar as possible, the biologic and social consequences of this innovation in terms of the community (and the outside participants); and (4) to see whether information of importance with respect to environment and disease in our present-day society can be obtained from study of a people who are emerging from a relatively primitive society and becoming part of the rural United States of today.

It was essential to establish a clinic remote from the general hospital at Fort Defiance in order to obtain the information basic to these four objectives. Such a clinic would enable the medical team working with a team of social scientists to investigate the total patterning of health and disease in a typical Navajo community. Furthermore, such a clinic could also be used for trying out new methods of extending modern medicine to the Navajo, as stated in the second objective. In fact, it would be necessary for the University research group to assume complete responsibility for the total health needs of the community if they were to have free rein in working toward the realization of all of these goals. This was quite in contrast to the earlier work of Cornell at Fort Defiance Sanatorium where the clinicians were concerned with only one line of investigation. Now the usual health services offered by the government at an outpatient clinic on the Navajo Reservation would have to be rendered; all research would be in addition to such service. As at other clinics on the Reservation, patients in need of hospitalization would be transported to Fort Defiance or one of the other hospitals. Likewise, women who preferred to have their babies delivered by a doctor rather than in the home environment would be taken to the hospital, but prenatal and postnatal examinations would be given at the clinic.

In short, in order to gain a better understanding of Navajo health and illness, what Doctor Dubos was later to call a "hospital without walls" was needed. Here the doctors, nurses, and social scientists would be living close to the Navajo home environment, thus enabling them to gain a better understanding of biologic and social processes in their natural setting.

Selection of the Community

A year and a half after it first mentioned to the Tribal Council the possibility of home treatment for tuberculous patients, the Cornell group once more consulted the Advisory Committee of the Tribal Council in the summer of 1955, and reviewed with them the advantage of studying means of further reducing this disease, as well as other diseases on the Reservation. He pointed out that a great deal of disease could be prevented if it was diagnosed early at a field clinic which would extend a service to the homes of the Navajo people. He proposed that the core of the group that worked at Fort Defiance tackle this problem. It was pointed out to them that all diseases would be treated at such a clinic, not just tuberculosis.

The problem of establishing a medical service on a pilot study basis in a localized area represented a new departure. Heretofore, the Cornell team had been identified with a central facility at the Fort Defiance Sanatorium which served the needs of the Reservation at large. Furthermore, it was evident that once the Council knew of plans for such a clinic, there would be a good deal of political pressure which might result in the location of the clinic in the community of an influential councilman, but in an area that was not necessarily suited to the research needs of the project.

The problem was presented by the Cornell investigators to the Advisory Committee, rather than to the full Council. They pointed out that the research group would like to select the best community for the pilot project as determined by various medical and social criteria, as well as certain practical considerations such as electric power, roads, water, and the availability of a nearby school, for much of the work would be with children, especially in preventive medicine. In addition, they explained in detail that the findings of the research group as to better ways of conducting a medical service in a remote area would be made available to the tribe, through their Health Committee headed by Mrs. Annie Wauneka, and such findings would also be known to the government health officials. The Advisory Committee granted their request.

In July 1955, an anthropologist (John Adair) was added to the medical team. He had had many years of experience on the Navajo Reservation, was well acquainted with both traditional Navajo culture and programs of technologic innovation made by the various government agencies in recent years.

The first decision which faced the anthropologist, working with his medical colleagues, was the selection of the community—a responsibility that had been delegated to them by the project director. Information was needed to answer the question posed by the medical team: Where will we find a community that is neither too "modernized" nor too "primitive"? In short, where would we find a "typical" Navajo community from which research findings might be generalized to a large number of other communities?

To the anthropologist, this called for the selection of a community that fell somewhere in the middle of the acculturation range. The social organization, economy, religion, housing, mode of transportation, in short, the total culture, had to be taken into consideration. This obviously ruled out the selection of a community in the northwest reservation where Navajo culture was the most primitive, and by the same token communities along the railroad, which had seen the most contact with the outside world. Communities such as Tuba City, Chinle, and Shiprock, which had been centers of government activity for many years, were also eliminated.

The whole reservation was surveyed with typicality given first priority. Secondarily, the physical facilities mentioned above had to be considered. After site visits at over a dozen communities, spread over most of the Reservation, five were finally selected as possible locations for the research project.

At this time an important decision was made by the survey team. Despite the fact that the project director had obtained a free hand in the selection of the project site, it was felt that representatives of the Health Committee should take part in the final decision. If a joint decision was made, that committee, representing the Council, would have a vested interest in the work of Cornell Medical College they would not have if the decision were solely that of the research group. Furthermore, there were many internal problems of politics and leadership that could not be assessed from the outside, and the advice of these leaders would help avoid pitfalls. This was in keeping with the participation of the Navajo in the earlier work at Fort Defiance. The anthropologist had seen many government projects fail because the Navajo themselves were not consulted.

Three of the communities were eliminated; one because it was off the reservation proper and there was a good deal of factionalism there; a second because it was in the home district of the Chairman of the Health Committee, and for this reason Mrs. Wauneka probably thought it an unwise choice. The third was eliminated because in the spring the population moved up onto the nearby mountain for summer pasture and would be difficult to reach from one clinic.

Eventually the Many Farms–Rough Rock district was selected (Map 2, inside back cover). This was a political constituency consisting of those two communities and Valley Store. Mrs. Wauneka favored this district as she had good political relations with its representative to the Tribal Council, Mr. Selth Begay. He was a Navajo man, about 40 years of age, with one year of college education, and a newcomer to tribal politics with a good record at both Window Rock and in his home community.

He lived at Many Farms, situated in the center of the reservation 14 miles to the north of the government community, Chinle, well known to many visitors to the Southwest as it is close to the famous National Monument, Canyon de Chelly.

The total district is 20 miles from north to south and 40 miles from east to west; there is a variety of terrain: a flat arid valley floor, bordered by rough badlands on the east, and mesa country on the west, covered with sage brush and sparse grass, and on the western edge piñon and juniper clad uplands surrounding the base of a tremendous mesa known locally as Black Mountain.

The natural terrain of the valley floor has been modified in the area immediately adjacent to Many Farms by a reservoir which impounds water from the Chinle Wash which runs northward, bisecting the valley. This water is used to irrigate a group of small farms. However, due to prolonged drought and administrative problems, this irrigation system had fallen into disrepair. Only a few farmers used the water for irrigating their corn patches and alfalfa fields. The elevation varies from approximately 7,000 feet at Rough Rock, on the western edge, at the base of Black Mountain, to 5,500 feet at Many Farms. There are no permanent streams in the area. Rainfall averages only 2 to 6 inches a year and often creates flash floods which drain into the Chinle Wash. The average annual temperature ranges from 40° to 60°F, but temperatures as low as 25°F in the winter to as high as 110°F in the summer have been recorded.

The population of this region is approximately 2,200. The families live in hogans (described in Appendix I) or in crudely built cabins. Four to five such household units make up a camp. Such camps are located close together in the area immediately surrounding Many Farms, but many miles apart in the outlying regions.

There are no villages in this district, but there is a considerable sense of belonging to a "community" such as Many Farms, Rough Rock, or Valley Store, 6 miles down the road leading to Chinle. Each of these three centers is marked by a trading post and a government elementary school. Additionally there are two Protestant missions, one at Valley Store and one at Rough Rock.

On September 16, 1955, the community of Many Farms was visited again, this time to announce the establishment of the clinic in that community. The meeting, called by Selth Begay, was held in the local irrigation office of the Bureau of Indian Affairs, the only structure in the community that would accommodate a sizable audience. Mrs. Wauneka had come out from Window Rock to introduce one of the Cornell doctors and his associates to the residents of the area. Her introduction was recorded and later translated:

> This Cornell doctor was at the Fort Defiance Sanatorium for several years. For a long time he has studied to find out how tuberculosis can be cured. Through study a number of medicines have been discovered which may either cure or prevent tuberculosis. These medicines can be taken by mouth or by a hypodermic needle. They can be given in the hospital or in the home. So far the only way a doctor can detect T.B. is by x-ray. We don't have that equipment close to our homes. As a result, many of our people have to be sent to faraway places where they are separated from their loved ones for as long as 2 or 3 years. People going away in this manner disrupt family life—the means of livelihood goes with them. The patients suffer loneliness, since they cannot speak English—so their suffering is twofold.
>
> Now an x-ray machine will be brought right here to the middle of the reservation—right in the midst of us. Then T.B. can be detected early. Home treatment will be given to patients by some of the finest doctors in the country. These medicines are going to be tested out here under the very worst conditions. Chinle Valley has a large population and is in the middle of the Reservation. It is accessible from all points. Some of you people live right here in the valley and others move up on to the mesa in the summer time and move back into the valley in the winter when it snows. A good deal of consideration has been given to other sites. But because of these factors Many Farms was thought the best. We members of the Tribal Council have discussed this clinic; we have considered all sides of the question and we have concluded that this is one of the best things being done for our people. So we are asking you for your cooperation.
>
> This clinic will not only be a T.B. clinic, it will also take care of other kinds of sickness from head colds to severe pneumonias. In some cases, if T.B. is not detected early enough it will not be treated here. These cases will be sent to the sanatoria. Because of the nature of the disease, often T.B. gets to a certain point so it has to be treated by rest, good food and fresh air. Such cases as that can't be treated under home conditions. That is the reason these patients will be sent away to the sanatoria. Then there are other cases which are in

the early stages—they will be treated right here at home. There are probably more of these cases which will not have to be sent away ... Perhaps there are unknown cases of T.B. which are spreading the disease among us. However, this is not only true in this valley but all over the Reservation.

Even among the white people there are cases of T.B. But they have reduced the number of cases considerably because they have put into effect such home treatment as we are going to try here, and because they have isolated those people with active cases. To a large extent this clinic is not an experiment—these methods have been tried elsewhere and shown to be very effective. T.B. can eventually be done away with. At first the clinic will be a small one, and later it may be enlarged. If it works well, some day there may be clinics like this all over the reservation.

One of the most important things about this project—as many jobs as possible will be given to Navajos.

Selth Begay had done a good job in getting the word around and talking up the possibility of such a clinic. The room was crowded with men, women, and babies from Many Farms and the adjacent communities of Rough Rock and Valley Store. One of its leaders, Atsidi Begay, was there, as was a delegate to the Council from Lukachukai, 20 miles to the east. Kenneth Dennison, a former patient at the tuberculosis sanatorium in Fort Defiance was in the front row. He had been especially invited by the research team to attend this meeting and had come down from his home at Round Rock. Kenneth had done a good deal of interpreting on the ward of the Fort Defiance Sanatorium and was the first Navajo to be hired on the project staff.

All the others were strangers. The older men wore moccasins, and their hair long, with a knot at the nape of the neck. The women were in velveteen blouses and colorful calico print skirts, ankle length in the traditional Navajo style, with Pendleton blankets over their shoulders. Some carried their babies on cradle boards. There were very few school girls in modern dress.

The traditional dress of Annie Wauneka—blanket over her shoulders, turquoise beads, long skirt, and velveteen blouse—belied her sophistication and excellent English. Selth Begay, too, presented a distinct contrast to the rest of the people with his fast nervous movements; he had a firm handshake for us, but like other Navajo who knew both worlds, he had a limp handshake in the traditional style for his constituents. Either Mrs. Wauneka or Mr. Begay could have been an articulate, effective, and dedicated leader in any American town, but each one lived a real Reservation life with feet well planted in their home communities, and both depended on their sheep and farms for part of their income.

Annie Wauneka had been able to convey the essential points to the community as she, more than any other Navajo, had a comprehensive knowledge of tuberculosis and its treatment. As we have learned, she had been educated in this subject by physicians and health educators for several years. Her contacts at the off-reservation sanatoria, where some 600 Navajo were hospitalized, also gave her a comprehensive knowledge of this disease and its effect on her people. Indeed, as her speech indicates, she had become very sophisticated as a layman in the problems of tuberculosis control and treatment and through her contacts with these physicians and others she was acquainted with the other major health problems of the Navajo. The Cornell investigators were thus aware of her grasp of the problem, but had taken the additional precaution of briefing her as to the nature of the service which the clinic would provide to the people in this area.

It should also be noted that tuberculosis had affected her own family. Her daughter had contracted the disease and had to be hospitalized far from home like the other Navajo. So she *felt*, as well as knew of, what she spoke, and personally shared the emotions of her audience.

Mrs. Wauneka was aware of the appeal of x-ray to the Navajo people. Going back to around 1940, the x-ray machine had become associated in the mind of the Navajo with success in treatment of this disease. Not that its use was well understood; in fact, many of the Navajo were of the impression that exposure to x-ray in itself cured the disease, and the more often you were x-rayed the healthier you became. Here, two deeply ingrained Navajo modes of thought are illustrated: (1) Post hoc, ergo propter hoc, a logical fallacy not, of course, confined to the Navajo but known to people everywhere, and especially prevalent among tribal peoples and societies as yet unexposed to scientific method; (2) the principle of spatial propinquity. One aspect of contagious magic which still influences Navajo behavior is that the part stands for the whole and possesses its power. By a related system of thought, contact is sought by the Navajo with the source of power (power in this case they construe as therapeutic power, i.e., the x-ray machine and the film). Acquainted with the folk beliefs of her people, as well as their views on modern medicine, she knew the positive appeal of this technology.

Also, she had the good sense to follow the age-old principle of good teaching: build upon what is positive, upon what the audience knows and accepts, rather than hitting negative cords of misunderstanding at the outset.

She went on to point up that this new home treatment relieved anxiety felt by all the people with members of their families away in distant sanatoria. Thus, she touched on a deeply *felt need* and one that had profound emotional appeal. Additionally she noted that the disruption of family life carried with it not only heartache, but economic deprivation, something again that these people well understood—a message which, of course, has meaning for poor people everywhere. Many Navajo were destitute when the male family head was unable to work for cash wages, or plant and harvest crops at home. Likewise, the children had to be sent to a relative when the female family head was hospitalized.

Dan Yazzie, Chairman of the local unit of Navajo government (see Appendix I), an older man wearing turquoise in his ears, spoke with great dignity—a dignity that the Navajo acquire as they grow to the age of respect among their own people. There was strength and force in his voice. He told of how his daughter had been ill, "her flesh was falling away"; she was taken to a distant hospital where the doctors used new medicine on her. "Now she has returned fat and healthy for the first time in many years." He spoke with pleasure of the prospect of a clinic being located in his community.

Kenneth Dennison, still emaciated from his long illness, was the last to speak.

> This doctor here saved my life. I had been working at the Navajo Saw Mill—but I refused to see the doctor. I felt worse and worse. Then I began to spit up blood. That was when I got scared—and I went into the sanatorium. He told me what would happen if I didn't go into the hospital for treatment. I would die. So I listened to him and followed his orders. I took the medicine you have heard about. I did just what he told me to—so here I am alive and able to tell you this story.

The meeting was closed with thanks to those who attended, and assurance that we would report what we had learned to our colleagues in New York.

Selth Begay continued to hold the interest of the community in the project and in turn the medical team was in frequent contact with him, reviewing the plans as they developed. The Cornell team consulted with him over blueprints of the clinic which had been drawn up in Albuquerque by a private builder.

At one meeting, held some months later, the public health nurse, Bernice Loughlin, was introduced. She had an easy manner with the Navajo and had had many years of experience on the Western Reservation.

The Cornell physician told the group of her ongoing work.

This nurse is now training the Navajo men and women who will work helping the sick people in both the clinic and out in their homes. We are also training a Navajo who knows how to run the x-ray in the things he will need to know in order to help the doctor in the laboratory. All of these people will come out and live at Many Farms when the clinic is opened.

We know how hard it is for the patient and the doctor to understand each other because of the two different languages they speak. We hope to overcome this in a number of ways. First, by having as many Navajo on our staff as possible who will be able to talk to the patients in their language and to the doctors in theirs. The clerk at the front desk, the Navajo assistants to the nurses, the laboratory technicians—all of them will be selected so they can speak both languages. Even now a Navajo nurse, Pauline McKinley, is helping . . . train the Navajo assistants. She is able to do this because she is a nurse herself and understands the ideas [which the public health nurse in charge] wants to teach. So they are taught in two languages—their own language and that of the doctors and nurses.

During the preceding months the core of the Navajo staff had been recruited. The first to be hired, as mentioned before, was Kenneth Dennison. The Navajo who had been mentioned for x-ray and laboratory training was Deswood Benally who had also been a patient at Fort Defiance. During these months, when the plans for the clinic and the staff housing were being developed, he was trained at the Lovelace Clinic in Albuquerque. At this time, the first two health visitors were also recruited and their training commenced at Fort Defiance.

The first resident physician recruited for Many Farms was a

temporary addition to the staff—for a period of 6 months. This doctor was serving a 2-year assignment with the Indian Division of the United States Public Health Service and came to us from Idaho, where he had been on duty in a migratory labor program. He spent a great deal of his time at Fort Defiance, where he worked closely with the public health nurse and Pauline McKinley, the Navajo nurse, in the training of the health visitors.

Many plans were made during these first months when the medical director of the Cornell project came out from New York for one week every 30 days. The land for the clinic site had to be approved by the government officials in the Bureau of Indian Affairs and by tribal officers at Window Rock, automobiles purchased, and the whole clinic, planned in New York, had to be constructed and furnished.

The rapidity with which all of this was accomplished astonished the Navajo at Many Farms, who were accustomed to the slow movement of the government. While we could, as outsiders, understand why the government took much longer to act, because of red tape and the nature of government contracts and regulations, from the local community's point of view, Cornell had produced a building almost by magic.

The dedication of the clinic on May 7 was a gala affair. Over 1,000 Navajo from all over the Chinle Valley and adjoining areas appeared and joined in the barbecue prepared by some of the Navajo women in the area. The project directors came out from New York City for the occasion.

Dan Yazzie was there in another role—as a medicine man who knew the House Blessing Songs from Beauty Way, one of the most sacred of the Navajo ceremonials. We had asked Selth Begay if it would be appropriate to have a medicine man bless the clinic, and his response was positive. He made the essential arrangements.

The waiting room of the clinic was filled on all sides. In the middle was Dan Yazzie, assisted by Yazzie Begay, also a singer.

In this case history (its chronologic story beginning with the work of the Cornell investigators at Fort Defiance described in Chapter 3) of how medical technology was brought to the grass roots level on the Navajo Reservation, a number of points should be emphasized.

The medical innovators were working in an area of great need. "We knew we were afflicted, but never knew to an extent what was ailing us," as Billie Bicenti had put it. Thus the stage was set for translating this felt need—essential for any program of change—into action. Additionally, the Navajo were favorably predisposed to modern medicine as a result of the great success in the use of antibiotics introduced only a few years before. The Navajo are slow to join in the support of a program based on glib generalities (often essential in getting any program underway), but quick to make up their minds when the results are demonstrated. Thus, as was exemplified by Sam Akeah, when he spoke to the Council of his trip to New York Hospital, for the Navajo, seeing was believing. The elaborate technology of medical research and the precautions used to safeguard patients taking a new drug could only partially be conveyed by word of mouth. For the Council at large, the eyewitness account of their own Chairman did much to build up confidence in the research.

In all probability, the reason there was never any dissension among the members of the Tribal Council, never any rumor that the "Navajo were being used as guinea pigs" was because the broader context of the medical work was conveyed by these means, and the leaders were able to see for themselves that the white man was using the same mode of treatment in his own community as he was using in theirs. It should be noted that the Navajo were very sensitive to the results of research efforts. Only 10 years earlier the government, in its attempt to control soil erosion, had set up many experiments which were linked with a livestock reduction program, a program that was carried through, but without sufficient understanding of its objectives at the grass roots level and without sufficient participation by the people. "Research," "demonstration," and "experiment" were loaded words which had to be used with caution, and always in context.

The pride of a newly emergent people is of tremendous importance in motivating them to take action. Only a few years earlier, the Navajo had been ashamed of the fact that many of their young men had been kept out of military service because of tuberculosis. Further, others were shunned by employers who knew of the high incidence of this disease among these Indians. Self-pity often sets in among people isolated in an underdeveloped economy out of the mainstream of national life. In this case, they no doubt felt that they were closer to the mainstream when they were made aware that they were participating in a program that involved people in another part of the country, victims of the same disease who were a part of the same experiment.

Basic to the success in gaining support for research in tuberculosis chemotherapy at Fort Defiance, as well as cooperation from the Tribe and the local community in the establishment and development of the clinic at Many Farms, was the way in which communications were handled. Scientific success from the biologic point of view, in order to assume the proportions of a true *innovation,* must be accepted socially and culturally.

Very often technology does not take hold because there is too great a conceptual gap between the innovating group and the ultimate recipients for whom the technology is designed. The practice of medicine, by its very organization, is so structured that there is a flow of information all the way from the clinical investigator at urban medical centers through a series of intermediaries: resident physicians, interns, nursing supervisors, nurses, and on down to the patient. In our urban society, as medicine is practiced, technical knowledge is passed from one level of practitioner to the next, and is reformulated and simplified to meet the level of understanding of the next group.

This is so commonplace in our society that we do not stop to note that the knowledge of the disease which goes with the technology is scaled down by each person concerned with medical practice, so that ultimately the "message" that was highly technical in the first place is communicated to the patient in very simple form. In the particular illustration at hand, important agents in this scaling down process were the Navajo interpreters who, knowing something of the medical concepts of both languages, were able to cross the language barrier to the patient successfully.

When the ultimate target for information about new medical technology is the community, we find it is passed along through a series of laymen who are not personally concerned with the practice of the technology but have an interest in its effect. While the route of information from the medical innovators to the patient is predetermined—"built-in"—to the practice of medicine, the route for such information out to the community poses a problem that the physician, especially the young physician, is not trained to solve.

This efficient vertical flow of information from top to bottom is so integral to the practice of medicine that it is apt to be taken for granted by those professionally involved. The young and inexperienced physician is unaware of the fact that a primitive society also has its structure and levels of knowledge through which communication must flow, and that comparable scaling down of information is essential in reaching the community level of understanding. Upon first entry into an underdeveloped area, he tends to address the same message to the political elite and to the rank and file, to the acculturated and unacculturated. As a result, the message about new technology does not reach its target and the people become hopelessly confused.

In the case under analysis, however, such confusion was avoided; the information was deliberately passed out to the political leaders, through the most skilled medical interpreter in the entire area, and then filtered down through lesser leaders, and ultimately this lay education reached the people of the community of Many Farms.

The top strata of this pyramid, the Tribal Chairman and his Secretary-Treasurer, had greater sophistication in the white man's world than the members of the Advisory Committee. As a group they, in turn, were better versed in English than the Tribal Council at large. In effect the educated Tribal Councilman was a link between the technologic innovator and the uneducated Councilman who in turn was a link between the educated leader and the local leader in the community. The well educated Navajo who has had considerable contact with outsiders, as have the leaders of the Tribal Council, shares not only the language of the outsider but many of his values. He is able to communicate effectively because of this identity brought about by the significant overlap in cultures. In turn, the members of this educated political elite are able to pass on information to those less educated than they, for they share many native ways with them. They can communicate knowledge of new medical technology in a meaningful way, again because of cultural sharing between them. In this way, knowledge flows out to the less educated people distant from the Tribal capital.

Thus, the highly acculturated Tribal leaders of the Advisory Committee formed a link between the Cornell group and the Council as a whole. Their level of acculturation placed them in the position of mediators and they were able to pass on knowledge to less educated councilmen who would have been at a loss to understand what the innovator said. By the same token, Annie

Wauneka and Selth Begay were able to form a useful bridge for conveying understanding out to the community leaders.

In effect, the medical team had, through its educational work, enabled lay information about this innovation to be passed up and down through the political organization of Navajo society in a way comparable to the communication of technical information in medical channels in our society.

Finally, it should be noted that in passing on knowledge about tuberculosis, the doctors, just as they do in their own medical teaching, relied on the cooperation of the patients themselves in educating the lay leaders, both on the top political level and in the community itself. The demonstrated recovery of health was most convincing for these laymen who might otherwise have doubted the word of an outsider.

In the preceding chapters, the broad background essential for the understanding of this pilot program in Navajo public health has been presented. The general and specific cultural framework as the context of analysis has been given; Navajo belief and behavior with respect to health has been presented in contrast to the physician's assessment of the health needs of these Indian people. We have seen how the Navajo have modified their behavior as a result of exposure to the superior medical technology of the white man. We have followed a change in the attitude and the behavior of physicians toward the Navajo methods of curing, and the realization that insofar as curing was central to their religious belief, such rituals had spiritual and curative value.

All innovations must be seen in cultural context, but, as has been pointed out, culture is in a constant state of change. That of course is true of the culture of the inventor, the innovating society, as well as the culture of the recipient society. Innovation which is, in final analysis, diffusion of knowledge—a classic problem in the study of anthropology—may take place at one time but be resisted at another. It is highly unlikely that Cornell University would have been as successful as it was at Fort Defiance if the technologic breakthrough that led to chemotherapy for tuberculosis had come about 15 years earlier when the Navajo were strongly resisting technology sponsored by the government. The time would not have been ripe for this innovation.

Finally, we have seen that innovation may depend on an awareness of the total *gestalt,* an awareness of when the time is right.

It is then that an innovator with a politician's sensitivity to timing and to the moods of a people is of paramount importance. The physician dealing with biologic change has one great advantage over the agriculturist, the educator, or the inventor of new technology in other fields. The demonstration takes place within the person of the potential recipient himself. If disease is arrested and the physician is sensitive to the emotional needs of his patient, then a favorable climate of opinion, so important for the acceptance of a new technology, may be built up very quickly. The arresting of pain and anxiety provides an immediate and strong motivation almost unknown in the introduction of other technologies, so that the conversion of biologic change to social cultural change can be relatively rapid if it is properly guided. But the physician who is insensitive to the patient and his needs, which are not only psychologic and religious but economic and political, may pass up a chance for introducing new medical practices, or indeed may even build up resistance. We have followed the way in which the climate of opinion was fostered by a group of Cornell physicians. The new drugs had been proven successful and the patients at Fort Defiance expressed their confidence in the new medicine to their political leaders. It was this use of political means that then diffused the knowledge throughout the society and what had heretofore been acceptance of a new means of treating tuberculosis by a few patients, became universally accepted by the Navajo leaders. Moreover, with the formulation of these goals, additional innovation was anticipated. The question, then, was: How far could the biologic change—arrest of tuberculosis—be used in bringing about sociocultural change in the Navajos' own environment? Motivating individual patients in the controlled environment of the hospital, which was the world of the doctor, was one thing. But devising new means for gaining acceptance for a total medical program beyond tuberculosis was another. Further, new forms of services and new means of bringing modern medicine would carry a program for an unknown length of time. But basic biologic change, additional medical breakthrough in other areas of the treatment of disease might be essential for gaining total acceptance of this new program of research among the Navajo in other communities as well as in the Public Health Service community.

1   At Crown Point, New Mexico upon seeing the
tubercle bacillus, Medicine Man Manuelito Begay said,
"I have seen the enemy of my people." *Courtesy of
Milton Snow.*

2   Annie Wauneka, chairperson of the Navajo Tribal
Health Committee. *Courtesy of John Collier, Jr.*

3   Physicians meet with Tribal officials. Kurt W.
Deuschle, M.D. (standing); Annie Wauneka (seated on
right). *Courtesy of Milton Snow.*

4   The Cornell physicians address the Navajo Tribal
Council. *Courtesy of Milton Snow.*

5   Drs. Kurt W. Deuschle and Walsh McDermott explain
medical treatment for tuberculosis to members of the
Tribal Council. *Courtesy of Milton Snow.*

6   Kenneth Dennison, a patient at the Fort Defiance
Sanitorium, talking to the advisory committee. *Courtesy
of Milton Snow.*

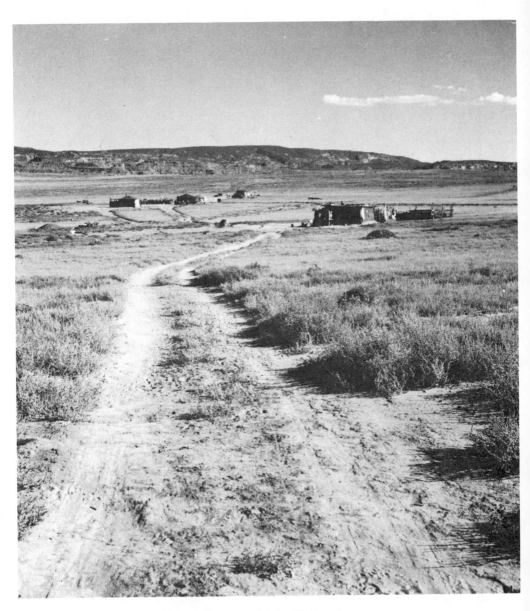

7 A Navajo camp. *Courtesy of John Collier, Jr.*

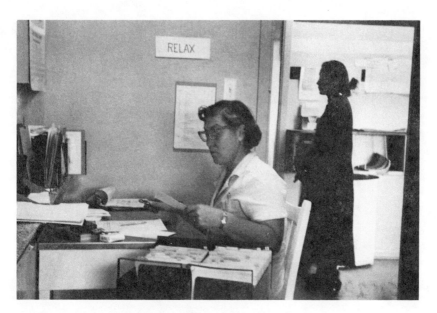

8 Bernice Loughlin, Public Health Nurse and Director
of the Health Visitor Program. *Courtesy of John Collier, Jr.*

9 Kenneth Dennison at work on the camp file of
medical charts. *Courtesy of John Collier, Jr.*

10   The clinic at Many Farms. *Courtesy of John Collier, Jr.*

11 Housing of the clinic staff. *Courtesy of John Collier, Jr.*

12   The clinic waiting room. *Courtesy of John Collier, Jr.*

13   Health Visitor Bess Tuchin leads a patient into the examining room. *Courtesy of John Collier, Jr.*

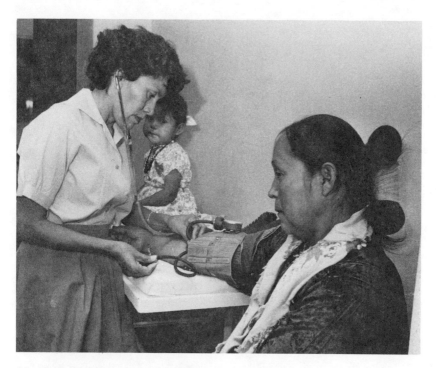

14   Bess Tuchin taking a blood pressure reading.
Courtesy of John Collier, Jr.

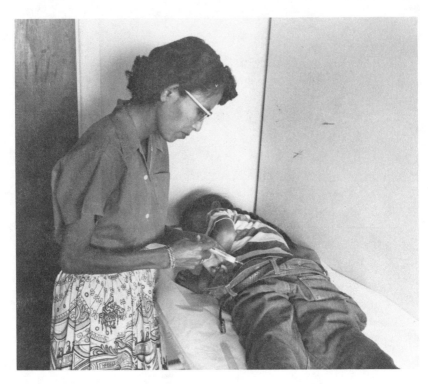

15   Health Visitor Ruth Anderson administering an
antibiotic. *Courtesy of John Collier, Jr.*

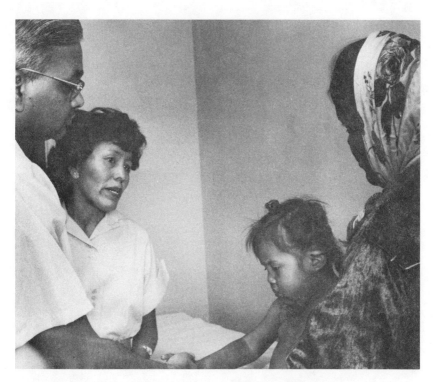

16   Bess Tuchin interpreting for Dr. Ramadwar, a visiting
physician from India.

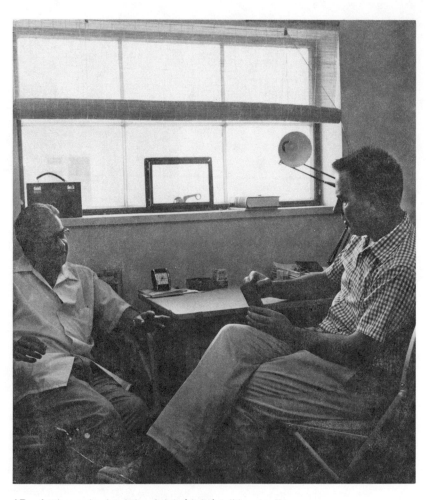

17   Anthropologist John Adair (right) talking to Dr.
Ramadwar. *Courtesy of John Collier, Jr.*

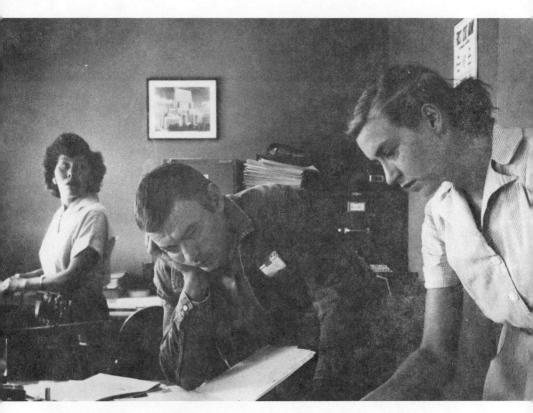

18 Anthropologist Don Rieder and Public Health Nurse
Ellen Mansell working on the camp file of medical
charts. *Courtesy of John Collier, Jr.*

19   X-ray and Medical Technician Deswood Benally.
Courtesy of John Collier, Jr.

20   Dr. Eugene Farley examining a girl with impetigo.
Courtesy of John Collier, Jr.

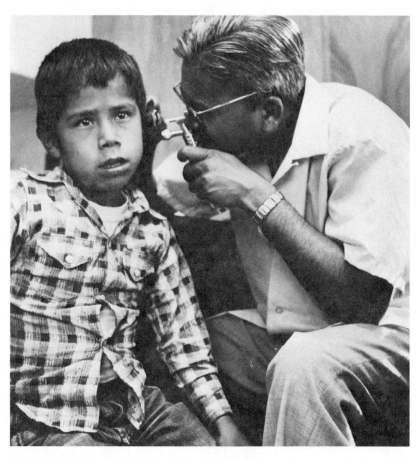

21 Dr. Ramadwar examining a boy with otitis medea.
Courtesy of John Collier, Jr.

22 Health Visitor examining the ear of a Navajo boy.
Courtesy of John Collier, Jr.

23a–c   Health Visitor Frank Ben George and the anthropologist Don Rieder interviewing a patient at her camp. *Courtesy of John Collier, Jr.*

5.

Training the Navajo Health Workers

Communicating Across the Cultural Boundary

When Scott Preston, the Vice Chairman of the Tribal Council, addressed a group of doctors at Fort Defiance, he said:

> There is a missing bridge between the Navajo patients and the [white] doctors. The bridge is adequate interpretation. The only way that you doctors can put across your message is through better interpretation.

> Do not rely on an interpreter who has had only a fifth or sixth grade education to translate a difficult message. It is most important that the interpreter have a good attitude for he must be pleasant and accommodate both parties, the doctor and the patient.

One of the very few Navajo registered nurses (Pauline McKinley), who had had many years of experience at the Fort Defiance Hospital, was asked for her opinion about this statement of Mr. Preston's.

> What he says is true. That happens all of the time—inaccurate interpretation. Several years ago a doctor right here at the best hospital on the reservation was in need of an interpreter. All of the

"blue girls"—they are the assistants on the wards to the doctors and nurses—were busy. So he called on a kitchen helper. Her English was just as good as those other girls, so he thought she could do the job. He asked her to interpret to his patient and she was too embarrassed to say no, so she went ahead and followed orders. She told the patient that she would have to have her appendix removed, while in reality the doctor had ordered a routine x-ray of the chest.

Medical diagnosis, patient management, and prevention of disease through immunization all depend on efficient and dependable communication between the doctor and the patient (and the nurse and the patient). These Navajo leaders had pointed this out in their own words. Indeed, it would not be possible even to *define* the patterns of health and disease at Many Farms without a reliable communication network.

In addition to this central concern, there were related problems in the administration of a health program that had to be solved if our program, or any future government programs, were to be a success. The expanse of the Reservation is enormous. Because the Navajo live in scattered homesites, it is necessary to use different logistics from those customarily employed in our own society, where most people live in tightly knit communities. Often it would take a highly trained public health nurse a full day to visit one or two hogans. She depended on a combination driver-interpreter to get her there and back and to put her in verbal touch with the patients in the hogans. Severe limitations as to the availability of trained public health nurses prevented the government field program from expanding to its full potential. Additionally, the rapid turnover caused by the hardships of living on the reservation, often many miles from other "anglos," aggravated the situation. There would *never* be enough trained "anglo" personnel to service the needs of the whole reservation, with its highly mobile and rapidly expanding population.

We reasoned that if Navajo assistants to the public health nurses were trained so they could do much of the routine work under direction, then the services of one such nurse could be increased three- or fourfold. The exact number, the type of training, and the degree to which the Navajo could be successfully taught to do such work were all subjects for careful study. Evaluation would follow and be turned over to the government, which would then be faced with the decision of the practicality of such personnel for their ongoing program.

We did not plan to develop a program of training "feldshers" or amateur physicians. We pointed out to the government authorities that we were convinced that the *health visitors,* as we call them, should at all times be under the supervision of the public health nurse. In fact, at a later date radiotelephones were installed in the cars, which enabled the health visitors to call back to the clinic and receive authoritative directions for dealing with situations which they were unqualified to handle on their own. It was apparent that if the program was to be a success, those tasks which occupied most of the working day of the public health nurse had to be turned over to her Navajo assistants so that she could greatly enlarge the area of her district by giving such supervision.

What were some of these tasks which took so much of her time? First of all, as pointed out, getting to the hogan and back. There would be no need for her to accompany each health visitor if she and the physician could *trust* him or her to do the tasks she herself would perform in the hogan. Broadly speaking, this fieldwork consisted of: tuberculosis control, administering and reading tuberculin skin tests, getting Navajo to come to clinic for roentgenographic and other laboratory work-up, well-child immunization in the school-health programs, follow-up medications after clinic treatment, and emergency nursing procedures.

The bridge of better communications between the doctor and patient, referred to by Mr. Preston, had to be built. But by going one step further and training the Navajo to render simple nursing procedures, much more could be accomplished. There was also the need of building a bridge between the clinic and the community. We have seen in Chapter 3 how the Cornell doctors used mediators for passing on knowledge when the conceptual gap was too great. Thus, the Advisory Committee of the Tribal Council performed that function between them and the full Council. The health visitors were needed for the same purpose; not only for better linguistic reformulation between doctor and patient in the clinic, but between the clinic and the patients and their families in the hogans.

The Cornell group (doctors, public health nurse, and anthropologist) all felt that the Navajo were perfectly capable of rendering all of these nursing procedures. Their faith in the Navajo and in the soundness of the program was attested to by their willingness to assume legal responsibility for the services performed by these health visitors.

The anthropologist knew that reluctance to transfer responsibility to Navajo working under government supervision was one of the principal things which held back technologic development in the agricultural and educational fields. However, in the last 10 years, wise government leaders, with faith in the political and administrative potential of the Tribal Council, had developed outstanding ability on the top level of Tribal leadership. Now responsibility had to be put to the test in the medical field, and on the community level, if real progress were to be made in health.

The Washington officials had demonstrated their faith in the Cornell team by giving them *carte blanche* in the Many Farms–Rough Rock area. We were free to conduct an experiment in medical innovation which the government itself, with its strict Civil Service codes, could not do. With this support behind us, we, as newcomers to the scene, were able to pass on to the Navajo Washington's faith in us.

Selection of Trainees

When we consulted Annie Wauneka and Paul Jones, the Chairman of the Navajo Tribal Council, about the selection of Navajo for this training, they told us not to choose people who were too young. "The Navajo needs a few gray hairs in his head to gain the respect of his elders," was the way the Chairman had put it to us. Additionally, those Navajo who were fully mature and had children of their own would be better able to understand the problems of parents with sick children.

From what level of education was it best to select? If we recruited high school graduates who had had work experience in an "anglo" community, communications between the doctor, or the nurse, and the health visitor would be greatly facilitated. Keeping accurate medical records would require knowledge of written English as well as the spoken language. Such Navajo would have those skills. But this ability to communicate with the professionals did not necessarily mean that such a person would be able to "accommodate the patient," as Mr. Preston had put it. In fact, the Navajo who had had a high school education and worked away from the

Reservation would, of necessity, have been away from home for long periods of time. In all likelihood, he would have forgotten a good deal of his native tongue. Robert Young had told us that when the returned student came back to the Reservation, he spoke to his parents and relatives with the facility of a child of only 12 or less. Often it took years for the individual to relearn enough of his own language to be effective in dealing with the older monolinguals. Additionally, he would be suspect by those elders as one who, after many years of living on the outside, had forgotten the ways and the religion of his own people.

Another practical reason for not selecting high school graduates who had lived away from their own people for a long time was that all of them were readily employed upon application at Window Rock or in other centers of government and Tribal activity. It would be hard to compete with these offices which offered many more of the comforts of our civilization that the young educated Navajo had come not only to enjoy, but to expect. There would be a minimum of such comforts at Many Farms, 100 miles from town.

As our first two trainees, we decided to select Navajo who we knew had had continuity of experience on the Reservation, even though they might not have facility in the English language. We could teach them that; but we couldn't teach the acculturated Navajo, who had these skills in English, how to get along with his own people in his own language and follow the dictates of traditional kin and clan relations. Without that ability, we would simply be introducing shadows of ourselves into the community, puppets in whom the Navajo had no faith. They would be just another version of what, in local parlance, was an "agency Indian" interested in promoting his own welfare, but too far over on the "white man's side" to know how to reach his own people.

There was another important criterion in the selection of these health workers—their emotional *set* with respect to disease. There had to be a positive motivation to work with the sick. The problem was not essentially different from that in our own society in the recruitment of health workers. The doctors and nurses, we felt, were the best judges of this motivation, so they looked among their own patients for potential trainees on the program.

All the trainees except one had had an extended period of hospitalization for pulmonary tuberculosis. Former tuberculosis patients were selected initially because Cornell physicians had had long-term acquaintance with them during their hospitalization and therefore could evaluate their basic interest and intelligence. Furthermore, previous hospitalization for tuberculosis helped these individuals understand the goals of medical care. Their own chronic illness had required their active cooperation and patience in order to complete successful treatment. They were therefore able to understand patients' reactions to diagnoses and the physicians' therapeutic plans. During the course of their own illness, they had found no quick or magic cure and had adhered to a long regimen of drugs, bedrest, and, in some instances, surgery before a cure was effected. They could testify that they had recovered from tuberculosis by following the doctors' orders and taking drugs. This, of course, did more to help the program get established than any amount of information on the germ theory, which was beyond the level of the Navajo educational experience.

The subjective knowledge of this paticular disease, and the motivation to help their fellow Navajo who suffered from it, was additionally important as this met the felt need of the Navajo leaders, who now thought of tuberculosis control as their number one public health problem.

Ruth Anderson had been such a patient, and so had Frank Ben George. But first, what had been the nature of their lives prior to hospitalization?

Frank Ben George was born in 1919 close to Piñon in a remote and relatively inaccessible section of the Reservation. He was the oldest of a family of 10 children. Neither of the parents was able to speak English. At the age of 6, he was sent away to a government boarding school. After a year and a half, he was shifted to another school, and then another. Summers were spent working on government projects, first on a Civilian Conservation Corps job, then on a soil conservation project. At the age of 14, he was needed at home to herd sheep (the accepted pattern for the oldest child in the family, especially in the years when Frank was growing up and the need for education was not recognized by Navajo parents). A series of off-reservation jobs followed: 2 years with the Ordinance Department of the United States Army, at the munition depot near Gallup, New Mexico; a few months in the Army at the very end of the war; and several years' work following discharge in a government warehouse in Los Angeles. Marriage had been early, at the age of 16, which is young even by Navajo standards. His wife and child did not follow him to off-reservation jobs and separation followed. He was married a second time, and this woman bore him four children, all but one of whom died in infancy. He went off Reservation again, this time to pick sugar beets in Idaho. In 1947, he returned to his home near Piñon. At that time he apprenticed himself to a medicine man (a fact that was revealed only after Frank had been hired and working at Many Farms for over a year). He learned *Apache Windway* from a singer by the name of Yellowhair.

I usually go around when he does the singing. We talk together and he teach me how the singing goes. It took me three years to learn. Then I became a medicine man.

Some time during the years off Reservation Frank acquired tuberculosis.

It started with a big cold and pneumonia. It was the second time I got pneumonia. The first time I had it was when I was a boy. I had a sing over me. It made me a little well. Then just coughing. Then diarrhea and fever. Then felt O.K. Went out on horseback. I was singing myself that time, *Apache Windway.* Also *Evil Way,* just learning. I went off to a *Squaw Dance* and nine night sings. My family got a medicine man in and he did a *Shooting Chant.* My pain in the shoulder stopped. But the cough continued.

I was pretty thin and tired. Not doing anything. My brother told me to try *Peyote Way.* Went over to one of those camps one night. It was about 30 miles north of my home at Low Mountain. That man he did that for me. Next day he told me: I did not know that you had T.B.! Go to the hospital. Have x-ray, have blood test. You might find out what was wrong. I tried Peyote on you but it won't do any good. They can only help you at the hospital.

The next morning I went to Keams Canyon. I had blood in my stool that time. And in my sputum. I had an x-ray there. The doctor was really impressed. Had a lot of white stuff in that x-ray. Told me to go to the hospital. I went back to my home until they had a bed available. In seven days had a bed. Went to the Fort [Defiance], where I was hospitalized in the tuberculosis sanatorium.[1]

This was a life experience typical of thousands of Navajo men who were growing up in the '20s and '30s. There had been some years of formal schooling, but Frank, like so many others, had dropped out to assist his family during the period of the depression when work relief everywhere made jobs easy to come by. Then the war came, and off-reservation employment, and marriage, so he never did get back to school. The years back and forth from home to one school after another, even at a tender age, was also typical of these Navajo. But Frank had been located back home for a sufficiently long time to be integrated once more in his community.

Ruth Anderson was the second candidate selected as a trainee. Ruth had been born and raised near Fort Defiance, in the most accultured region on the Reservation, where contact with "anglos" goes back over 100 years. Many of the Navajo in the area work for the government in various capacities. However, Ruth's parents did not speak English. She went through the fifth grade in school. The summer of her 14th year was spent in the employment of a Navajo family as a housekeeper. In all probability it was a family in which the father and the mother worked for the government. Work in a restaurant followed and then Ruth worked off-reservation at Winslow for 2 years, where she was employed as a maid for the Fred Harvey Company. She returned to Fort Defiance when she was 19, and got a job as a nurse's aide at the hospital. Marriage followed when Ruth was 21. The next 9 years were spent as a housewife, and in raising a family of three boys. Ruth had been ill for some while before her trouble was finally diagnosed as tuberculosis. She had been hospitalized for some months at Fort Defiance where she was again working as a blue girl, but her condition up to that time had not been revealed by x-ray. Finally, when she knew the nature of her trouble and made arrangements for her children's care, her mother tried to get her to have a sing.

> I told my mother the sing didn't do any good on me. If I have a sing on me the sing won't help, I said. Then my mother got mad at me. "It might help you some way," she said. I told her I had tuberculosis. "Nobody can cure tuberculosis except when I go to the hospital," I said.

While Ruth had had sings before as a younger woman, she had seen enough of tuberculosis and its treatment to believe that the white doctors were more effective in curing that disease than the medicine men. Some years later, when Ruth was asked where she thought she had acquired the disease she said:

Well, this disease is contagious. We had a grandma, but we didn't live with her. We used to go see her once in a while. She died with tuberculosis. She used to have lots of sheep. One of my brothers, he used to stay with her over there. After she died with this tuberculosis my brother had tuberculosis too . . . He got no place to go so my mother brought him back. He stayed with us and he got hemorrhage at home.

Ruth entered the tuberculosis sanatorium in Fort Defiance in September of 1953.

Shortly after their discharge from the sanatorium, Ruth Anderson and Frank Ben George were recruited as the first two trainees. During a period of 4 years, six other trainees were selected. One of these (Bess Tuchin) had a full high school education, but had been in close touch with Indian communities during the years following. In two cases, we selected trainees who had not themselves experienced prolonged disease. They were, however, residents of the community and one had come from a family in which the disease was widespread. Of this total number of eight, four were women and four were men. The first two were started on their training prior to the opening of the clinic; two more, this time with more advanced education, were trained after the clinic had been in operation for a year, and the last four were trained as a group in 1959.

Training

At the onset of the training program, four goals were established for the health visitors. They were expected:
1. To understand the basic facts about health and disease and to be able to interpret them in the Navajo language and in terms of the Navajo culture;
2. To carry out selected nursing procedures intelligently under the direction of the public health nurse in the field, clinic, home, and school;
3. To collect demographic and health information and to keep accurate records of the information collected and of the simple medical instruction and procedures that they had carried out;

4. To recognize emergencies and administer first aid until the patients could be taken to a physician or nurse.

Training the first two Navajo, who had been away from school for many years and who had only a fifth and sixth grade level education, proved to be much more of a challenge than was anticipated. While the techniques of nursing, such as temperature, pulse taking, and so on, were quickly mastered, the basic concepts of why temperatures were taken, what the pulse rate indicated, and what respiration rate meant were not understood by these people. So the public health nurse revised her lesson plans and started on a much simpler level. The first week was spent on basic anatomy of the chest and abdomen as these were the parts of the body for which the health visitors had the best understanding from their own experience as patients at the sanatorium. Physiologic functions were also taught. Each student made drawings of the organ-systems as they were studied. Again, they proved that they were very deft with their hands, much more so than the student nurses in our own society.

But the students were not grasping either the English terminology or the concepts which were basic to an understanding of what they were being taught. Even though our public health nurse director had had years of work with the Navajo, and even though the trainees were all able to speak adequate English, the barrier between the teacher and the students was still too great. An intermediary was needed, and Pauline McKinley was called in.

She was the Navajo nurse who had worked for many years at the Fort Defiance hospital, but was now retired from the service with a physical disability. She knew the English terminology and, furthermore, could, by working in her own language, put across the concepts without which just the anatomical and physiologic vocabulary would be so many empty words that could only be repeated parrot-like by the students, without comprehension of what they were saying.

During the next 3 months, the doctor and the nurse taught this first class of health visitors the elementary principles of anatomy, physiology, nutrition, and disease entities. After the doctor's or the nurse's presentation of a fresh unit of material in the English language, the class would be handed over to Pauline McKinley and there would follow a thorough discussion in Navajo of what had been presented. Mrs. McKinley recalled those first days of teaching:

> I took the class over and we reviewed the terminology on chest anatomy, abdominal anatomy, and the names of diseases such as diabetes, gall bladder, etc. Our greatest need I realized then was that the students that we had, really had no idea as to the first precepts of anatomy, disease, and other health teachings. Therefore, we had to start from the bottom up.

> They told me at the time that it was very hard to understand without having it translated, being very limited in their own English knowledge. So we had to start way from the beginning and work our way up the ladder.

By this method of bilingual teaching, a breakthrough was achieved in terms of the transfer of medical concepts (discussed in detail in Chapter 7) which, in effect, was crucial for the whole of the program and all of the service and research which was to follow at Many Farms.

This breakthrough was possible because we had selected highly motivated individuals who were given all of the personal attention they needed, and because we were aware from the start of the program of how the concepts had to be conveyed by working through the native as well as the acquired language.

Another important reason for this approach lies in the fact that the Navajo people are tremendously sensitive to shame sanctions. (Leighton and Kluckhohn, 1947).

> Control of the individual is achieved in Navajo society primarily by "lateral sanctions" rather than by sanctions from above. That is, the Navaho from childhood on is brought into line more by the reactions of all the people around him rather than by orders and threats of punishment from someone who stands above him in a hierarchy. "Shame" is the agony of being found wanting and exposed to the disapproval of others, as opposed to the fear that some single superior person will use his power to deprive one of rewards and privileges if specified tasks are not carried out according to instructions. (p. 105)

In the schoolroom, teachers have a difficult time getting the children to recite. There is a reluctance to stand out from the rest of the group, and to exhibit more knowledge than the others exposes the individual to the jibes of his classmates. This sensitivity to the reaction of others does not disappear when the individual grows up. It remains a part of his personality and accounts for his shyness in the presence of strangers. "A Navajo who speaks some English will indicate assent or comprehension when he has not understood at all—lest he be 'shamed.'" (Leighton and Kluckhohn, 1947).

It was difficult for the doctor and the nurse to find out what the trainees knew and what they didn't, as they were reluctant to speak up in the classroom. Without any feedback of the student's reaction to what she or he had learned, it was of course impossible to know what to stress and what to pass over more quickly. The public health nurse hit upon the technique of depending on Pauline McKinley for this information, and as long as names were not singled out, Mrs. McKinley was able to mask the identity of the individual, who otherwise might be reluctant to admit to his or her shortcoming. This technique was also used by Kenneth Dennison at Many Farms when he was made responsible for carrying on the teacher-interpreter role.

The first phase of the clinical training had been conducted at Fort Defiance and in Gallup at a government clinic, until the opening of the Many Farms Clinic in May made it possible to carry on the training there. Our public health nurse director has described this phase:

> A large amount of time has been spent on sterile techniques, both asepsis and antisepsis, the packaging of medication under supervision, cleaning and sterilizing of equipment, needles and syringes. In addition to gaining confidence in the skills already enumerated, the health visitors were taught the techniques of giving hypodermic injections, recognizing chest sounds, and observing eardrums. They were also instructed in how to assist the doctor with the physical examination. They were cautioned again and again about not diagnosing or attempting to evaluate signs and symptoms, but rather they were taught that these observations are an integral part of the interpretation and history taking.

After their many weeks of classroom work, the actual interpretation for the physician and the performance of nursing procedures were much enjoyed by the health visitors. Ruth had this to say about that period in her training:

> We help with all kinds of examinations, and take temperatures,

pulse and respiration again here. They taught us, too, about giving shots when the doctor orders it, that includes penicillin and DPT shots for immunizations. Sometimes we take urine specimens from the people to take it to the laboratory. Sometimes when the doctor orders to give a bath to these little Navajo kids when they need it, so we give them bath here. I enjoy my work here with the staff. I think that we learn more here. We teach the people how to be better and how to take care of themselves. We have a lot of babies with diarrhea coming into this clinic. We teach those mothers how to take care of their babies.

And Frank:

After the dedication of the clinic was over, then we started working on the patients. Day after day more patients were coming in. I really had fun working with the patients and they enjoy it too. These people coming in with headaches, coughs, and some pain in the chest, legs, arms and things like that. I examined them first by looking in the throats, and in the eyes, ears and listening to their hearts. After I finished with the patients, talk with [the doctor] and give treatment that the doctor orders.

The same basic technique of instruction was used in training the second group of health visitors in 1959. The curriculum included personal health in relation to community hygiene and aspects of normal growth and development, including prenatal, infant, preschool and school health, and geriatrics. Elementary principles of epidemiology, immunology, sanitation, nutrition, dental care, and family life were presented. Following this background material, teaching was focused on disease conditions, such as infant diarrhea, congenital malformations, and tuberculosis. The curriculum was designed so that the theoretical and conceptual material was given first. The teaching materials were developed by the field medical "faculty" and were later assembled into a teaching syllabus which each trainee had available for continued study and reference.[2] (Loughlin et al., 1960).

An anatomical laboratory demonstration proved to be a vivid experience for both trainees and faculty. A sheep was dissected, and the similarity between sheep and human organs was carefully pointed out (Fig. 5.1). Navajo, in butchering a sheep, remove the organs above the diaphragm *en masse*. Since there is no separation of one organ from another, the contents of the thoracic cavity are, understandably, described in a single Navajo word and are thought

DIBÉ BITSÁADI
CH'IYÁÁN BÁ NAHAZT'I'GI

THE DIGESTIVE SYSTEM
OF SHEEP

PALATE
PHARYNX
TONGUE
EPIGLOTTIS
TRACHEA
'AZÁGÍ
(ESOPHAGUS)
'AJÉÍDISHJOOL
(HEART)
'ACHÁSHJISH
(DIAPHRAGM)
'ATŁ'IZH
(GALL BLADDER)
'AZID
(LIVER)
'ACHÁ' ÁSH K'AZHÍ
(RIGHT KIDNEY)
'ALOHKE'
(PANCREAS)
CAECUM
'AJILCHII'
(RECTUM)
ILEUM
VAGINA
'ALIZH BIZIS
(BLADDER)
'ACHʼíʼDOOTʼIZHÍ
(SMALL INTESTINE)
'ACHʼíʼDIIL
(COLON)
DUODENUM
'ABID
(STOMACH)
DORSAL SAC
OF RUMEN
VENTRAL SAC
OF RUMEN
ABOMASUM
OMASUM
RETICULUM
(RIGHT SIDE OF SHEEP)

Fig. 5.1. Drawing of digestive system of sheep. (From Loughlin et al., 1960. Courtesy of the Navajo Tribal Council.)

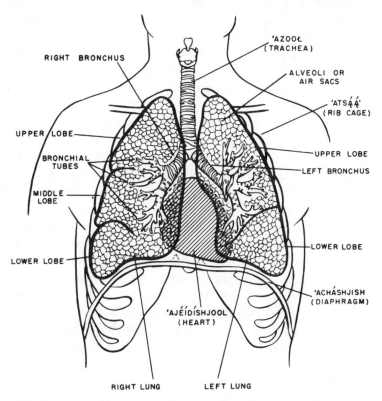

HAYI'DI
NÍŁCH'I BÁ NAHAZT'I'GI

THE
RESPIRATORY SYSTEM

RIGHT BRONCHUS

'AZOOŁ
(TRACHEA)

ALVEOLI OR
AIR SACS

'ATSĄ́Ą́'
(RIB CAGE)

UPPER LOBE

BRONCHIAL
TUBES

MIDDLE
LOBE

UPPER LOBE

LEFT BRONCHUS

LOWER LOBE

LOWER LOBE

LOWER LOBE

'ACHÁSHJISH
(DIAPHRAGM)

'AJÉÍDÍSHJOOL
(HEART)

RIGHT LUNG   LEFT LUNG

Fig. 5.2. Drawing of human respiratory system. (From Loughlin et al., 1960. Courtesy of The Navajo Tribal Council.)

to act as a single unit. The anatomical and physiologic differentiation of the trachea, heart, and lungs was a new concept which required the invention of new words to make the translation into Navajo practical (Figs. 5.1 and 5.2). Navajo trainees listened to tape recordings of their interpretative work during discussions between non-English-speaking Navajo patients and the doctors and nurses. Review of how scientific medical concepts were presented to the patient and how the patient's response was translated for the physician and nurse served to emphasize their problems and progress. Through the necessity of revising material for the vocabulary of the lower educational level of the Navajo as well as for the cultural differences, professional workers were able to perceive how, in the past, many of their explanations were complex and unusable to Navajo patients. The professional staff had not realized previously, despite long experience on the Reservation, how ridiculous many of their scientific explanations sounded when translated, and the Navajo trainees had not realized how many medical words and phrases they had accepted while they were hospitalized without the slightest notion of their meaning.

Training in numerous nursing procedures was another vital part of the auxiliaries' preparation. They learned to conduct and record the initial health interview in the clinic for the physician's review, direct patients in and out of examining rooms to appropriate laboratory and x-ray examinations, and obtain simple measurements of height, weight, and blood pressure. They administered visual and auditory tests, operated the electrocardiograph machine, and cleaned and sterilized medical instruments and equipment. They administered, under supervision, intramuscular and subcutaneous injections of streptomycin, penicillin, and a variety of vaccines. They administered and read tuberculin skin tests. They demonstrated sterile techniques and the proper method of administering nosedrops and eardrops. They learned how to record their observations and the procedures performed on the official medical records of patients and how to operate and use appropriately the radiotelephone which provided two-way communication between the field vehicle and the clinic.

It had been the experience of many physicians who had worked on the Navajo Reservation that the medical history was the most difficult part of the medical work-up because of the language barrier. It was decided that the health visitors could very well take the medical history, if it was simplified in its presentation and if the physicians took the history of the presenting complaint. This too was an innovation in medical practice on the Reservation, an innovation that we, as a contract group, could afford to experiment with, while the government could not.

The form, as it was finally adopted, was divided into seven parts. First, the physical measurements. The second part was reserved for a recording of the complaint which brought the patient into the clinic. Then followed the history proper, which touched on the major systems in a systemic review—concerning previous hospitalization and injuries; head and neck; cardiorespiratory; gastrointestinal; genitourinary; and finally, a section for infants. The form was closed with a section for summary and remarks. (See Appendix II.)

Insofar as a great many of these questions could be answered by simple yes or no answers, the completion of the questionnaire was not straining the training of the health visitor. Positive replies could then be followed up by further questioning from the doctor. But it did get at the same facts that could be obtained only by working tediously through both languages.

Trainees began clinic duties within the first month of training and thereafter spent increasing amounts of time in supervised clinic work. Field visits began after about 4 months and, under the constant supervision of the public health nurse, the health visitors were trained in the methods of extending services out to the homes of the Navajo. The nurse accompanied each health visitor on a round of such calls; gradually she withdrew from the direct supervision, and they went out on their own.

They were encouraged by the public health nurse to get to know the problems of each of the families they served: the hogan environment, economic circumstances, off-reservation work patterns, infant feeding practices, and so on. Only through such contacts in the home and the feeding back of such information to the clinic staff could the health service to the community be made truly comprehensive in terms of total needs.

The health visitors were instructed in how to fill out a report on each of their home visits. These reports were reviewed by the nursing supervisor upon their return to the clinic. They were then fastened into the same files that contained the medical charts, thus enabling the physicians to have more extensive knowledge of the patients than would otherwise be possible. Several comments from these reports follow:

(Rena) Made a quick visit to Rena Benally to get another urine specimen for testing again. Rena had moved from their regular camp to another place, had difficulty finding the place. Meet someone on the road told me where I can find Rena's camp. So I did but Rena was out herding sheep with the grandmother. I went out and find where Rena was herding. Asked her grandmother about what I came for as the doc's order and explain to her about Rena's physical finding that she has pyelonephritis. Her grandmother said she knows that Rena suppose to return to clinic about in two weeks but the problem was transportation. Rena gave me her urine specimen and her grandmother said she would like to know the result again as soon as it is done. I told them that we'll be very glad to do that as soon as possible.

(Charlie Badoni) 9/8/58 Patient was home complaining he has some skin infection on the back of hand and some on right cheek. Was seen here at Many Farms and at Piñon where the Public Health Nurse was given medicine for it. But it didn't help, only help to relieve the itching. Patient was advise to go to Many Farms soon.

2/12/58 Hogan visit Lucy Begay. Just to check on isoniazid. She still have some INH yet enough for another week. We just talk with her there for while. She told us she had headaches and sore ear on left side. She been like that now for 3 months now. Sometime she got weak. We told her to come down see the doctor. She said she been try to come down but she has no way to come down.

The trainees also collected vital statistics and census data during the visits, and they provided preventive services such as immunization, advised on the feeding and care of infants and the aged, occasionally provided simple nursing services to the sick, and checked on the progress and effects of treatment. Assistance in the school health program was also part of the field activity.

In 1958, the anthropologist was asked to make a comprehensive study of the total health visitor program. Such an evaluation would be useful to the staff in the training of the four new health visitors who would soon be brought into the program, and would serve as a preliminary report for the government.[3] One of the Navajo patients expressed the following opinion during an interview:

It seems to me that those interpreters are more at ease where they are working down there in the clinic. . . . Only thing is they ask more questions in the clinic. And we ask more questions of them there too. We usually think that these people who come out here as being in a hurry—when we see them looking at their watches we don't want to hold them back in their work.

This opinion was confirmed by others in the community and also by the health visitors themselves. All four of them stated they preferred to work in the clinic. How can this be explained? One would think that these Navajo would rather work with their own people, in their own language, and enjoy the freedom that comes with working out in the field.

This preference for work in the clinic can be understood if we examine the two contrasting roles these acculturated Navajo were asked to play. In the clinic the health visitors were in the role of *mediators,* for which they were admirably suited because they shared the cultural "worlds" of both societies—that of the white man, carrier of the new technology represented by the doctors and nurses, and that of the Indian—the recipient society represented by the patient. They shared the language of each and participated at the clinic in our society, yet maintained contact with their own families and communities; and shared the medical values of each group. They knew how their fellow Navajo perceived illness and depended on traditional medicine as well as modern medicine (they never discouraged a patient from seeing a medicine man). By virtue of their training (and former illness), they had complete faith in the ability of the doctors and wanted to help them understand the patients. This bicultural understanding, sharing, and participation proved to be of basic importance in achieving the goal to which Scott Preston had referred when he talked of the need "to accommodate both the patient and the doctor."

In the clinic, the health visitors felt secure as part of a closely knit organization with well defined job relations toward other members of the clinic team. They had a reference group which helped to shape their own role in the clinic. There they were seen by the patients as fellow Navajos and assistants to the nurse and doctor. They had the security of their backing, which gave them confidence in performing the unpleasant and culturally unsanctioned duties required of Navajos in medical work. An excellent illustration of this is the fact that the health visitors learned to ask questions, without embarrassment, about bodily elimination and sexual matters, which run against the grain of their native culture.

Out in the field, the health visitor was in the role of an *innovator.* Traditionally, aides to the public health nurse did not go out to the hogans unaccompanied. This was initially a more difficult role for the acculturated individuals to play, as it emphasized their marginality to the conservative ways of their people. Or, stated in other words, their education was to their advantage in the clinic but was a handicap in the field where they were judged by the

Navajo norms, and not in the context of the white man's society. As an illustration, men and women out in the community viewed the request for a sample of urine as aberrant behavior and often refused. No Navajo in his sane mind would make such a request, as urine was used in witchcraft. But in the clinic, where the patients perceived the health visitors in terms of their roles as assistants to the doctor, such requests were granted routinely.

This same dichotomy of roles was clearly exemplified in the training period, when the supervision of work in the hogans involved personality and cultural factors that extended beyond those relevant to training in the clinic. The public health nurse was faced with the problem of teaching the Navajo, whom she had known in the clinic and classroom within the framework of our society, how to extend medical services to a society which was known to her only superficially, but well understood by the trainees. As a result, though the nurses had been effective as a reference group in the clinic, they became much less effective in the Navajo world where the health visitors tended to identify with their own people and ways more than with the white nurse. She could teach techniques, but some of these became subject to modification as the expectations of conduct shifted from the Anglo to the Navajo world. For example, it might be good technique for a public health nurse always to enter the home of the patient and explain the reason for the visit, coming directly to the point soon after gaining entry. But this behavior is bad manners from the Navajo point of view; one usually waits until the person comes out of the house rather than gaining immediate entry, and then one takes one's time and talks about other things first. To force the health visitors to adopt the former technique would be to place them in an uncomfortable position. So the questions for the health visitors arise: How much should they pattern their behavior after that of the Anglo teachers who know so little about the way of life of the Navajo people? How much should they model their behavior after that of their own elders? The teachers, too, are in an ambivalent position. To what degree should they attempt to modify these Navajos' behavior in their own society in order to follow conventional procedure? An interesting comment on this situation came from one of the health visitors. During the course of an interview, he was describing the behavior of the nurse who went out on a visit with him:

Sometimes she would hit them just like with a needle. But I wouldn't interpret for her. Then I explain to her later what I didn't say—because we don't want any hard feelings. . . . Like the time out in camp 61 there is an epileptic. . . . We talk that over about him. That woman, his mother, she had objections to us. We went out there just to find out more about that case, but they wouldn't tell us much. She [nurse] asked about that too abruptly, later I explained to her why I hadn't interpreted all she said.

Experience at Many Farms showed that with close supervision during the training period, it was possible to hold rigidly to the critical points of technique, and at the same time to relax discipline on points which fell more within the realm of custom and etiquette.

These role conflicts which arise and handicap the Navajo during their training period are severe in the first months in the field, and the health visitors tend to become overdependent on supervision, and the public health nurse, sensing this lack of security, tends to be overprotective. The roles already established in the clinic predetermine those in the field. However, once the health visitors do start to go out on their own and establish firm relations in the hogan, they are able to restructure their behavior in accordance with Navajo norms; that is, if they have lived sufficiently close to traditional Navajo life to know what they are.

The Navajo who was the first to break through and establish himself in this new role was the one who had many relatives in the community. This he did by building on the recognized kinship behavior that would be normal in any traditional setting. Nemore described his situation as follows:

In every single camp up on top [of Black Mesa] they call me by a relationship term—and around Rough Rock too . . . When I go to a hogan the first thing they ask is "What clan are you?" then "What is your father's clan?" and "Where are you from?" I ask them the same thing. When they know what clan you are in they know how to greet you.

He might also have added, "and how to act towards you," for in traditional Navajo society the use of a kinship term such as "grandfather" describes for the user the behavior of a grandson towards that clan-related person, so that he behaves toward him as he does to his own "blood grandfather." Likewise with the other kin terms—each denotes a specific kind of behavior, which may be one of respect, or perhaps a joking relationship. If one does not know how one is related, one's role is uncertain. Positive relations can be built up without "kinship" but it takes, as one health visitor said, "at least three or four calls before they act friendly."

Another aspect of the program which served to modify the marginal role the health visitors experienced in the field was the use of the radiotelephones. Essentially they brought the authority of the doctor out to the hogan, thus reestablishing the health visitor in an intermediate role between the physician and the patient. This function was well illustrated by an incident witnessed by the anthropologist when he was observing a hogan call. There had been an outbreak of streptococcal infection in one of the camps. The doctor wanted throat smears taken on all the members of the family, and penicillin injections given.

The health visitor explained why he had come and was asked in by the mother of the family. He proceeded to obtain the cultures from all of the members of the family in a very orderly manner. He then properly identified each culture dish with the patient's number and then phoned the clinic to verify the number of shots to be given and these were administered with no incident. When he got to the mother, who was very obese, she asked if she could have the shot in her arm rather than in the buttocks. He complied with her wishes. "She had real fat arms and I thought it wouldn't hurt her to have the shot there," he later explained.

But then he met with resistance. One of the daughters (possibly following the example of the mother) also asked for a shot in the arm. "I don't think she should have one there," he explained to the family. The mother and father tried to persuade her, but she would not change her mind.

The health visitor then went out to the car and phoned the doctor at the clinic. He described the situation in detail and asked him what he should do. The doctor said if the family couldn't get her to take the shot in the buttocks, it would be safe to give the penicillin in the arm. This he proceeded to do.

Breaking through to the field role was much easier for the last four health visitors. They had the model of the earlier trainees before them and received direct guidance from them. Further, expectations of their field activities had already been established in the community. "They had become accustomed to us," is the way one health visitor put it. "They ask us questions right away— what we have come to their homes for."

Another of our theories of selection was substantiated in further interviews in this evaluation study. One of the questions asked of the health visitors was: "Was your previous history of tuberculosis actually of benefit to you in dealing with your patients?" All of the health visitors stated that their experience as patients gave them confidence in dealing with the Navajo in the community. One went so far as to say: "I think my experience in the sanatorium is the best teaching I got."

Frank Ben George, who had practiced as a medicine man prior to hospitalization with tuberculosis, said:

Only if a person is really sick and I want him to go to the clinic do I tell him my own story.

Like Tsinajinnie Begay. Two times he took his wife to Ganado. She had a pain in her abdomen. They couldn't help her. They also did a lot of singing over her.

I went there one time . . . the old lady—she wanted medicine . . . Her folks said, "We took her two times to Ganado to see the doctor. Then we quit. Thought it would be best to treat her in the Navajo way." Then I used my story.

Upon questioning, Frank said he had "used his story" three times, and each time the Navajo to whom he told it followed his advice and came to the clinic to see the doctor.

A third answer to this question included the comment: "I think that all of the people know that we are ex-san patients, that is all of us health visitors." It may be inferred that, from the patients' point of view, the fact that the health visitors had had the disease and were there to tell them about it in all probability was a more convincing argument for submitting to hospitalization and in taking isoniazid at home than general statements about germs.

In sum, the opinions of the professional staff emphasized a number of strengths and weaknesses of the health visitor program. Their ability to interpret for the physician in the examining room was appreciated by all of the doctors and nurses who worked with them. One physician who worked with the health visitors for almost 2 years wrote:

Having been away from the program for six months, I find the role of the health visitors has grown in importance in my mind rather than lessened. I would hate to work in a clinic without them because they help not only in the diagnoses and treatment, but in giving more meaning to the doctor-patient relationship.

It was unanimously agreed that they did an able job in carrying out nursing procedures and performing the numerous manual tasks essential to running the clinic.

Several of the physicians thought that the weakest point was in obtaining a chronologic history, even of the chief complaint. One commented: "Whenever you would get into a history which required a reasonably detailed description of symptoms, there was a good chance of having difficulty."

All agreed that it would have been impossible to carry out the field program without the assistance of the health visitors, that their understanding of the ways of the people, their home life, religion, methods of child care, and so on, were invaluable to the clinic staff. An example of a specific medical program that could not have been successfully conducted without the aid of the auxiliary was the tuberculosis control program. Extensive studies were carried out on the prevalence of tuberculosis, and all school and preschool children were tuberculin tested. With the help of the Navajo auxiliaries, it was possible to supervise closely the domiciliary tuberculosis chemotherapy program. The auxiliaries were able to enlist the cooperation of the individuals, the families, and the entire community for this work.

In retrospect, one most important fact must be pointed out. The quality of the health visitors' performance depended to a large degree on the quality of their supervision. When the nurses and doctors took an active interest in their training and worked closely with them in reviewing their performance in the field and the clinic, they responded by doing a good job. But, as is universally true, if interest and motivation lagged on the top level, it was immediately reflected in an indifferent attitude on the part of the health visitors.

6.

Developing a Cross-Cultural Approach to Medical Files

A vital aspect of the art of cross-cultural medical service and research, or of any newly introduced technology, is ascertaining which of the native institutions are still vital and highly valued in their present form by the recipient society. These must be taken into consideration by the innovators in designing their program.

It was the responsibility of the anthropologist, as part of the research team, to determine such valued institutions and the all-important linkages between them in the native culture. These in turn had to be related in a practical way to the basic, going needs of the program. For example, the matrilineal social organization of the Navajo has a direct relationship to family composition, residence patterns, economy, and decision making. All of these had relevance to the medical service being planned. Furthermore, there was a relationship between naming practices and bilingualism. These too were of importance in the design of the program. If these vital aspects of culture and their intercommunications are ignored by simply superimposing our institutions on theirs, there will be inefficiency in the service and resistance is likely to develop.

The problem of organizing a useful system of medical records to be used in the clinic became one of applying this principle so that the records would reflect the patterns of living of the Navajo, rather than the cultural heritage of western society.

When the clinic opened its doors in May 1956, we had no satisfactory medical or public health records on the residents of the area.

The Many Farms–Rough Rock Navajo had been served by the Chinle Clinic maintained by the government, and by the Ganado Hospital, over 50 miles to the south. A public health nurse worked out of Chinle, but she had had such a huge area to cover that programs had been limited to school immunizations and tuberculosis case findings and follow-up. We did have these records and the results from a mobile unit x-ray survey of tuberculosis. We also obtained from the Education Office of the Bureau of Indian Affairs a rough map of the area with approximate location of families (and hogan sites) which had children in school.

The clinic at Chinle had had an overwhelming load—it serviced an area some 50 miles wide, extending from the southern border of the reservation to north of Lukachukai. Consequently the doctor, like the nurse in the field, could take care of only the most pressing needs. While the clinic at Chinle was supposed to have two doctors, the government had never been able to keep it staffed with more than one. He often saw as many as 100 patients a day. Under such conditions only the major complaints could be treated. Nor was this exceptional; all of the clinics on the reservation had to be run under similar conditions.

Records kept at Chinle were adequate for such a service, but were of little value beyond keeping track of each patient's diagnosis, treatment, and medications. The public health nurse kept her own records of her field case load. The medical officer in charge reported incidence of all diseases treated on standard forms used throughout the reservation, and by the entire Indian Division of the United States Public Health Service. The public health nurse rendered her own set of reports to her own superior. Such a system was, of course, geared completely to government service needs. There was no time for research even if the doctor or nurse had such interests. If a particular piece of research was needed, such as determining the tuberculosis prevalence in the area, a special survey group, organized at higher headquarters, was sent out.

At Many Farms, we had a different type of assignment. Our area was much smaller than the government clinic areas, but we were responsible for determining the total health needs of this sample population. This called for a very different clinic procedure which would allow for a complete physical examination on as many of the people as possible. We were also equipped and staffed for complete x-ray and laboratory tests.

Additionally, we were responsible for four schools in the area and eventually, after the clinic service was well established, for work in the hogans, especially in tuberculosis chemotherapy and in the broad area of preventive medicine.

The clinic staff started out for the first 5 months using records that were derived in part from an urban hospital outpatient practice with which the medical officer in charge and the project directors had had their experience, and also from the local government record system. We too were responsible for monthly reports to higher medical and nursing headquarters. It had been agreed at the planning meeting in Albuquerque (March 1956) that we would render to the government all the customary reports required of all field installations.

Each patient was given a number, and this ascending number system was cross-filed alphabetically so that any given patient could be located by name. Such records were initiated by the Navajo clerk at the front desk.

It was not many months after this system was inaugurated that we found ourselves in complete confusion. There were countless duplications of records (just as there were at the hard-pressed and understaffed government clinics), and sometimes two patients shared one record due to mistaken identities. Such conventional information as "occupation" called for in virtually every form filled by United States residents everywhere, in this case was of little use as it was filled out as "farmer," "sheepherder," and the women were automatically recorded by the clerk as "housewives."

The face sheet data included as well: name, date chart was opened, Bureau of Indian Affairs census number, marital status, birth date, educational level, and immunization data. A home evaluation sheet was set up for work out in the area with provision for information on the home recorded by a number system. This included the names of household members, water supply, waste disposal, and trading posts used, all data deemed useful by the public health nurse from her previous experience.

While this modification of the record system contained several times more information than that carried elsewhere on the reservation, it was the opinion of the anthropologist, with the concurrence of the public health nurse, that the forms were not sufficiently complete.

Numerous meetings were held between the doctor, the public health nurse, the anthropologist, and the head of the Navajo staff. We felt the problem to be basic to the whole working of the clinic, and that the record system must reflect our total approach. All service and research would have to be coordinated and recorded in order to achieve any goal, and this system would have to meet the dictates of time pressures and practicality when used by Navajo with limited education. Furthermore, records which coordinated work in field and clinic had to be devised.

Setting up this record system, and carrying it through, was one of the first challenges to the staff. It was essential to work out a solution which would be agreeable to the professions involved. Each had his own bias; each had his own vested interest; and each brought to this program his own set of values and body of knowledge based on prior experience.

The doctor's experience, in this case, had been limited to dealing with hospital records in urban centers, including those of the outpatient clinic. His professional competence allowed him to speak for the records which would be kept on the clinical examinations and the laboratory and x-ray services which would be part of the routine work in the clinic. Certain modifications had to be introduced to work effectively cross-culturally through an interpreter.

The nurse had kept track of all community, school, and home services in all her work in the past. Now we were faced with combining these records from the field with the clinic records on each patient, so that there could be a comprehensive medical service rendered to this rural population.

From the very start of her training, the nurse had been taught the importance of accurate records, but in nearly all cases her interests were confined to service. She did not have a research frame of reference. She knew a great deal about Navajo culture, but she had never thought of it in a research context. Never during her years on the Navajo Reservation had the public health nurse been as closely tied into clinical medicine.

The head of the Navajo staff was most obliging in giving us all the information needed on Navajo culture as related to this problem of medical records, and in spite of his complete lack of experience in medical work—his total experience with medicine had been limited to being a patient—and his unaggressive Navajo personality, he was very useful in helping to solve problems once they were pointed up by the others. In other words, he did not know the significance of the Navajo way of life as related to medical service and research. His home was only 15 miles to the north, and his knowledge of the local population was, of course, extensive.

The resident field anthropologist had never, prior to joining the staff, had experience with the Navajo, but he had had experience in cultural analysis and field experience in several other areas. Furthermore, he had never had experience in working with a medical team. But he was sensitive to subcultural differences within our own society, including contrasting values, beliefs, and behavior of the public health nurse and the young doctor trained only in clinical medicine.

His point of view was expressed in a report he wrote on the problem of medical records at Many Farms and the solution of that problem:[1]

> ... medical records must represent an abbreviated outline of the patterns of day to day living in a particular society. For much of the past century the predominant thinking in the medical sciences has been European and, more recently, American. Consequently, the medical recording practices in general use have tended to reflect the cultural patterns of Western society. The environment of the individual patient can vary considerably within the outlines of these patterns, but can almost always be adequately represented by "standard" recording procedures.

> When, however, modern medical services are to be extended to peoples outside of Western society, the recording procedures present many new problems. When the medical practitioners and the patient groups share a common cultural heritage, a great part of the communication provided by the record system rests upon shared assumptions and shared values. Such items as where in the city a patient lives, his occupation or grade of school completed can reveal to the physician a great deal about the patient's background. When that physician is dealing with people among whom residence does not indicate social class, and where occupations are not specialized, the same information would be of little assistance. In the typical United States family the father and mother share equally in the discipline of the children; uncles and aunts have little to do with it.

The physician or nurse, therefore, is interested in the relationships between the child and his parents, and is not concerned with aunts and uncles. If, however, one is dealing with a society in which the maternal uncle is more often the disciplinarian than the father (as is the case in traditional Navajo society) then a new set of relationships must be noted.

Designing Medical Files with Cultural Relevance

The doctor delegated the responsibility of working out a suitable system which would serve these overall clinic needs, and the public health nurse and the anthropologist, consulting with the Navajo staff, carried on from there.

Those areas of Navajo culture which were functionally interdependent and therefore necessary to consider were examined and dealt with under the following headings: location of residence, identification of individuals, structure of family and kin groupings, and vital statistics such as marriage and divorce, parentage, births, and deaths.

Residence

Only the broadest facts as to residence and settlement on the land were known. These could be ascertained by a quick trip through the area. The population was thinly scattered, especially as one went out from the valley floor to the higher steppe and mesa land to either side.

During those months when these records were being designed, the field project had not gotten underway, so it was not possible to ask the health visitors where a particular hogan was, nor were they familiar with the landmarks such as a particular arroyo or sand flat. Most of them were from out of the area, and the terrain was as new to them as it was to us. At this state of the project, they no more knew where the residents of the area lived than did a nurse in training in any hospital. They knew the Navajo at this time only as patients in the clinic.

Furthermore, the means of communication whereby such data could be gathered were few, as there were no fixed centers of community life beyond the trading post and, to a limited degree, the school. This made it difficult to contact more than isolated segments of the population at any one time.

Other devices useful in locating residence in our own society were of only limited value. Mail address would help in our rural areas with the rural route number; or in a city, of course, an address could be exactly determined. Here the mail address was the trading post most frequently used—and this by Navajo living 50 miles in all directions.

The enormous problem of determining residence which in turn required mapping the area was solved by our resident anthropologist (Donald Rieder) doggedly working with Kenneth Dennison and Wilfred Slivers, the maintenance man at the clinic; both were familiar with the area.

The resident anthropologist constantly went over the records with the clerk and with Wilfred Slivers as they were accumulating and recorded where each person lived. The inadequate map that we had obtained from the schools division was then modified in accordance with this more accurate firsthand data and all the essential information was projected on a wall map. Not only were the hogans placed more accurately, but drainage patterns, land contours, windmill sites, and other landmarks were adjusted.

Once the health visitors went into the field regularly, they reported back when a camp site had been misplaced and gave such data to the clerk.

Identification of Patient

The anthropologist was able to point out that naming practices were not what they are in our society. Most of this was knowledge gleaned from the anthropologic literature and checked with Navajo on the staff. He wrote, in summarizing this aspect of the problem:

> The accurate identification of the individual is often difficult because of the vagaries of present-day naming practices. Traditionally, the Navajo individual has only one true name. This name is known only to one's family and perhaps by a medicine man. It should never be used either to refer to the person or to call him by except in certain ritual situations and in times of great danger. This name (often referred to as a "war name") is considered part of the person almost a part of his being, and he could become ill or weakened if it were used indiscriminately. In the same tradition, people are called by the appropriate kinship term (an easy thing in a small group of related persons) and referred to either by a kinship designation or by a nickname, the nickname often being known to everyone but the person bearing it. Thus a woman would be called *Shima* (my

mother) by her children, *shadi* (my older sister) by her sister, *sha'esdzaan* (my wife, literally, my woman) by her husband and so forth. Others outside the family might refer to her as Ben *bima* (Ben's mother) if her son, Ben, happened to be well-known. Or she might be called *bidaghagai bitsi* (white mustache's daughter) if her father were well-known. Yet others might refer to her by a nickname, often based on some physical circumstance or event. Thus, she might be widely known as *'asdzaatsoh* (big woman).

Today most Navajo carry an Anglo or Spanish name or an anglicized version of a Navajo name. Until quite recently such names were arbitrarily assigned by traders, government personnel, or missionaries. A further complication arises from the Navajo reluctance to abandon what they consider a perfectly functional naming system. The result of this, especially in dealing with older people, is often an unwillingness or actual inability to "name" the members of one's family. . . . At the present time there is some stability in naming practices, especially with the educated young people, but quite often people will use one name on one occasion and another name on a later occasion.

Our biggest problem has arisen either from spelling variations or from overcommon surnames. For example, *baada-ani*, a kinship term meaning one's in-law, was early picked up as a surname and given a dozen spellings. Begay, a corruption of the Navajo *biye'* (his son) is proportionately much more common than Smith in English or Martinez in Spanish.

The consequence of name confusion has been to preclude the use of the name as an important identifying device. The government, in its more important dealings with the Navajo, has for years used a census number. These must be obtained by registering at one of the subagencies and are necessary for many of the dealings between the people and the tribe or the government. However, one of the problems of relying upon census numbers is that few Navajo remember the number or carry the metal tag on which it is stamped. Its use is generally restricted to obtaining grazing permits, getting emergency relief and the like, and few people think to bring it along on a visit to a health installation.

We have tried a number of partial solutions to the name difficulties. One of these was to record Navajo names in Navajo, an attempt soon abandoned because of the difficulty in training staff members to use Navajo spelling. Another has been to cross-index all names and variants of names held by individuals. When done, this has considerably alleviated the problem. However, it has been generally impossible to institute cross-indexing as a routine procedure. Our best answer lies in peripheral information such as clan and kinship, location of home, age, and so forth. In one instance we were able to straighten up a particularly difficult identification problem by recourse to a considerable difference in weight between the two persons involved.

Structure of Family and Kin Groupings

The structure of the Navajo family and kin groupings is based on the matrilineal and matrilocal extended family. This extended family usually makes up what for lack of a better name is referred to as a "camp"—geographically distinct residence area containing from two to as many as 10 separate households. Typically, one house will be occupied by the old father and mother and their unmarried children and other dependent kin: the surrounding houses will be occupied by their married daughters and the daughters' husbands and children.

It is this camp that gives geographic stability to the extended family. In some instances it becomes necessary to record both a summer and winter location, but in the great majority of cases, one particular camp is occupied by at least a portion of the family throughout the year. A records system using the camp as the basis has an advantage of geographical stability that could never be obtained from a system based upon individual or even the nuclear family.

The camp, furthermore, is sufficiently isolated so that its inhabitants constitute an infecting group. There is constant contact, both day and night, among the members of any one camp and while visits to other camps, attendance at group events and at school serve to override the geographical isolation to a considerable extent, one can act on the assumption that the members of any one camp will share each other's infections.

Beyond the limits of the camp are the social units of the clan and other kinship groups. The Navajo do not share the general Anglo-American pattern of associative groups based on proximity (job and neighborhood, for example), but use instead associative groups based on kinship. Navajo kinship is divided sharply along maternal and paternal lines, with the clan being the chief determinant of relationship.

Every Navajo belongs by birth to one of the 40-odd clans.[2] He is born into his mother's clan, which means that he is a "blood" member of that clan and therefore closely related to every other member.

Such relationship is considered fundamental and overrides biologic relationship to the extent that one cannot marry a member of one's own clan regardless of how distant the biologic relationship might be. Every Navajo is also related through his father's clan and cannot intermarry with members of that clan. Appropriate kinship terms, depending upon sex, generation, and relative age, are applied to clan members on both sides so that, for example, a female clan relative of the generation of one's mother's mother will be called grandmother even though no biologic relationship can be traced and she resides 200 miles away on the other side of the Reservation.

The extension of kinship terms to one's clan relatives is an indication of the importance of the clan as a social unit. Its major function is the regulation of marriage and this provides an invaluable device for positive identification. The clan never changes, regardless of vagaries of names and shifting residence. Beyond that, the clan fills for the Navajo many of the functions filled for non-Indians by friendship groups, job companions, neighbors, clubs, and the like. It serves as a socializing unit, a mutual assistance group and, by providing a wide circle of respected older kinsmen, as a powerful agency of social control.

The public health nurse with her field experience had learned the importance of the Navajo extended family, although she might not have called it by that term, but as "all of those relatives." She was also well acquainted with the importance of clan in Navajo society—again because she had worked on the field level. Yet many administrators on the Window Rock level regard clan as something that has no application to administration or the world of practical affairs—something that can be relegated to the Indian past along with their legends.

For the doctor, the argument that "the members of any one camp will share each other's infections" was a convincing one. It translated family sociology into family medicine. Thus, during epidemics persons who might be the next to be infected were easily located, and when a patient who came to the clinic was diagnosed to have an infectious disease, the members of his living unit could be immediately sought out for home visits and possible immunizations.

The nurse and the physician saw the relevance of Navajo family structure, kinship, and clanship to the overall medical records problem. Interestingly enough, resistance was met with only among the Navajo staff. This resistance could be accounted for because we were dealing (in our clerks) with Navajo who were a bit ashamed of clanship. As well educated members of their society, they did not like to admit to the importance of this practice among their own people and, even more important, no one had ever asked a patient for his clan upon registering at a clinic in the experience of our patient population. Rebuke by elders: "What do you want to know that for" or: "What business is that of the doctor's?" or shaming and kidding by others no doubt made the clerks reluctant to get such information. This was a situational factor: While it would be quite proper, indeed mandatory, for the acculturated Navajo to ask this question out in the hogans as part of normal behavior, this clinic was not of their world but of the white man's, where such things were not considered important. Indeed, many white administrators and teachers had ridiculed such customs along with the Navajo religious practices. Since such teachers and administrators were often the only models of conduct of a Navajo in white man's society, the very acculturated Navajo took on similar attitudes, at least in the presence of Anglos.

The clerks became less embarrassed when they learned that we did not look upon clans as a curiosity but as important to our clinic records system, and once the utility was demonstrated they were won over.

This type of resistance is encountered constantly in working with American Indian people, and no doubt with peoples in many areas of the world where Western technology is bringing about a change in native institutions. The stereotypes held by the bulk of the society to which there is an acculturation trend are taken over and make it difficult to work through native institutions which are still functional to the implementing of innovations. The educated Indian is placed in a position where conflicts between the new and the old affect his behavior. This ambivalence and role conflict is at least partially resolved only when he realizes that all people in our society do not feel the same way about what he considers to be the old-fashioned customs of his people. He learns to discriminate between those who scoff and those who appreciate, and models his own behavior in their presence accordingly.

Marriage and Divorce: Vital Statistics

Marriage and divorce, the anthropologist pointed out, "have always been considered the business of the families and clans involved rather than matters of tribal or government regulation." However, the State Welfare Office and the administration of the Aid to Dependent Children and other state and federal programs increasingly demanded information regarding marital and parental status. The Navajo had become accustomed to such questions being asked when they went to one of these offices seeking aid—a mother for the support of a child in the absence of a father, or for help in supporting aged members of the family who could not work.

We, in contrast to the government agencies, did not extend cash benefits and such information was harder to come by. Again it was situational. "What has my being divorced have to do with this sick child I have brought to the clinic?" Likewise, there was no linkage in their thinking between birth, a natural process, and the clinic which tended to the ill. Deaths among families were difficult to get data on, even though there was a linkage between disease and death, because of a very strong cultural taboo against reference to the dead.

The anthropologist and the public health nurse recognized that we were not getting as full information on these matters as we needed. But they agreed that we would get much more information from the routine home visits and that in the meantime we would have to rely mainly on chance information. That did prove to be the case, and with a change in the situation and in the role of the person seeking out the data, it became much easier to find out essential facts about marriage and divorce, births, and deaths. The proper place to talk about such things was in the home, where in the context of family life the mothers and fathers were only too pleased to talk about such matters.

Changes Made in Medical Records

The anthropologist and the nurse took into consideration all of these cultural factors, including role and situational problems, and recommended the following changes:

1. That a place for clan be established on the records.
2. That the relationship between individual, his or her place in the family, and the relationship between that nuclear family and the extended family be made evident in the records.
3. That further attempts at designating location of house be

made in terms of nature of surroundings and additionally, by nearest neighbor.

4. That all aliases be used in addition to the name given to the clerk upon request.

Then, the most important change of all was inaugurated. The whole ascending number system was scrapped and a *campfile* system of filing was inaugurated. This system also involved filing in one place all of the individual patient's clinic records and school immunizations as well as all data on camp visits in one place. Each camp folder would contain a list of all those resident in the camp, with the charts of the various members filed by household. Thus, in terms of records, the patient would be seen in the context of the natural social units in which he lived, and not just as a separate individual. The master folder would include pertinent information on the entire camp (the smallest face-to-face living unit) so that it could be used for case evaluation on any particular individual in that camp. Disease would be coded so that the physician or nurse could quickly check the health conditions of the entire camp.

This system, then, provided as complete a record as possible of the health picture of an individual in his or her living unit, or the health status of the unit as a whole, thus facilitating the prevention and treatment of illness and at the same time offering a compact body of research material based upon social and medical environment.

In evaluating this particular facet of the Many Farms Project, the physician members of the Cornell team wrote:

> The camp file system will allow us to know which members of any particular camp have come to the clinic and which haven't. This is one of the most important aspects of the system as far as research is concerned and one, we think, that is almost unique in Indian medical service. We will have, in effect, a social census of the area that should tell us whom we have been contacting and whom we have not. . . .

> We expect it to be of primary importance in evaluating Navajo receptivity of modern medicine; in planning and conducting health education programs; in collecting data on Navajo health, and in epidemiologic studies.

> Once we have mastered our area in terms of incidence of sickness the camp files should provide fertile grounds for research in nutrition, medical practices, economic behavior, sanitation and other

pertinent areas of health research. Both researcher and the practitioner in these fields will have two-thirds of the ground work accomplished and can from the beginning have an idea of the social and medical background of the people being studied.

And, in more general terms, they spoke of the value of using such a cultural approach:

One of the greatest problems today in bringing better medical service to such peoples as the Navajo is the refusal—conscious or unconscious—of the average medical professional to recognize the peculiar conditions under which his program must operate. Persons from one culture tend to view another culture in terms of their own. Variations are seen as oddities to be ignored or reserved for conversational anecdotes and the whole complex of customs and behavior systems peculiar to the other culture is put out of consciousness. In the end, the ignorance of these customs and behavior systems results in confusion, inactivity or frustration and the program breaks down because of blocked communication, lack of response or antagonism.

In the simple mechanics of public health work a lack of recognition of the cultural differences makes impossible adequate information on vital statistics, morbidity, epidemiology and makes the planning and carrying out of health education and preventive medical programs extremely difficult. Case finding, an important part of public health work in the behind-the-times Indian reservation, cannot succeed if elementary social, demographic and geographic facts on the population are lacking.

7.

Bridging the Gap of Language and Culture:
Conceptual Transfer

In the chapter on the health visitors we have seen how Navajo aides to the doctors and nurses were trained to bridge the gap between the Western world of medical research, practice, and technology and the less developed medical world of the Navajo Indians. In this chapter the linguistic aspects of this cultural gap will be examined in some detail.

At the outset of the project, consideration was given to the question: To what degree should the language of the Indians be utilized by the physicians and the nurses? For the most part, the individual members of the staff would be in the field for only 2 years. Thus our situation was much the same as that of the staff in the United States Public Health Service. They too were limited to 2 years of service for the young physicians under the federal military draft act, while the career officers were frequently moved from one reservation to another, each with different languages. On the broader scene, the situation was also comparable to that which faces administrators from the United States and Europe who are responsible for developing medical programs in Africa and Asia, where many languages are spoken by tribal peoples in each country, and where residence among the speakers of a given language is of short duration.

We were fortunate in having the consultation of Mr. Robert Young, who not only knew the language of this tribal group, but was well acquainted with problems of communication across a language barrier in technologic aid programs carried on by the Bureau of Indian Affairs. In his opinion, even if our personnel had marked aptitude as language learners, in 2 years they could expect only imperfect control of the language, and never sufficient mastery to warrant dispensing with medical interpreters in the clinic. He encouraged us to learn as much of the language as possible, as that was of considerable importance in establishing rapport with the community as well as with patients. Additionally, such rudimentary knowledge served as a check on the interpreters themselves.[1]

Furthermore, we were encouraged to pay particular attention to systematic training of our medical interpreters. Mr. Young was well aware of the crucial importance of *conceptual transfer* to the process of technologic development in such diverse fields as agriculture, mining, forestry and, in more recent years, industrial development. In most of the government's effort, including its medical program, there had been little systematic attempt to educate interpreters in the *concepts behind* the vocabulary they would use in interpreting for agricultural scientists, engineers, and physicians. In nearly every case, the interpreter was expected to learn concepts in each of these technical fields while on the job.

In fact, there was no Civil Service job category of interpreter established in the medical field. In the hospitals, ward orderlies and nurse's aides were called upon to render this service. In the field, driver-interpreters assisted the public health nurses. There were occasional meetings in which they discussed problems of interpretation, but no systematic training program had been developed. Further, no standards for adequate interpretation had been established or methods of evaluating the accuracy or effectiveness of an interpreter's job performance. It was agreed that development of methodology and teaching materials was much needed, as well as methods of evaluation.

The Language of the Navajo Indians

In order to understand the problem of interpreting from Navajo to English and from English to Navajo, it is important to know something about the language of the Navajo people, its relationship to other languages, its sound system, and a few facts about its grammar.

The Navajo Indians speak one of the Southern Athabascan languages, a group known to linguists as Apachean. That group of languages is in turn related to Northern Athabascan spoken by various Indian tribes in Alaska and Canada. So here in North America we have a situation analogous to the distribution of such a large linguistic stock (or superfamily) as Indo-European, or Aryan, as it is popularly called. That family of languages has a spread in the old world all the way from Spain to India, and within the overall family are languages which are closely related, i.e., Spanish, French, and Italian; or German, Dutch, and Norwegian. Again an analogous situation exists in the old and the new world. There are peoples living in India, for example, the Telugu of east-central India, whose Dravidian language is totally unrelated to their neighbors who speak Hindi, the language of descendants of the Aryan invaders. So, too, in the American Southwest, the Hopi, who live alongside the Navajo, have linguistic affinities to the Ute and other Shoshone tribes, but have no linguistic ties with the Navajo, who came to the Southwest many centuries later.

Sound System

Even the insensitive ear will immediately catch the singsong up-and-down sound of the Navajo language. Like Chinese, the Athabascan languages depend on pitch, and failure to place a vowel in proper register—high, low, falling or rising—may make a major difference in the meaning of what is said. For example, 'áníí' (with the vowels in high pitch) means nostril, while 'anii' (low pitch) means face.

In addition to pitch, nasalization plays an important part in the language (as it does in French). As to other features of the phonology, the phonemes—or basic units of sound—are not as difficult to master with training as the complexity of the grammar. Perhaps the most difficult feature of the sound system for the speaker of English to master is the glottal closure, a clutching in the glottis which may be illustrated in English by the expression "uh huh." The hesitation between the two units of sound is such a glottal closure. While such a closure is rare in English, it is basic to Navajo. In fact, no Navajo words start with a vowel—all are preceded by such a glottal closure.

Verb System

Some of the major differences between the structure of English and Navajo can best be illustrated by the verb system of the Navajo language. Robert Young (1961) writes:

> The Navajo verb is extremely complex and morphologically is totally dissimilar to the familiar verb structures and categories which characterize English and other Indo-European languages. The complexity of this feature of the Navajo language has frustrated many teachers and other Bureau employees in attempting to learn to speak Navajo, even when a working knowledge of the language would have been invaluable to them. (p. 455).

The nature of these differences in the two languages is well illustrated by Clyde Kluckhohn (Kluckhohn and Leighton, 1946, a few editorial additions to this quotation are indicated by parentheses):

> How the Navajo and English languages dissect nature differently perhaps comes out most clearly when we contrast verbal statements. Take a simple event such as a person dropping something. The different "isolates of meaning" (thoughts) used in reporting (the following) identical experience will be (quite) different in Navajo and in English. "I drop it." In English the subject is specified: "I" the type of action, *drop,* and the time of action, while speaking or just before. In contrast the Navajo language specified: the subject, sh; the direction of action, downward—*naa;* definite or indefinite object (verb form), the type of object (verb stem), here a bulky roundish hard object *naa,* and the amount of control of subject over process: in act of lowering, in act of letting fall and finally where the object is falling from—the area of the hand. Thus we find that the Navajo utterance, *naash'anh lak'ee* means translated into English: "I am in the act of lowering the definite bulky, roundish, hard object from my hand." While the utterance *naashne' lak'ee* means "I am in the act of letting the definite, bulky, roundish, hard object fall from my hand." (pp. 204–205.)

This brief description touching on some aspects of the Navajo language points up the fact that it is not possible for the interpreter to parallel English lexicon in translation, as is possible in translating from closely related European languages, such as French and Spanish. Rather, the interpreter must choose terms which are only roughly equivalent. In the words of Young, the interpreter "must translate *concepts*, not words, and to do so he must understand fully the material he is called upon to interpret." The quality of interpretation is not determined as much by whether or not "there is a word in Navajo for a given idea or thing, as by the degree to which the interpreter understands the subject matter and the extent to which he has command of both languages." (Young, 1957, p. 184).

Motivational Factors

Motivation to language learning is, of course, of key importance in determining the language to be used in any technologic aid program, including medicine. It is readily apparent that from a logical point of view it is just as difficult for a Navajo to learn English as it is for us to learn Navajo. But in the case of the Navajo learning English, the individual's behavior is shaped by the actions, desires and values of his parents, his age mates, and even by local and tribal leaders. On all levels of Navajo society, education, and especially learning to speak and understand English, and to read and write it as well, has become in recent years a prime value. Thirty years ago this was not the case. The brightest children were held out to herd sheep, considered to be of greater importance than communicating with the white man. The experience of the war years, when some 8,000 men were forced out of their language community and into a new economy based on off-reservation job employment, accounts in large part for this change in motivation towards the learning of English. Today the Navajo knows that the individual who can converse with the white man gets a better job and those with skills in the written language are hired at an even higher rate of pay.

These pressures are all in accordance with the general and rapid drift of the people, an important aspect of the acculturation process, and as such are to be taken into consideration in the training of interpreters and in mapping better communications in technologic aid.

On the other hand, high motivation to learn Navajo on the part of outsiders has been present only when it is absolutely essential to one's work. Thus, traders are forced to learn the language, at least enough of it to carry on business, and the missionaries find the native language vital in conveying the gospel. But government employees whose length of stay in the Reservation is uncertain and whose job promotion does not depend on speaking the language are low in motivation and as a rule learn very little Navajo.

Knowledge of these motivational factors reinforced Mr. Young's advice to put major emphasis on systematic training of the health visitors as our major effort in simplifying medical communication between the medical team and the patients.

An Experiment in Conceptual Transfer

In order to define the problem of conceptual transfer of medical knowledge more precisely and to understand the problem better from a practical viewpoint, a simple experiment was performed. We wanted to ascertain what happens in communication when the medical interpreter is confronted with new medical concepts. Such a demonstration would illustrate what happens every day when interpreters without sufficient training are used in hospitals and clinics. Such a demonstration could then be compared to communication when the interpreter was well trained and had an understanding of the concepts involved.

In order to illustrate the first situation, a disease rarely seen among the Navajo—myocardial infarction—was selected. A passage from the standard medical textbook (Cecil and Loeb) was considerably simplified by one of our physicians and then reviewed by Mr. Young, who eliminated all figures of speech and complex constructions, and in several instances recast the English in language more comprehensible to the average interpreter. This twice edited version follows:

> There are several different kinds of disease that may affect a person's heart. One of these heart diseases is called "Coronary Occlusion" or "Coronary Thrombosis" in English. This name means that one of the blood vessels in the heart has become plugged by a clot of blood, and the blood cannot flow through the heart freely. It is like when something plugs up a pipe so the water cannot flow through it.[2] This heart disease could be called *ajeitsoss da'deeshjah* in Navajo.

Symptoms—How we know a person has Coronary Occlusion. When a blood vessel in a person's heart becomes plugged by a blood clot he suddenly becomes very sick. It is said in English that he had a "heart attack"—(that is *t'aadoo hooyani hajei d'ishjool baah dahoo'a*). When this happens, the person suddenly gets a terrible pain in his chest, and sometimes this pain spreads upward to his left shoulder and then down into his left arm. Sometimes the pain spreads upward to his left jaw. Some people who have a heart attack of this kind say that their stomach hurts and they feel like vomiting.

The pain in the person's chest, arm, jaw or stomach may last quite a long time. Sometimes it lasts for several hours. When the severe pain stops, the person often has a dull aching pain in his chest for several hours. Sometimes it feels as though there were something heavy lying on his chest. He may feel that way for several days.

When the blood vessel in a person's heart becomes plugged up, he suddenly becomes *pale* (yellow?). Some people's faces become blue, and some look gray like ashes. Some suddenly become wet with sweat. The person cannot get his breath. He feels weak. He feels very sick and thinks that he is about to die. Some people feel like vomiting and some do vomit time after time.

The above passage was read to our health visitors and to employees in government clinics. Their interpretations into Navajo were recorded on sound tape. These tapings were translated into written Navajo by William Morgan, who then back-translated the passage into English.[3] Mr. Morgan is a highly trained Navajo interpreter-translator who had been an assistant in linguistic work to Mr. Young.

One of the subjects of this experiment interpreted the first part of this passage as follows:

Now with regard to this, there are several *contagious* diseases that affect people, it is said here. Now these things that affect the lungs— I mean the heart—are called coronary occlusion and coronary thrombosis. They affect it that way, it is said. Now this thing that affects it that was just named means that in the blood vessels the blood seems to clot, it is said—in the vessels that spread about in the heart it is said, and then the unclotted blood is blocked off and doesn't seem to flow freely and strongly inside a person. Now what he just told about—when a water pipe becomes plugged so the water gets so it won't flow through it—our heart vessels spread about just like that—so the meaning is "plugged heart vessels" in Navajo.

There are several words in Navajo for "disease," one of which carries the connotation of contagiousness, the others of which refer to condition (i.e., ailing condition, pain, fever, and so forth). The interpreter mistakenly chose the term "contagious disease," although she was well educated and had had considerable experience in medical interpretation.

A second interpreter with considerable previous experience began the same passage with the statement that coronary occlusion means that the heart *stopped*. The English term "heart attack" may be translated into Navajo either as *the heart stopped* (in which event the patient has probably died) or as "the heart was attacked by a disease" (in which case the patient is still alive).

A relatively uneducated nonmedical employee referred to coronary occlusion as a "fever" and the remainder of her version was a painful effort to grasp and express those concepts through guesswork, translating the passage:

> This (acute myocardial infarction) is a condition that is sometimes referred to as a "heart attack." This disease usually begins with severe heavy "choking" kind of chest pain located in the area under the breastbone. . . .

> Now this is heart ailment. Sometimes it affects a person very strongly; when it does that, it is called heart stopped. Now this *fever* which bothers a person—if it bothers one severely, it sometimes nearly chokes him. . . .

> Now this thing that affects the thoracic organs, this thing called *tuberculosis* this truly causes pain. Now here it pops up suddenly or his face gets blue, that's the way he appears when looked at from yonder.

A third untrained "interpreter" (employed as a cook in one of the government sanatoria), who is occasionally asked to assist the doctors on the wards, rendered this same passage:

> Now this sometimes causes the heart to stop when the heart is ailing—which is called right in the right side a pain is felt—. . . .

> —and sometimes when one's upper abdomen is affected in this way his stomach becomes abnormal it is said, and it keeps his stomach sick and at the place where it hurts it keeps hurting for 30 minutes, or else for several hours it customarily hurts, it is said.

In order to demonstrate the opposite situation, that is: what happens when the interpreter *is* well acquainted with the concepts used by the physician, a disease commonly found among the Navajo was selected: rheumatoid arthritis. Again the passage was read, recorded on tape, transcribed into written Navajo, and back-translated. The two versions may be compared. Original English:

> Rheumatoid arthritis is an illness that strikes mainly at the joints. It occurs most often in people between the ages of 20 and 50, although it may be found in children. This disorder usually comes on slowly—beginning with some aching or discomfort in the arms or legs; there may be some loss of appetite and weight, there may also be some fever, tiredness, and decreased vigor. Then the joints become affected and there is pain, swelling, stiffness, and heat in the joints.

Interpreter's version translated from Navajo:

> There is a disease that affects mainly the joints. It affects especially persons from 20 to 50 years of age. However, it sometimes affects children and old people. When this affects one, its effects usually come on gradually, one's arms or legs hurt and he has no appetite and his weight usually decreases. Sometimes one is feverish (lit. one's body is hot) and he tires easily (lit. he goes futilely) and he has no energy (vigor). The one becomes aware of the condition (and appearance) of the joints for they are painful and they become swollen. They do not move easily and they become feverish (hot).

In the first experiment we duplicated a situation that is to be found in the hospitals and clinics all over the Navajo Reservation. Doctors new to the Reservation, and often those with experience, call upon interpreters unfamiliar with the concepts which are basic to the medical vocabulary used. In fact, very often hospital orderlies and clerical personnel are asked to interpret, often with disastrous results.

With reference to these experiments, Mr. Young (personal communication) pointed out:

> Medicine is a field as highly specialized as chemistry, physics or astronomy, and many medical concepts are as unfamiliar to the average Navajo as molecular weight or the quantum theory. Terminology in these fields, as well as medicine, can be simplified to minimize that aspect of the interpretation problem related to vocabulary, but simplification of the concepts is, of course, faced with serious limitations.

The interpretation from English to Navajo calls for artful paraphrasing of technical terms. However, simplification of the technical
vocabulary can be carried only so far, and beyond that meaning is
entirely lost.

In other words, this was a demonstration of the fact that if we
were going to have good communication, technical vocabulary
should not be avoided but, on the contrary, the interpreter had to
be given an understanding of such a vocabulary. The problem that
faced us was how to develop a training course which would give
the health visitor understanding of such vocabulary, and of medical
concepts in a relatively short length of time, that is, an alternative
to the usual hit-or-miss learning over a period of many years on
the job.

Training for Conceptual Transfer

The content of the course given the health visitors has been
outlined in Chapter 5. *How* that content was conveyed to the
health visitors in the classroom is relevant to the matter of conceptual transfer.

The health visitors were educated in anatomy, physiology, disease resistance, and so forth, by both the doctor and the nurse,
with one important link between them and the students, one of
whom, it will be remembered, had no more than a fifth grade
education. This link was a Navajo registered nurse who had had
many years of experience in converting medical concepts from the
one language to the other. Thus, when the concepts did not get
across, she was able to rephrase them so that they would understand them. In fact, her participation in Navajo culture and in the
subculture of our medical world as it exists in hospitals and clinics
on the reservation placed her in a similar mediating role to that
of the health visitors between the patients and the doctors. But in
this case the mediation took place on a higher level of acculturation—between bilingual Navajo on the one side, and monolingual
English speakers on the other. It was our experience that even
though the doctor and the nurse could readily converse with their
students, when concepts new to them were introduced, it was
essential to have this additional link in the communication chain.

This role, which might be called that of the teacher-interpreter,
was also taken by Kenneth Dennison, after Mrs. McKinley withdrew from the program due to illness. Although he did not have

her background in nursing, he had had considerable experience as an interpreter when he was a patient in the Fort Defiance Sanatorium (see Chapter 4). Additionally, he had sat in on the sessions conducted by her and observed the way in which she transferred medical concepts from the one language to the other.

In the Navajo language there are very few loan words taken over from English. Doctor Herbert Landar, who served as a linguist with our project (1959 to 1961), has said (Landar, personal communication):

> Instead of borrowing terms from the English medical lexicon, some of whose phonemes are lacking in the Navajo inventory anyway, the average Navajo speaker operates with *ad hoc* relative expressions which may or may not gain currency and become familiar to other speakers. A femur is not called a "femur" for example; it is referred to as a *'ajaad* ("one's leg") *bita'* ("inside it") *sitan* ("it sets, it is in position as a thin rigid object") *i* or *igii* ("the one")—the relative expression *'ajaad bita' sitan igii* is used by some, the relative expression *'ajaad bita sitan i* is used by others; similarly, a humerus is not a "humerus"; it is *'agaan* ("one's arm") *bita sitan igii*, or simply *'agaan ta' i*, "the thin rigid thing in the arm." Technical terminology from English is translated or transfigured into explanatory relative expression to conform to a pattern which makes a signal and profound impress in a multitude of semantic fields. Terms which are familiar to Navajos from everyday usage relating for example to plants, colors, kinship, or religion, offer them no conceptual difficulties. With unfamiliar concepts, however, the transfiguration without support of competent explanation may be confusing: viruses and microbes, for example, are classified with worms and insects as *ch'osh* "bugs"; they are lumped together as "the bugs which are not visible."

The selection of such "explanatory relative expressions" was a principal concern of the teacher-interpreter. It was her job to convey to the students those expressions which had already become standardized in the Navajo vocabulary, and her job to agree upon the most accurate descriptive phrases for conveying in Navajo new concepts, such as a term for myocardial infarction.

The teacher-interpreter's conceptual command of technical vocabulary in English is, of course, basic to his ability to recast such terminology into grammatical Navajo through the use of such *ad hoc* relative constructions. Thus, the inadequately trained interpreter, in some contexts, might well confuse the patient if he used the Navajo term for tuberculosis, "dwindling lung," without further explanation when tuberculosis of the bone was the topic of interpretation. Likewise, basic understanding of poliomyelitis is needed to use the Navajo word for the disease, "shriveled limb" in the proper context. "Bigtwist," the term for arthritis, might be confusing to the patient who has an incipient stage of the disease.

> In interpretation some confusion of terms owes to loose usage in English. "Stomach" is often used in English, both with regard to the specific organ or to describe the general area in which the stomach is located. In Navajo, one term refers to the stomach proper, and another to the abdominal area. On the other hand, confusion sometimes arises because of nonspecific terminology in Navajo. Thus, the thoracic cavity and its organs are all included in a single term in Navajo, whereas English specifies lungs, heart, trachea, etc. These organs may be distinguished in Navajo also by the use of adjectivals (neuter verbs which describe the specific organ involved), but many persons do not make the distinction unless pressed to do so. It is like using the term "chest" to include the area and all of its organs instead of specifying heart, lungs, etc. (Young, personal communication.)

Anatomical charts were prepared and labeled in both languages to assist the health visitors in learning the vocabularies. As mentioned in Chapter 5, Navajo knowledge of human anatomy is largely derived from knowledge of the anatomy of sheep and goats, and to a lesser extent the anatomy of cows and horses. They have made gross observations of these animals in butchering, especially the women whose job it is to kill the animals and prepare the meat for cooking. As a result, the health visitors brought to the classroom a fairly adequate knowledge of the skeletal system (Fig. 7.1), a crude knowledge of the digestive system (where, of course, there are major differences in comparison to the anatomy of the sheep) and next to no knowledge of the circulatory or nervous system. This became very evident when the human anatomical charts were labeled; specific terms were available for the digestive system; relative expressions had to be coined for the circulatory and nervous systems (Figs. 7.2 and 7.3).

The Language of Pain

Herbert Landar, who had made a study of Navajo syntax, and who had a particular research interest in psychological aspects of language, made a study of the language of pain. It was recognized by the anthropologist that while the perception of pain neurologically probably did not differ from one racial group to another, nor from one cultural group to the next, the verbal *expression* of pain was quite possibly related to the structure of the language and the conditioning of the individual Navajo by the culture in which he was born and raised.

It has been noted in the literature, and confirmed by the observation of many physicians, that the Navajo are stoic in the presence of pain. The school children do not give way to crying at inoculation clinics as do children in our society. Mothers in the delivery room likewise do not express their pain by screaming as do women in Western society.

It had also been noted that there were only a few terms in the vocabulary customarily used for the description of pain. There was *diniih,* used to express internal sharp pain, and there was *neezgai,* used to express dull pain or aching. Pain as such is something that has little interest for the Navajo, and in their own medical system diagnoses of the cause of illness by the hand trembler do not depend on a close questioning as to the nature of the pain, its exact location, periodicity, quality, and duration, as is the case in modern Western diagnosis. This restriction in the Navajo vocabulary for ways of expressing pain is, for example, in contrast to the culturally valued knowledge of plants. Hundreds of species of plants are known to the Navajo by precise terms as they are important to native medicine.

The question then remained: Did the paucity of terminology inhibit communication with the patient? In effect, did this lack of terminology act as a language barrier? The diagnosis of angina pectoris is largely dependent on a careful questioning of the patient as to the exact nature of his pain. Were cases being missed due to a language barrier?

Landar investigated the matter by two methods. First, he took standard descriptions of pain as given in medical textbooks, read them to William Morgan, who transcribed them into Navajo and then into English. From the analysis it became evident that a great variety of questions regarding pain posed by the physician or nurse

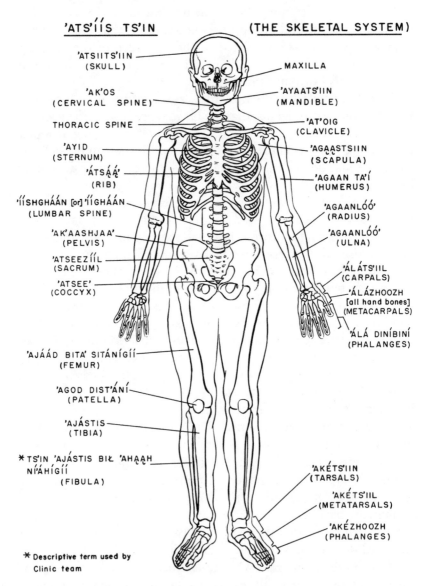

'ATS'ÍÍS TS'IN (THE SKELETAL SYSTEM)

'ATSIITS'IIN
(SKULL)

MAXILLA

'AK'OS
(CERVICAL SPINE)

'AYAATS'IIN
(MANDIBLE)

THORACIC SPINE

'AT'OIG
(CLAVICLE)

'AYID
(STERNUM)

'AGAASTSIIN
(SCAPULA)

'ÁTSÁÁ'
(RIB)

'AGAAN TA'Í
(HUMERUS)

'ÍÍSHGHÁÁN [or] 'ÍÍGHÁÁN
(LUMBAR SPINE)

'AGAANLÓÓ'
(RADIUS)

'AK'AASHJAA'
(PELVIS)

'AGAANLÓÓ'
(ULNA)

'ATSEEZÍÍL
(SACRUM)

'ÁLÁTS'IIL
(CARPALS)

'ATSEE'
(COCCYX)

'ÁLÁZHOOZH
[all hand bones]
(METACARPALS)

'ÁLÁ DINÍBINÍ
(PHALANGES)

'AJÁÁD BITA' SITÁNÍGÍÍ
(FEMUR)

'AGOD DIST'ÁNÍ
(PATELLA)

'AJÁSTIS
(TIBIA)

*TS'IN 'AJÁSTIS BIŁ 'AHĄĄH
NÍ'ÁHÍGÍÍ
(FIBULA)

'AKÉTS'IIN
(TARSALS)

'AKÉTS'IIL
(METATARSALS)

'AKÉZHOOZH
(PHALANGES)

* Descriptive term used by
Clinic team

Fig. 7.1. Drawing of human skeletal system. (From Loughlin et al., 1960. Courtesy of The Navajo Tribal Council.)

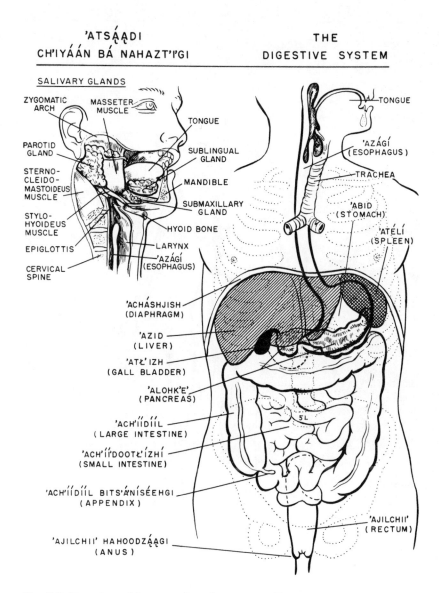

Fig. 7.2. Drawing of human digestive system. (From Loughlin et al., 1960. Courtesy of The Navajo Tribal Council.)

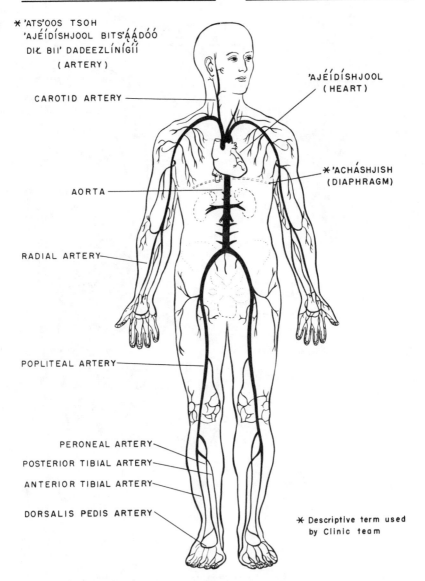

'ATS'ÍÍS TAH DIŁ NIDAAZLÍNÍGÍÍ   THE CIRCULATORY SYSTEM

* 'ATS'OOS TSOH
  'AJÉÍDÍSHJOOL BITS'ÁÁDÓÓ
  DIŁ BII' DADEEZLÍNÍGÍÍ
  (ARTERY)

CAROTID ARTERY

'AJÉÍDÍSHJOOL
(HEART)

* 'ACHÁSHJISH
  (DIAPHRAGM)

AORTA

RADIAL ARTERY

POPLITEAL ARTERY

PERONEAL ARTERY
POSTERIOR TIBIAL ARTERY
ANTERIOR TIBIAL ARTERY

DORSALIS PEDIS ARTERY

* Descriptive term used
  by Clinic team

Fig. 7.3. Drawing of human circulatory system. (From Loughlin et al., 1960. Courtesy of The Navajo Tribal Council.)

could be asked *through a well trained interpreter.* Likewise, the patients' responses in Navajo could be interpreted into English with accuracy.

Furthermore, the graduation of pain, its radiation, periodicity, and locus could all be described with sufficient accuracy to permit the full range of application of modern medicine.

The second method for the investigation of pain was to subject Navajo on the clinic staff to a series of painful stimuli, and then record their descriptions of the pain. Pain in its various dimensions (aching, pricking, burning, itching) was produced by the following means: The subject held his hand in ice water for a minute or more; a tuning fork was held to the elbow; the upper lip was brushed lightly; tetanus toxoid was injected into the muscle of the arm.

The verbalization of these types of pain was completely adequate to communicate the various characteristics of the pain patterns produced in these test situations.

Landar, in this investigation of the language of pain, found that "individual Navajos ... fell into two classes, those who consistently used simple terms, without qualifications (e.g., 'it hurts,' 'it itches,' 'it burns,' all one word predications in Navajo), and those who consistently used complex sentences worked by one or more subordinate clauses (e.g., 'it hurts while it burns slightly')." However, such varying levels of abstractions were "a trivial barrier to medical communication."

Other Grammatical Factors

Landar pointed out that lack of generic terms for "color, shape, form, material and other cognitive categories forces interpreter and patient into circumlocution." Thus, when the doctor asked the patient, "What is the color of the spit?" the interpreter phrased the question, "I'd like to know then how is it, he says."

This vague interpretation did not elicit the response called for, and it was only after the question was posed a second time by the physician: "What color is it?" and the interpreter said: "How is it usually, either what you spit out time after time, or your nasal mucus which you haul out (as a load) time after time?" that the patient responded: "The nasal mucus that's usually nasty yellow; a little blood is red within it."

Such a long exchange, however, could have been avoided, had the physician been aware that there was no *generic* word for color, in which case he could ask, "Is the mucus greenish-yellow with streaks of red?" or he could have elicited a series of "yes's" and "no's" by narrowing down on the color by a series of precise questions: "Is it dark yellow, is it light yellow . . . ?" and so on.

It was discovered that the Navajo concept of time did not allow for a few minutes. That is, he had no way of expressing such a short period of time directly but could again, by resorting to analogy and circumlocution, express this concept if asked to do so.

In the judgment of Landar, such differentials in the grammar of English and Navajo did not constitute a true block to communication. However, from the point of view of one of the doctors, "the danger in this situation is that, quite without knowing it, the physician has transferred to the interpreter the responsibility for deciding how deeply this particular question of color should be probed." In other words, such differentials certainly imposed a potential hazard to good doctor-patient communications and thereby restricted good medical practice, unless the physician was instructed as to this linguistic difference between the two languages.

In this chapter we have gone into considerable detail describing the training given the Navajo intepreters which enabled them to transfer medical concepts. This methodology may serve as a model for those administrators of public health programs in many parts of the less developed world.

In the operation of cross-cultural and cross-linguistic medical programs, such as those carried on by the World Health Organization or by the Central Government of India extending services to its millions of tribal peoples, there is no doubt that the ideal condition is for the physician and nurse to speak the language of the patients fluently. But programs that allow sufficient length of time in one place for such learning to take place, are the exception. Most, like the service rendered to the American Indian by our national government, are built on the basis of rapid professional turnover. Such a short term makes it quite impossible to master the language to a point where the physician feels confident in addressing the patient in his own language without an interpreter present.

Additionally, as pointed out at the outset of the chapter, it requires less of an expenditure of time and effort to give specially designed training to the acculturated native so that he can learn such concepts than to give the doctor or nurse sufficient knowledge of the language.

Another important consideration is that from the point of view of the patients, the presence of a more or less permanent skilled corps of interpreters minimizes the break in communications which takes place when new physicians and nurses come to the community.

8.

Community Response
to the Clinic

Given the efforts described in the preceding chapters to modify the standard medical delivery system according to the cultural and geographic characteristics of the community, it is reasonable to ask to what extent the clinic was used by the community. Since there was no clinic present at Many Farms before the introduction of the Navajo–Cornell facility we have no baseline that would allow us to compare clinic usage before and after the adaptive changes made by the project staff. Further, we have no comparable data on a matched control community at the same period of time with which to make a comparison. The clinic usage figures presented in this chapter thus are not a definitive test of the utility of the innovations, but they do provide an indication of the responsiveness of various segments of the community to the establishment of this type of clinic. There are of course other indicators of community response aside from the statistics presented here. During the course of the clinic's existence there were several attempts by community leaders to expand the facility so that it could serve as a hospital. Further, during the last year of operation, several community meetings were initiated by the community in an unsuccessful attempt to convince the Public Health Service that the clinic should be maintained after the departure of the Cornell group.

Another important reason for examining the clinic usage data is that the morbidity findings presented in Chapter 10 derive from examination of Navajo patients who visited the clinic. Analysis of the characteristics of the population which used the clinic provides a partial answer to the question of whether the pattern of disease diagnosed by the physicians was a reflection of disease extant in the population or simply of that segment of the population seen in the clinic.

The Clinic Attendance Record

Gross Clinic Usage

On May 9, 1956, before approximately 1,200 members of the total community, the Many Farms Clinic was inaugurated at ceremonies conducted by a prominent Navajo medicine man from the community. The services also were attended by important tribal officials and by the local delegate to the Navajo Tribal Council. From its inception, therefore, the medical facility and its peripheral services were well known throughout the 700 square mile area.

It was not until several months after the inauguration of the clinic, however, that radiographic equipment and other necessary facilities were fully operative. Considerable time also was required (as described in Chapter 6) for the development of an identification system and a census base which would permit establishment of population based rates of clinic usage, morbidity, and mortality. The introduction of the first clinic in the community could also be expected to motivate a number of visits just out of curiosity. For these reasons, the clinic usage statistics presented in this chapter start with 1957, the first full calendar year of operation. This year also provides reliable base data for the population and excludes the novelty effect of the first months of operation.

During the first three years of operation there was a rise in the number of individuals seen, the proportion of the population seen and in the total visits made to the clinic (Table 8.1). During the last two years of clinic operation a decline was registered in these same categories. The decline took place independently of any known marked change in morbidity or mortality. Indeed, the peak usage year of 1959, as measured by the proportion of the population seen and the total visits made, was a year with extremely low morbidity and mortality. The years of 1957 and 1960, however, were marked by measles epidemics and associated complications of pneumonia and otitis media. Therefore, the reduction in clinic usage in 1960 and 1961 can most probably be attributed to three obvious administrative and external factors.

In the latter part of 1959, the Public Health Service opened a modernized clinical facility at Chinle, 10 miles from Many Farms. In early 1961 the road to the clinic from Many Farms was paved. In the fall of 1960 the Many Farms facility was closed one day per week so that the staff could service a community outside the study area at the request of the Public Health Service (resulting in a five percent drop in the number of days the Many Farms Clinic was open). The one day closing was viewed by the clinic staff as a phase in the process of planned withdrawal from the community. From 1960 on, the community was advised at a number of open meetings in the Chapter House that the research group would leave the community in June 1962 and it would be up to the Public Health Service to operate the clinic if such maintenance fit their plans for the area. The process of gradual disengagement was continued in August 1961 when the Many Farms Clinic was closed two days a week in order to provide increased services outside of the community. By the end of 1961, physicians at Chinle reported they were seeing many more patients from Many Farms than before. The 14 percent decline in the proportion of the population seen at the Many Farms Clinic, however, was far less than the 28 percent decrease in service days open (Table 8.1, Column 5).

As is evident from the five year record of clinic attendance the accessibility of the clinic and the Navajo need and desire for the services offered permitted the examination of a minimum of 55 percent of the community population in any year. With the exception of 1961, over 60 percent of the population was seen each year. These figures do not indicate, however, the proportion of the population which was seen over the entire five year period. To establish this proportion, the charts of all those resident in 1961 (the last full year of clinic operation) were checked for visits over the previous year. Of the 2,299 people resident in 1961, 2,079 or

Table 8.1. Patient visits,[1] by year.

Year	Patients seen	Days open[2]	Index days open[2]	Total population	% pop. seen	Total visits[3]	Visits per person/pop.[4]
1957	1,223	260	100	1,936	63	4,964	2.6
1958	1,362	260	100	2,044	67	5,378	2.6
1959	1,453	260	100	2,127	68	5,582	2.6
1960	1,386	246	95	2,221	62	5,050	2.3
1961	1,265	186	72	2,299	55	3,539	1.5

[1]Excludes non-Navajo patients and patients not residing in the study area.
[2]As part of the process of planned withdrawal from the community, the clinic was closed one day per week starting in the fall of 1960, and two days per week beginning in August 1961.
[3]This figure includes multiple visits made by the same individual. The number of individuals seen is shown in Column 1. Excluded from these figures are "administrative visits," i.e., visits made at the request of clinic staff for study purposes and visits made to obtain physical examinations required for fire fighting, food handling or relocation off the Reservation under auspices of the Bureau of Indian Affairs.
[4]Computed by dividing total visits by total population for each year.

Table 8.2. Clinic usage by age groups compared to total population, 1957–1961.

	1961			1960			1959			1958			1957		
	No. in clinic	Percent clinic population	Percent total population	No. in clinic	Percent clinic population	Percent total population	No. in clinic	Percent clinic population	Percent total population	No. in clinic	Percent clinic population	Percent total population	No. in clinic	Percent clinic population	Percent total population
Under 1 year	60	4.7	3.7	81	5.8	4.5	74	5.1	4.2	78	5.7	4.5	59	4.8	4.4
1–4	274	21.7	15.6	280	20.2	15.3	301	20.7	16.1	287	21.1	16.3	237	19.4	16.7
5–9	226	17.9	17.0	266	19.2	17.3	275	18.9	17.2	270	19.8	17.1	236	19.3	16.6
10–29	314	24.8	36.6	368	26.6	35.9	391	26.9	35.0	340	25.0	34.5	321	26.2	34.9
30–64	318	25.1	22.4	321	23.2	22.5	342	23.5	23.0	332	24.4	23.4	302	24.7	23.1
65 & over	73	5.8	4.6	70	5.1	4.5	70	4.8	4.6	55	4.0	4.3	68	5.6	4.1

90.4 percent had been seen in the clinic at least once during the five year period.

With regard to age, there was a consistent pattern of differences in clinic attendance over the five full calendar years of the study (Table 8.2). In comparison with their representation in the total population, infants under one year of age and those in the 1–4 and 5–9 age categories were over-represented in the clinic population.

Heavy clinic usage by those in the 0–9 age groups appeared to reflect the morbidity pattern. This is the age group most prone to be ill with common acute conditions, i.e. diarrhea, measles, otitis media and pneumonia. Mothers, in a sample of 40 residents interviewed intensively by Dr. Tom T. Sasaki, indicated that they tended to bring their children to the clinic without delay for treatment of acute childhood conditions. The high usage in this age group thus appears to be the result of a combination of the morbidity pattern, which affected this age group more than others, and the willingness of parents to utilize the clinic for treatment of the potentially serious conditions which affected this group.

The clinic attendance pattern for the younger age groups was consistently reversed for the 10–29 age grouping. This age group comprised a proportion of clinic users significantly smaller than their representation in the population. A substantial portion of those who had never attended the clinic during the five year period 1957–1961 were between the ages of 10–24. They made up 59 percent of all non-clinic users but only 31 percent of the total population. A large proportion of non-users in this age group were only technically residents of the community. They were absent most of the year attending boarding schools. Males in this age group were more heavily under-represented in the clinic population than females. The absence of community members in this age group to attend school also explains the sex differential in clinic attendance in this group. Of the 31 students at boarding schools in 1961, 21 were males.

In each of the five years, the total population was almost evenly divided between males and females, but males were consistently under-represented in the clinic population and females were over-represented (Table 8.3). Part of the explanation for this difference is indicated above—more males than females were absent from the community due to employment out of the community or off

Table 8.3. Clinic users, by sex, 1957–1961.

Year	Male			Female		
	No. patients	Percent clinic pop.	Percent males total pop.	No. patients	Percent clinic pop.	Percent females total pop.
1957	558	45.6	49.4	665	54.4	50.6
1958	633	46.5	49.7	729	53.5	50.2
1959	659	45.4	49.8	794	54.6	50.2
1960	633	45.7	49.8	753	54.3	50.2
1961	592	46.8	49.6	673	53.2	50.3

the Reservation. Another reason for the male-female difference in clinic usage probably rests on the generally greater need of women for medical care in the childbearing years, a pattern evident in the United States generally and not peculiar to the Navajo. The clinic at Many Farms tended to accentuate this pattern because it did not have a separate pediatric facility and women who brought in their children for care could just as easily be seen by the same physician.

It was expected from observations of the community and the pervasive transportation problem that the location of a patient's camp would have an important bearing upon attendance at the clinic. Residents of camps along the valley highway (Zones 4, 5, and 6, see Map 8.1) could reach the clinic by pickup truck or horse and wagon in a matter of minutes. Some were within walking distance. From the more distant zones of the study district, such as Black Mountain (Zone 1), it was more than an hour and a half to the clinic by truck. During the winter months the road up the mountain was passable only in the early morning or late evening when the surface froze. Generally, the more distant the zone from the central highway, the more traditional was the mode of life of its inhabitants. Distance of course is but a crude measure of physical isolation. Travel time is a far better indicator. Far East Mesa, for example, was closer to the clinic (and the highway) than Black Mountain (12 miles as compared to 20 miles), but the travel difficulties were as great from Far East Mesa during rainy and dry seasons.

The residence zones also provided differential access to other communities and medical facilities. The families in Black Mountain could easily stay on the high plateau and reach such communities as Piñon. During 1960 and 1961, when the clinic at Piñon was serviced by physicians from Many Farms, a number of patients from the Many Farms study population were seen at the Piñon clinic (their visits were not placed in the records of the research facility). Similarly, some of the families in Zone 2 had access to facilities at Rock Point or Chilchinbeto, while those in the South Valley (Zone 6) could easily reach Chinle. While the residents of Far East Mesa had almost as much difficulty reaching Many Farms as residents of Black Mountain, the main road out of their zone required them to pass by the Many Farms Clinic.

Despite the variations in time and travel to reach the clinic, and the attraction of other facilities on the periphery of the study district, over 78 percent of the population from the most distant area of Black Mountain was seen at least once in the clinic (Table 8.4). The residence areas closest to the clinic (Zones 3 through 6) sent a larger proportion of their population to the clinic, but the more distant areas were not far behind. The same pattern was evident in a review of the camp affiliation of those who had not attended the clinic even once during the five year period. There were camps which had five or more non-users of the clinic. Four of these camps were on Black Mountain, two on Far West Mesa and four in the South Valley which were oriented more towards Chinle. There was no indication that traditional bias played a part in the aloofness of these camps. Only 50 percent of them had a resident medicine man or diagnostician, for example, and this same ratio existed in the total study district.

A follow-up study of a random sample of 40 non-users of the clinic, stratified by residence areas, was conducted in the spring of 1962 by Dr. Mark Nammacher, then a fourth year medical student. Each respondent was questioned about reasons for not utilizing the clinic (Table 8.5). Lack of transportation, combined with distance, was cited by only one respondent as the reason for not using the Many Farms Clinic. The largest group of those in the sample were away at school most of the year, while four others were absent for varying periods in order to work or fulfill their military obligation. Ten respondents utilized other medical facilities at Chinle, Piñon, Ganado, Kayenta and Rock Point. Of those

LEGEND

▬▬▬ Zones	●	Camps
▬▬▬ Paved roads	○	Clinic
╌╌╌ Dirt roads	⌂	Schools
⋯⋯ Trails	T.R	Trading post
∿⋯ Intermittent drainage	◖	Reservoir
∿∿ Permanent drainage	╌╌╌	Fences
⌇⌇ Rims	⟷	Airports
⌇⌇ High cliffs	╌╌╌	Irrigation ditch

ZONES WITHIN THE
NAVAJO-CORNELL FIELD HEALTH PROJECT
1961

Table 8.4. Clinic attendance by residence area.

Residence area	Total population[1]		Clinic users		Percent of total pop. seen in clinic[2]
	No.	Percent	No.	Percent	
1. Black Mountain	219	9.5	172	6.7	78.5
2. Far West Mesa	336	14.6	291	18.6	86.6
3. West Mesa	475	20.7	444	22.4	93.5
4. Clinic Cluster	241	10.5	232	11.3	96.3
5. North Valley	357	15.5	347	19.9	97.2
6. South Valley	285	12.4	249	12.1	87.4
7. East Mesa	238	10.4	211	9.4	88.7
8. Far East Mesa	148	6.3	133	5.6	90.0
	2,229	99.9	2,009	100.0	AV. 90.4

[1]Total population as of December 31, 1961.
[2]Percent of those resident in 1961 who had been seen in clinic at least once during the period 1957–1961, inclusive.

Table 8.5. Reasons given for non-attendance at Many Farms Clinic by a sample of 40 non-users.

Reason	No.	Percent of sample responses
Attending school out of area	17	42.5
Used other medical facilities	10	25.0
No illness	6	15.0
Often away from community	4	10.0
Lack of transportation	1	2.5
No answer	2	5.0
TOTAL	40	100.0

who reported an illness during this period of time, two had occasion to use a native practitioner.

In summary, the level of clinic usage was very high over the entire five year period. The age, sex and residence characteristics of the population seen in the clinic was remarkably constant during the study period. With over 90 percent of the district population attending the clinic, the significance of such selective factors as transportation and cultural traditionalism was minimized.

The Nature of Clinic Visits

Measures of clinic usage have been presented to: provide a basis of judgment for evaluating the morbidity findings; and demonstrate the response of the population to the presence of the clinic and its outreach activities. Ordinarily the patient's motive for making a clinic visit would not be relevant for these purposes. But the special nature of the Many Farms Clinic, which was not instituted as a service clinic but rather as a research facility, demands some consideration of the effect of the research activities upon attendance at the clinic.

In order to assess the representativeness of the clinic population and more thoroughly describe their use of the clinic, a chart review was instituted after the clinic was closed. A fourfold categorization was established based upon the chief complaint or reason given by the patient for the visit and recorded in his chart by the health visitor. This information did not provide for depth analysis of the motivations of the patient or the nature of the decision-making process which finally brought him to the clinic. Such probing was carried out on a sample of patients who were interviewed in the clinic immediately after they saw the physician or shortly after they returned home. Findings from these interviews are reported in a later section and were not used for the portion of the study described below.

The four usage categories established were: Administrative Visit; Visit with Presenting Symptoms; Preventive Visit; and Chronic, Voluntary Visit. The first category was designed to gauge the effect of the special nature of the clinic. During the course of research, members of the community in selected age, sex and family groups were invited to visit the clinic by the health visitors, and in some cases transportation was provided. All such visits were coded as administrative visits unless the patient appeared with a presenting complaint or stated that the visit was made for the purpose of a preventive check-up or procedure. Also included in this category were visits made to satisfy requirements set by the tribe or the government. All candidates for relocation, applicants for food handler licenses and those desiring fire fighting duty were required to obtain a physical examination and their visits for these purposes were coded as administrative.

The second category, Visit with Presenting Symptoms, is self-explanatory. This visit is one during which the patient reported some physical complaint to the health visitor. Immunizations might have been given during the course of the visit, or a radiograph taken for research purposes, but in such cases, the visit was counted only once as a "Visit with Presenting Symptoms" and was not counted in any other category.

In the third category were tabulated visits for which the patient desired a preventive procedure, such as immunization, or a physical examination (in the absence of symptoms and for no administrative purpose). All pre-natal and post-partum examinations of women without presenting complaints were included in this category. The same rules applied to this category as to others, i.e. though an immunization might be given in the course of a visit with a "presenting complaint," only those visits made for this purpose as stated by the patient were coded as preventive visits. Also excluded from this and all categories of visits were immunizations given periodically by the physician and public health nurse at the schools.

The last category of visits encompasses voluntary visits made for periodic treatment, examination, or re-medication for chronic or semi-chronic conditions. The bulk of visits in this category were made by patients under treatment and observation for tuberculosis who visited the clinic for a periodic chest film or refill of their isoniazid. Again, the categorization of a particular visit was based upon the patient's reported view of the visit. Thus, the twelve visits made by a rheumatic fever patient for monthly prophylactic injections of penicillin were coded in the fourth category, rather than as preventive visits, because from the patient's point of view this was protracted treatment for a condition originally coded as "Visit with Presenting Symptoms."

The results of this analysis (Table 8.6) show, first, that the research nature of the facility did not greatly influence the volume of clinic visits. Over the five year period, administrative visits (which include those made at the request of governmental units as well as the research facility) constituted a little over 3 percent of the total visits. The great majority of patients who made administrative visits also used the clinic for other purposes. Only 1.2 percent of all those who ever attended the clinic did so exclusively to satisfy administrative requests. The clinic usage pattern then may be viewed as a response to a service-oriented facility in this area.

Table 8.6. Number and percentage of visits by type and year.

| Year | Total visits | Type of visit | | | | | | | |
| | | Presenting symptoms | | Chronic voluntary | | Preventive | | Administrative | |
		No. visits	Percent of total visits	No. visits	Percent of total visits	No. visits	Percent of total visits	No. visits	Percent of total visits
1957	5,245	4,423	84.3	379	7.2	162	3.1	281	5.4
1958	5,578	4,533	81.3	255	4.6	590	10.6	200	3.6
1959	5,748	4,292	74.7	225	3.9	1,065	18.5	166	2.9
1960	5,120	4,435	86.6	209	4.1	406	7.9	70	1.4
1961	3,669	3,144	85.7	182	5.0	213	5.8	130	3.5
TOTAL	25,360	20,827	Av. 82.1	1,250	Av. 4.9	2,436	Av. 9.6	847	Av. 3.3

It is not surprising in a population with a disease pattern dominated by acute infectious disease, that the largest proportion of total visits (82 percent) were made by patients who presented with symptomatic complaints. If the two categories of visits, Presenting Symptoms and Chronic Voluntary are combined to make them comparable to the "complaint" category in the U.S. National Health Survey, the proportion is increased to 87 percent as compared to the U.S. national figure of 75 percent. The figures for the United States, however, represent multiple coding so that a visit for treatment and for immunization would be counted twice, i.e. once in each category. On this basis, the difference is not great.

The most striking finding concerns the proportion of preventive visits (9.6 percent of all visits). Anthropologists have suggested that Navajos look more to the present than to the future, therefore, inducing them to act to prevent some future event would not be very successful (Kluckhohn & Strodtbeck 1961). It is debatable whether the orientation to the present is so overwhelming in the health area. There are many preventive avoidance behaviors practiced by both a woman and her husband during a pregnancy to prevent the future birth of a deformed infant, such as not making a weaving comb with more than five prongs or not castrating an animal. Our findings suggest, that under certain conditions, preventive care will be actively sought.

The rise in preventive visits in 1958 and 1959 can be explained largely by the operation of a satellite facility for well-baby care from March 27, 1958 to March 24, 1960. The facility was opened in a converted railroad boxcar at Rough Rock, 22 miles from the main facility, and was staffed once a week by the Public Health Nurse and a Navajo health visitor. Visits to this facility were coded as if they were visits to the main research clinic, but they were not included in the morbidity tabulation because no physician was present to record a diagnosis. An analysis of visits to the well-baby clinic showed that during the two years of operation the nature of the facility was never clear to the community since many children and adults visited the boxcar for treatment of symptoms. Such cases were referred to the Many Farms Clinic. Nevertheless, making a facility easily available to the residents of Zones 1, 2, and 3 significantly increased the number of preventive visits and the level of immunization in the population.

While there was some increase in the delivery of preventive care by making the services more readily available, significant gaps in such care remained. During the years 1958 through 1960, only one-third of the 290 children under the age of one year received diptheria-pertussis-tetanus immunizations and only one-fifth received polio vaccine. Similarly, only one-third of the children aged one to four years received these inoculations each year. When it is recalled that each of the injections should be repeated several times in order to achieve optimum levels of immunity, it is clear that these children did not have adequate levels of protection from these diseases.

A similar picture emerged in the area of preventive pre- and postnatal care. During her fertile years, 15 to 45, a Navajo woman spends much of her time in a pre- or postnatal state and the population sustains one of the highest fertility rates in the world (232 per 1,000). The health visitors in the field and the physicians in the clinic encouraged those who were pregnant to obtain pre-natal care. Nevertheless, of 486 successful term pregnancies recorded over a five year period (1957–1961), only 54 percent of the mothers were seen at the clinic before giving birth. Of those who were seen, most visited but once, usually in the last trimester of pregnancy. Of those seen in the last trimester, 45 percent were anemic with hematocrit readings of less than 36 percent. The situation was little better in the postpartum period. Despite tribal encouragement, in the form of a free layette for mothers bringing themselves and their child in for postnatal examinations and census registration, only 24 percent of the mothers and 23 percent of the children made postpartum visits.

The health visitors and physicians encouraged expectant mothers to plan to deliver their children at a hospital. Referrals were made to the Fort Defiance Indian Hospital, some 90 miles away and when birth was imminent, transportation was provided to Sage Memorial Hospital at Ganado, 50 miles away. During 1958 and 1959, a small mission-operated clinic at Rock Point, some 38 miles away from the Many Farms facility, but closer to district families living on the periphery, was equipped to handle deliveries. Other hospitals of course could be used by the population, such as the United States Public Health Service Hospital at Tuba City, or Gallup, or any other hospital near which the family found itself when temporarily away from the community.

Over a five year period, 282 births (59 percent of the 482 births

Table 8.7. Physician-attended births by year.

	All births			Physician attended	
Year	Total	Attendance unknown	Percent unknown	No.	Percent known
1957	95	0	—	43	45.3
1958	100	0	—	63	63.0
1959	94	1	1.1	55	59.1
1960	105	2	1.9	63	61.2
1961	92	1	1.1	59	64.8
Total	486	4	Av. .08	83	Av. 58.7

about which the circumstances were known), were physician-attended (Table 8.7). Only six of these births were attended by physicians at Many Farms; the remaining 276 occurred at a hospital or other health facility. It is evident that the proportion of physician-attended births rose significantly after 1957, but the rise in 1958 and 1959 cannot be directly attributed to the Many Farms facility. Twenty-seven of the physician-attended births in 1958–59 occurred at the Rock Point Clinic and at facilities off the Reservation where families had gone for temporary work, as compared to three such out-of-district births in 1957. In 1960 and 1961 combined, however, all but 14 of the 122 physician-attended births occurred at the recommended facilities, Fort Defiance or Ganado.

The medical effect of the rise in physician-attended births was not discernible. During the entire five year period there were no maternal deaths. Further, neonatal deaths were extremely low in all years and there was no significant relationship between neonatal deaths and whether a birth was or was not attended by a physician.

In summary, the clinic was well attended and the patients seen were representative of the community population. Analysis of the charted reasons for visits demonstrated that the clinic usage pattern was not skewed by the research nature of the facility. As in the general United States population, a greater proportion of women than men were seen in the clinic and a smaller proportion of the population between the ages of 10 and 24 were seen by clinic physicians since they were at school, away from the community, much of the year. Accessibility did influence clinic usage, with only 79 percent of the most distant population visiting the clinic in 1961, while 96 percent of the population in the immediate vicinity of the clinic were seen. There were no systematic cultural barriers to clinic usage that could be identified. Indeed, as will be seen in the next chapter, the indigenous system also functioned actively during this time and in the last year of the project an estimated 1,350 curing ceremonies were held.

9.

The Indigenous Curing System and Modern Medicine

Modern or Western-style medicine is never introduced into a vacuum. Every culture has its long established system or systems to deal with the crisis of illness. The presence of a heavily utilized Navajo curing system was known to the researchers when the Many Farms facility was established in the community. It also was known that members of the community utilized ceremonies of the Native American Church for curing and had recourse as well to nearby Hopi diagnosticians and indigenous therapists. What was not known, however, was the affect the indigenous system or systems might have on the use of the facility, either to reduce clinic usage or as a major selective factor determining who used the clinic. There was concern that the indigenous system might affect the outcome of an illness by causing a patient to delay seeking medical care. Resort to native curing practice, it was believed, also might cause the patient to neglect the treatment regimen prescribed by the physician. These were all practical problems of direct interest to the research staff.

There was an additional, ethical reason, for examining the indigenous medical system. As conceived by the research staff and conveyed to the community, the facility was to operate for a limited time, yet it might have a more lasting impact on the indigenous system. The ethics of the situation then, as well as scientific interest in culture change and the nature of our clinic patients required that we investigate the interrelationship between the indigenous curing system and the innovation of a modern medical facility in the community.

The Traditional Systems

Diagnosticians

The most commonly used method of diagnosis at Many Farms was hand trembling. While in a trance-like state, the hand trembler makes involuntary hand movements, producing and erasing designs on the floor of the hogan. At the end of the trance he interprets symbols remaining on the ground and determines the ceremony that is necessary.

Another known but not so widely practiced diagnostic method was that of star gazing. Traditionally, this is a more elaborate procedure and sometimes involves the use of a sand painting. None of the nine star gazers at Many Farms, however, made use of sandpainting. The gazer sings the appropriate songs for star gazing and then stares fixedly at a star until he can see what is causing the patient's illness. Two star gazers at Many Farms reported that their vision was "something like an X-ray." The same purpose can be served by gazing at a quartz crystal or other rock but there was no one versed in crystal gazing at Many Farms in 1961.

One other method of diagnosis has been described in the literature, that of "listening," during which sounds are interpreted to make the diagnosis. Many Farms residents were aware of the existence of such a method but the one man who practiced the art utilized it only to locate lost people, animals and objects.

The patients in the study district had 69 diagnosticians from whom they could choose[1] (Table 9.1). There was one diagnostician for every 33 residents, or one for every 2.6 camps. Nearly a third of the 21 diagnosticians were singers as well. It was common and expected practice at Many Farms for the diagnostician to also perform the recommended curing ceremony if he was able even though traditionally this was not the customary practice.

Table 9.1. Singers/curers and diagnosticians, by sex, 1961.

Functions performed	Male	Female	Total
Singing/curing only	28	—	28
Singing/curing and hand trembling	13	1	14
Singing/curing, hand trembling and star gazing	3	—	3
Singing/curing and star gazing	4	—	4
Hand trembling only	13	33	46
Hand trembling and star gazing only	2	—	2
Summary			
Singing/curing	48	1	49
Hand trembling	31	34	65
Star gazing	9	—	9

Of the 69 diagnosticians, 66 were hand tremblers; 5 of the 66 could also star gaze and an additional 3 specialized in star gazing exclusively. In contrast to the singers (only one of whom was a woman), the diagnosticians were almost equally divided between men and women. Of the 48 individuals who functioned only as diagnosticians, 33 (69 percent) were women.

Singers/Curers

In contrast to the diagnostician, the medicine man or singer must serve a long and therefore costly apprenticeship in order to learn the complex interweaving of prayers, chants, sandpainting, body painting, cutting and decoration of prayer sticks, and the mixing and administration of herbal infusions—which in proper sequence make up a Navajo ceremonial. The full fledged singer of a particular ceremonial also must learn the full chant for that Way which includes the origin story of the ceremonial. The proper performance of the ceremonial compels the Gods to restore harmony and health to the individual patient, and the accolade of singer is reserved for the individual who has learned the total complex of a ceremonial.

Nevertheless, portions of a ceremony can be learned by individuals from watching or assisting a singer. The individual who learns in this way often is referred to as having "stolen" the ceremony. In the Many Farms area, individuals who knew little bits

Table 9.2. Selected ceremonies known to Many Farms singers/curers.

Ceremony	No. of singers
Blessing Way	23
Shooting Way	23
Chiricahua Wind Way	16
Flint Way	9
Navajo Wind Way	8
Red Ant Way	6
Enemy Way	2

and pieces of ceremonies, particularly the herbal preparations and a few of the songs, were called curers. They often referred to themselves as short form singers, or reported, "I only give herbs and blacken the patient," i.e. referring to one part of the Ghost Way ceremony during which the patient is painted with a mixture of ground charcoal. There were four such men in the community, in addition to 45 others who were referred to simply as singers (Table 9.1). Among the singers a distinction was often made between those who knew only the Blessing Way Ceremony, which protects the individual from future harm, as opposed to those who knew the other ceremonies which are used to re-establish health in an individual who is already sick. Two of the 49 singers/curers were Blessing Way singers only, and a total of 23 singers included Blessing Way as part of their repertoire (Table 9.2).

There was one singer/curer for every 47 residents or one for every 3.3 camps. Singers are not as interchangeable as diagnosticians, since no singer is able to perform every ceremony. But at Many Farms there were a number of singers versed in the most common variations of the major ceremonials (Table 9.2). In addition to the 23 singers of Blessing Way, 23 knew Shooting Way and there were 16 singers of Chiracahua Wind Way. These data are based upon interviews with the singers since people in the community would sometimes report an individual as a singer of a particular chant, but that person would respond, "I only know a few bits and pieces."

It should also be noted that while the study was confined to this particular district of the reservation, the population was not confined to that district when it sought medical or indigenous curing treatment. Just as patients could seek Western-style medical treatment at Chinle, Ganado, or Fort Defiance, so they could consult and use diagnosticians and singers outside of the study area.

Other Curing Systems

The Many Farms population also had access to two other curing systems. The Hopi Indians live approximately 85 miles away from Many Farms by paved highway and 35 miles away via backroads over Black Mountain. From the Hopis, they were able to obtain diagnostic services as well as treatment, particularly with herbal remedies. These services were used extensively, usually for cases that did not respond to Navajo or clinical medical treatment.

A third curing system was introduced into the area around 1931 in the form of the Native American Church. The ritual and beliefs of the church combine elements of Christianity with Indian religion, particularly that of the southern plains where it first developed. As it moved into the Navajo country, elements of Navajo ritual were added and six of the Blessing Way singers in the study area were road priests in the Native American Church. Communicants of the Church take peyote (containing the drug mescaline) as a sacrament and this feature of the religion has created a great deal of controversy in the states involved.

The use of peyote was outlawed by the Navajo Tribal Council in 1940 (Navajo Tribal Council, 1940). The ban was rescinded by the 1967 Navajo Tribal Council, 1967, but the legal prohibition in effect during the research reported here made it difficult to directly question informants regarding their adherence to the Church. In several homes, however, communicants who owned prayer rattles and feathers used in the ceremonies proudly displayed them on their wall and some willingly discussed their participation. Sometimes, members wore distinctive jewelry bearing symbols from the Church ritual in the design. Despite the illegal status of the Church, there was a general consensus in the community about which camps housed at least some members of the Church.

An estimated 25 of the 143 Navajo camps in the study district, or 16 percent of the camps, contained adherents to the Church. This figure, while rough, does give some indication of the strength of the movement in the community, and more pertinent to the discussion here, a measurement of the importance of an alternate healing system. As was true with Hopi medicine, a patient did not have to be a firm believer in the Native American Church in order to utilize the ceremonies for curative purposes. Thus, individual patients shopping for cures could make use of Navajo curing, Hopi medicine, the curing potential in ritual of the Native American Church, in addition to visiting the clinic.

Medical Co-Existence

The Existence of Dual Systems

The response to the introduction of a modern medical facility into the community, as measured by clinic usage, clearly was one of acceptance. But did this "acceptance" involve use of both the indigenous and the Western systems?

The dual use of systems is best demonstrated by analysis of the behavior of two groups at the extremes of the two systems—the Navajo health visitors trained by the clinic staff and the singers in the community. The health visitors were all in the 20–30 year age group and most had the equivalent of at least an eighth grade education. Almost all of the health visitors had been former tuberculosis patients who had been treated by some of the same physicians engaged at the research facility. They therefore had extensive personal contact with medical science (see Chapter 5). It is essential to note here that they had received more education in concepts of disease and the nature of modern medicine than could be given to other members of the community even if the entire resources of the project had been channeled into a community-wide health education program. Nevertheless, the health visitors utilized the clinic only as often as did others of the same age and sex in the community. Most significantly, when they and other members of the family were ill, they also utilized the services of a diagnostician and singer as frequently as other members of the community.

In contrast to the health visitors, the singers were of an older generation, nearly 90 percent were 50 years or older, and they had little formal schooling. The singers had well defined roles to play in the indigenous system and were committed in belief and behavior to that system. Yet, of the 49 medicine men in the area, only three had not visited the clinic as patients during the five year period. As a group they utilized the clinic as frequently as others in the population of the same age and sex.

Medicine men and diagnosticians not only used the clinic but also referred patients to the physician. Eighteen of the 42 medicine men who were interviewed also were diagnosticians; of these, 14 (78 percent) reported that there had been occasions when their hand "had pointed towards the clinic." Of the non-diagnosing medicine men interviewed, one third stated that they had suggested to patients that they consult a physician. The medicine man was less likely to suggest an alternate mode of treatment because as several explained:

> If people come to me for a sing, I would never refuse them. I don't want those people to get angry with me. If she didn't get better, I would recommend that she go to another diagnostician who would tell her to go to the clinic.

It is reasonable to ask at this point whether the indigenous system was being "pushed out" by the Many Farms Clinic and the other Western medical facilities available to the population. In order to investigate this question, 42 of the 49 singers in the community were interviewed by the author in the spring of 1962 and were asked, among other things, about the number of ceremonies they had performed in 1961, the last full calendar year of clinic operation. Many of the singers found the question difficult to answer because they do not keep records. All attempted to distinguish between major ceremonies of five nights duration, and "short form" ceremonies. A few found it easier to compute the number of patients they had performed over during the past winter, "from the time of first snow [in December] to the first lightning [in March]," rather than remember back the entire year. The number of ceremonies performed each month varied over the year, as did clinic attendance. Certain ceremonies, however, such as the Mountaintop Way could be performed only during the winter, while others, such as Enemy Way, could be performed only in the summer. But in an emergency, parts of any ceremony can be performed no matter what the season, in an effort to save the patient.

Twenty-six of the 42 medicine men gave responses that could be usefully tabulated. The number of ceremonies performed in a year ranged from five to thirty, with the upper figures reached by those singers who perform the Blessing Way. The singers performed over an average of 2.3 patients per month. When these findings were extrapolated to the activities of all 49 singers, it was found that on a conservative basis a total of 1,350 sings had been performed in 1961, or one sing for every two residents. It should be recalled here that medical services were provided without charge at the Many Farms Clinic, but diagnosticians and singers received a fee, in addition to the substantial expenses incurred by patients and their families incident to having a curing ceremony.

It is unfortunate that a similar figure on the number of ceremonies performed was not obtained at the beginning of the study in order to compare it with the last year of clinic operation. The medicine men were asked in 1962 whether they had experienced a decline in the number of patients during the tenure of the clinic in the community. All of the singers reported that there were variations from one year to the next, based chiefly they felt on the amount of illness in the community, but none reported an overall decline in the number of patients seeking treatment from them. While the medicine men expressed great concern over what they foresaw as a future diminution in the number of singers (discussed below), none, under direct probing, saw the use of Western medical facilities as a factor in this potential decline.

Other data collected at Many Farms also demonstrated directly that ordinary clinic patients—not singers, diagnosticians or health visitors—were utilizing both curing systems. In 1961–62 the author followed up 100 patients who had been seen at the Many Farms Clinic within the preceding year. Selection was made on the basis of diagnosis to insure that there would be an equitable division between patients with acute, chronic and semi-chronic conditions. Of the 100 patients, 82 were found to have undergone a curing ceremony for the same complaint before or after their clinic visit.

It is clear then that clinic usage did not occur at the expense of the indigenous system. The two major curing systems in the community, Navajo medicine and modern medicine, were able to co-exist in a non-competitive relationship with a minimum of individual or institutional conflict. How did this relationship come about and how was it maintained?

The Nature of Medical Co-Existence

Clinic usage at Many Farms reflected the fact that Navajo patients, under certain conditions, decided that the physicians at the clinic could alleviate their physical pain and discomfort, even if that discomfort had its etiology in the Navajo belief system, rather than in germ theory. The activities of the clinic staff were directed towards research, treatment and encouraging use of the clinic. One important condition for the development of medical co-existence at Many Farms was that free patient choice among systems was not inhibited. Health education was carried on by the physician on an individual patient basis, as dictated by the medical problem at hand. But there was no organized community program to alter basic beliefs regarding health and disease. Similarly, clinic physicians were instructed never to denigrate or ridicule the indigenous curing system or attempt to prohibit patients from using it. Thus, the resident staff actively strove to stimulate wide use of the clinic while making clear that the Navajo patient could choose to use the facility—before, after, or while undergoing treatment in the indigenous system.

When choice of treatment is possible, the relationship between two systems can best be described by ascertaining the conditions under which one system or the other is the preferred, or first choice. In order to study this question Dr. Tom Sasaki conducted a series of 40 interviews in the community in 1958. He found that treatment at the clinic was the first choice of 60 percent of his respondents when the onset of symptoms was sudden and pain was acute. When the onset of illness was slow, lingering and produced a general malaise, 38 of the 40 respondents preferred treatment first by the medicine man.

As mentioned above, in 1961–62 the author also conducted a survey of 100 patients seen at the clinic. Of those patients, 82 had been treated by a singer before of after their clinic visit. Fifty-eight of the patients had been treated for acute conditions, and of these, 74 percent underwent ceremonies *after* visiting the clinic. Of those with chronic conditions, however, only 54 percent waited until after a clinic visit to seek treatment by the medicine man. The difference was in the same direction as that reported for 1958 but the differences were not statistically significant.

When the singers were interviewed in 1962 regarding the nature of the conditions for which they felt patients should be referred to the clinic, they cited tuberculosis, pneumonia, appendicitis, acute cholelithiasis, injuries, fractures and painful dislocations. It is obvious that all of these conditions, except tuberculosis, involve the sudden onset of acute pain. Intensive interviewing, however, did not uncover a simple listing of diseases best treated by the clinic and another set best treated by the medicine man. Rather, the cases cited by the singers and those followed by the clinic suggested a more complex relationship between the two systems.

First, from the Navajo point of view, the two systems perform very different functions. Navajo patients and practitioners believed that the physician treated the symptoms of illness rather than the underlying etiology of disease. An illustration of this dichotomy is the case of a two-year-old child seen at the clinic during 1961. The child was successively treated over the year for gastroenteritis, impetigo and pneumonia. In the view of the family and the physicians, treatment for each episode had been successful and the child soon became asymptomatic. But, the family felt that the three episodes, unconnected in occurrence from the physician's point of view, actually were part of one syndrome. Their child was a sickly child and the clinic was treating a variety of symptoms of a generalized sickness that would continue to cause trouble. According to the hand trembler to whom the child was taken, she had been in contact with lightning and a Shooting Way ceremony was prescribed and performed. As the family phrased the situation, "If we did not get at the root of this the child would be in the clinic every week with a different problem."

This case is one of many that were recorded at Many Farms. But the division of illness into symptomatic and etiologic components is not peculiar to the Many Farms area. In 1978, at a meeting of Navajo curers and physicians it was "agreed that both traditional and modern types of medicine are necessary, for while the physicians treat the disease, or the patients' ailments, medicine men treat the illness, or the physical and mental problems (Kayenta Community Based Cancer Control Project 1978:13)." It is important to realize that this is not a simple dichotomy between conditions that the indigenous system can cure and those that can be cured by the "White man's medicine." Rather it is a recognition that illness in the individual involves many components needing treatment and both systems are necessary for complete treatment.

Thus, in many situations the indigenous system and Western medicine are considered to have *complementary* functions. Illustrative of this type of thinking and behavior is the case of a prominent medicine man who was diagnosed with an acutely inflamed appendix in 1959. The diagnosis was made at the Many Farms Clinic and he was sent immediately to Ganado Hospital where an appendectomy was performed. After his stay in the hospital (which was extended because of a post-operative infection), he had a curing ceremony performed. According to his account, "We used to do things like surgery but that knowledge has been lost, so I had it taken care of at the hospital. Afterwards, I had the Flint Way ceremony [usually for wounds or internal injury], in order to help heal the incision made by the surgeon."

It has been pointed out by writers on Navajo culture that Navajo rituals provide positive psychotherapeutic benefits to the patient (Leighton & Leighton 1941; Sandner 1978). When the medicine man returned from his hospital stay, relatives, friends and neighbors gathered around him for the ceremony and all participated in "thinking only good thoughts" for him and expressing their pleasure at having him back in the community. From a Western point of view, it provided a means of community "re-entry" and was probably an excellent method to prevent the "hospitalism" syndrome so common to long-term patients in the U.S. population.

The physician ordinarily provides some psychological support and relief to the patient by explaining to him and his family the nature of his condition, listening to his fears, and helping to plan for the future. It is an extremely difficult service to perform, however, across cultural and linguistic barriers. Much of this supportive help can be provided through the indigenous curing system, thus freeing the hard-pressed physician in an underdeveloped area to handle the heavy disease load. Both the patient and the physician stand to benefit in this situation. Since patient choice determines which system is used as a first treatment for a given episode, and acute episodes are most often seen first at the clinic, neither system is excluded from seeing a patient, and care is delivered optimally and holistically.

The Maintenance of Medical Co-Existence

The state of medical co-existence documented at Many Farms might be considered a stage in the innovative process which Ralph Linton called "a period of trial." According to Linton, "During this period both the new trait and the old trait or traits with which it is competing become alternatives within the total culture complex. They are presented to individuals as different means to the same end" (Linton 1936:280). Linton saw this period as one which precedes "full acceptance" of the new element that has been introduced. Our data suggest, however, that the Navajo do not perceive the two systems as different means to the same end. Rather they have different functions. Further, there are good reasons to suggest that the period of trial may actually produce a long term equilibrium between the new elements and the old, an equilibrium which will change as the result of further innovations, rather than by full acceptance of the new and rejection of the old.

First, it must be realized that this is not a situation of competing alternatives. Rather, there is belief on the part of patients that both systems have something to offer, they both "work." Approximately 60 to 85 percent of all illness episodes are self-limiting, which means that for any curing system, the odds are in favor of the "house"—the system is bound to win more times than it loses. In fact, the individual will be cured, or the pathophysiological process will stop at a certain point, whether treatment is initiated or not. The reasoning of patients in both Western and Navajo systems is similar, based upon their clinical experience, "I took the medicine, or had the proper ceremony, and I got well. Therefore, it works."

What this means in a situation of medical co-existence is that, as we have seen, both systems are likely to be used for a given illness. In some cases, it is felt that both systems are necessary either to provide a cure or to prevent a recurrence of the illness. Since both systems are utilized, if the patient wishes to assign credit for a cure, then, even if it is assigned arbitrarily or randomly, one of the systems will be credited, whether it deserves the credit or not. It is possible, for example, as in the case cited of the child with gastroenteritis, pneumonia and impetigo, that *we* might conclude the clinic provided cures. But from the point of view of the family, the medicine man is credited with the cure. In other cases, the clinic might be credited by the patient, even though, from the medical work-up the diagnosis was a mystery and the prescription was palliative. The result of medical co-existence then is not a situation typified by competition over efficacy, but rather one of mutual reinforcement. Thus, the two systems can persist in this relationship over a long time if other factors do not intrude to weaken or destroy one of the systems.

The medicine man is the heart of the indigenous system. He has

Table 9.3. Singers/curers by age groups, 1961.

Age	No.	Percent	Cumulative percent
80–89 years	4	8.2	8.2
70–79 years	11	22.4	30.6
60–69 years	18	36.7	67.3
50–59 years	10	20.4	87.8
40–49 years	3	6.1	93.9
30–39 years	2	4.1	98.0
20–29 years	1	2.0	100.0
Total	49	100.0	

Table 9.4. Diagnosticians by age groups, 1961.

Age	No.	Percent	Cumulative percent
80–89 years	6	8.7	8.7
70–79 years	14	20.3	29.0
60–69 years	16	23.2	52.2
50–59 years	17	24.6	76.8
40–49 years	11	15.9	92.7
30–39 years	4	5.8	98.5
20–29 years	1	1.5	100.0
Total	66	100.0	

specialized knowledge in a systematic form. As each generation of medicine men ages and dies, if that knowledge is not transmitted to the next generation of medicine men, then the indigenous system, as a system, surely will perish. As we shall see, the system is vulnerable in other ways as well, but this is one of the most clearly bounded vulnerabilities of the system.

On these grounds, the medicine men expressed fears for the future of Navajo healing, since they were aware of the data contained in Tables 9.3 and 9.4. Of the 49 singers at Many Farms, 43 (88 percent) were 50 years or older. The diagnosticians tended to be in the same age group, with 77 percent 50 years or older. While the singers did not lack for patients, they did not have pupils to whom they could pass on the tradition. The 49 medicine men

in the area had a total of only 6 pupils who were learning ceremonies, and one of these pupils was already a medicine man who
was adding to his repertoire. The aging and consequent decrease
in the number of medicine men has been documented for other
areas of the Reservation as well (Henderson 1982).

No single cause can be assigned to the failure of the younger
generation to choose to become singers. The medicine men mentioned three reasons for the decline in their numbers, in the following order of importance: economic problems; absence of children
at school; and direct attacks made on the system by the missionaries. None of the medicine men, even with direct probing, saw
the increasing use of medical facilities as a factor in the declining
number of medicine men and apprentices.

The medicine men in the area date the beginning of decline in
the number of apprentices to the 1930s when the entire economy
of the Reservation and indeed, the country, was depressed. An
apprentice must pay not only the medicine man for the knowledge
transmitted, but he must be supported by his family while he is
learning. Further, if he is married and has a family, they too must
be supported during the training period. In an economy based
upon herding, rather than wage labor, it was possible for the
extended family to provide support for the apprentice's family.
Once he has learned a ceremony, the apprentice must then obtain
his medicine bundle—the necessary paraphernalia to perform the
ceremony. The bundle may be inherited or if it is to be collected,
the time and resources required would total today several thousand
dollars. After all of this effort, the medicine man might not be able
to support himself and his family with income derived solely from
curing. Few young men today, the medicine men feel, are willing
to make the sacrifices necessary to achieve a status that will not
provide an income for them and their families.

Another economic factor, not alluded to by this older group of
medicine men, was the difficulty of maintaining a practice while
engaged in wage work. As traditionally constituted, being a medicine man is a part-time occupation. In the traditional economy
it was possible for the medicine man to be a master of his own
time and move from subsistence activities to curing and back
again. As the economy has shifted increasingly to wage employment, it has become difficult for medicine men to have a job to
return to when he absents himself from that job to work as a curer.

This group of problems is not insoluble. In the spring of 1962, for example, a group of leading medicine men at Many Farms appointed a spokesman, Frank Mitchell, to present to the author their suggestion for increasing the number of apprentice medicine men:

> We have talked over this situation that you have learned about and which we all know, that the present generation is not interested in learning these songs. We have been wondering how we can continue to do these sings and carry on our customs. We know that the Tribe is sponsoring our young people to go to school and get an education. We would like the Tribe to know of the situation here and to sponsor young people to learn the sings. We are not thinking of young people who have not been to school. We have in mind several young people with an education, some who have worked off the reservation but then have come back in order to return to their people. It is this type of person we feel would do very well as a singer, if he was sponsored so that the medicine man could be paid and a medicine bundle assembled for him. We would like you to report this to the Tribal Council.

The tribe did not act upon the proposal at the time. But in 1967 a training program for medicine men was started at the Rough Rock Demonstration School and in 1969 the program obtained federal support from the National Institute of Mental Health. The first group of trainees graduated in 1972 (Bergman 1973, 1983). The school has demonstrated that the traditionally long training period can be shortened by use of training films of ceremonies and through printing of some texts. What effect this will have in the long run, for example, codifying practice and perhaps stifling innovation and change in the system, is not clear.

With regard to the second problem of part-time employment as a medicine man, this too is subject to some adaptive adjustment. Most medicine men at Many Farms tended to specialize in one or two major curing ceremonies. Given the long time necessary to become fully conversant with the complete ceremonial cycle for a given curing complex, this was understandable. The common practice was for a singer to learn all of one of the ceremonies and then in later years perhaps go back into training to increase the number of ceremonies he could perform, as was true for one of the apprentices at Many Farms. By foreshortening the training time necessary to learn any one ceremony it would be possible for a singer to have a large enough number of ceremonies under his command so that his services could be utilized on a full-time basis.

Singers concerned over the role of the missionaries expressed the view that missionaries were attacking the premises of Navajo religion. They reported that many who converted to Christianity in the Many Farms area continued to use their services, but the true convert, particularly to the Protestant sects and the Church of the Latter-Day Saints (Mormon) was lost to Navajo religious life. Fifteen years after this concern was expressed to the author, in 1976, an evangelical minister encouraged his congregation to bring medicine bundles and other religious paraphernalia to be burned. The evangelist was expelled from the Reservation and the Tribal Council passed a resolution prohibiting the destruction of such material (Shepardson 1982:205). There is, however, no systematic data available on the differential use of Navajo curing or the state of belief in the Navajo curing system of those Navajos who have joined various Christian religious groups (Kunitz 1983:143). Certainly, differential use on this basis was not evident at Many Farms.

With regard to the role of the schools, the medicine men noted that almost all school-age children are away at school during the day and many are at boarding schools for most of the year. This leaves limited time for indoctrination into the basic beliefs and practices of Navajo culture, according to the medicine men. Thus, when the educated young adults return home, they have enough traditional background to feel the need for the diagnostician and medicine man, but they are insufficiently motivated to actively perpetuate the tradition and become singers. Again, there is insufficient information on the role of education in relationship to the beliefs held by the educated population. The Rough Rock Demonstration School provides one solution to this proposed problem, by bringing medicine men to the school to teach the children about Navajo culture. In the long run, this is a critical area since if the general population is not socialized into Navajo culture, of which the curing system is but one part, singers will come to lack for patients (Aberle 1982:229).

Economics may also come into play in relationship to the curing system if patients cannot afford to pay for ceremonies. It should be noted that the system continues to exist despite uneven economic competition—the Public Health Service does not charge but the medicine man does. Part of the expense of the indigenous system comes from the length of the ceremonies, which also can have a secondary economic cost by significantly disrupting the wage employment of a patient. A number of adaptations have modified costs. Starting in the 1920s, food stands started appearing at ceremonies so that the patient's family did not have to feed all participants. There is increasing use of the short forms of ceremonies and they tend to be scheduled on weekends. Medical insurance for some Navajo workers also covers part of the cost of curing ceremonies (Shepardson 1982:206).

It is clear that the locus of change in the Navajo curing system does not lie in the present interrelationship with Western medicine. Disturbances in the equilibrium of non-competitive medical co-existence must be sought outside of the two systems under consideration. Focusing just on the two systems, the present situation has developed and can be maintained because there is no interference by either system in the choices to be made by the patient. Choice then becomes a question of which system is utilized first for a given episode, rather than which system will be used and which rejected. This is in stark contrast to other systems of *competitive* medical co-existence where there is interference by either system in the choices to be made by the patients.

In a situation that is structured competitively, specialists in either or both systems will insist that patients utilize their system exclusively and will denigrate the efficacy of the competitive system. Under these conditions, the patient's choice becomes politicized. Specialists in the indigenous system will clearly see themselves and the culture as threatened by the competing system and the result is likely to be increasing polarization of the community. Patients find themselves unable to utilize both systems for a given episode of illness and are out of reach of the system not chosen. If a patient chooses the indigenous system, for example, this fuels the competitiveness of the physician and encourages feelings that the patient's health is threatened by the indigenous system, because he cannot be treated by the physician. The two systems then, co-exist, but for any given illness there is no interaction. This situation is very unstable and one of the systems is likely to become dominant—but the outcome will be decided on political grounds, rather than on factors related to the relative efficacy of the two systems.

In contrast to competitive medical co-existence, the non-competitive co-existence at Many Farms means that choice is more likely to be made on an individual basis with reference to the condition of the patient. In the majority of cases both systems are used and the result is that each system reinforces the other. Since the framework for choice is non-exclusive, the specialists in each system are less likely to feel that patient health is being jeopardized. So long as other factors such as economic conditions or major changes in cultural transmission do not intervene, both systems will continue to be utilized and the population will benefit from the services that each system can provide.

10.

Health Care Experiment at Many Farms[1]

by Walsh McDermott,
Kurt W. Deuschle, and
Clifford R. Barnett

Medicine and the other health professions are undergoing wide-ranging scrutiny as parts of a total health care system. One part is the system for primary health care consisting of a university-connected health center manned full time by physicians and nurses, with the aid of well-trained indigenous, auxiliary personnel who work both at the center and in the homes.[2] A chance to measure the impact of such a system on the endemic disease pattern of a poverty-stricken rural, and traditional tribal society was provided as part of a larger series of studies on a Navajo community (Adair and Deuschle, 1970). Naturally, the human support components of medical care were heavily involved in this activity. However, these aspects have been purposely excluded from this analysis, which is concerned solely with the influence of the technology. By technology is meant the capability to alter disease in a predictable fashion by such entities as drugs, vaccines, diagnostic equipment, or surgery. In a community with satisfactory health services, those services delivered to the individual and those delivered to the group operate simultaneously; hence it is difficult to separate their respective effects. Such a separation is necessary, however, if rational choices are to be made in setting up systems of medical care in communities where the existing systems are ineffective or non-existent. In the present study, the circumstances were such that the influence of one of the systems—in which the technology is selectively applied by a clinical physician to one patient at a time—could be evaluated free from significant influence by the other system—in which the technology is applied by a variety of professionals to the community as a group.

Background and Methods of Study

The Navajo–Cornell Field Health Research Project was organized by the Navajo Tribe, Cornell University Medical College, and the U.S. Public Health Service in 1955, when the responsibility for the health of the U.S. Indian was transferred to the Department of Health, Education, and Welfare. The stated purposes were four-fold: To develop effective methods for the delivery of modern medical services to the Navajo people; to see to what extent these methods could be applied to other people in similar socioeconomic circumstances; to study discrete diseases, particularly in light of their possible shaping by Navajo culture; and to find out whether the sudden apposition of modern biomedical science and technology and the disease pattern of a nontechnological society could provide valuable knowledge in the attack on contemporary medical problems.

The research on these questions covered a wide range. There were studies of such familiar entities as infant feeding (French, 1967), congenital hip disease (Rabin et al., 1965), coronary heart disease (Fulmer and Roberts, 1963), tuberculosis (Omran and Deuschle, 1965), and accidents. There were also studies of an immediately practical nature, such as effective cross-cultural training for paraprofessional field health workers and the development of a manual to be used as a text in training them (Deuschle 1963a; Adair 1960; Loughlin et al. 1960; Mansell and Loughlin 1958; Loughlin and Mansell 1959; Wauneka 1962). Finally, there were studies in such sharply focused areas as the discovery of a new, genetically determined transferrin (Parker and Bearn 1961) and ethnolinguistics (Landar et al. 1960; Landar 1962; Lander 1967).

It is unlikely that any of this research, with its requirement of continued and enthusiastic community participation, could have been conducted in a remote, non-English-speaking tribal society unless there were clearly visible, immediate benefits to the people living there.[3] Indeed, without the capability of supplying substantial benefits, it would have been inappropriate even to propose the project. The procedure chosen, therefore, was to create a comprehensive system of primary health care and, as a major corollary, to organize various programs of research (McDermott et al. 1960). Thus, the introduction of a complete system of personal medical care to a community in which only a rudimentary system had existed became, in itself, one of the major experiments.

A natural and political unit of some 800 square miles, known as the Many Farms–Rough Rock community (hereinafter called Many Farms), near the center of the 23,000-square-mile Navajo reservation was selected jointly by project and tribal representatives. The community was considered to be reasonably representative of Navajo society and was thought to contain about 2,000 people.

The System

The system of primary health care was in actual operation from May 1956 to July 1962. It included a well-equipped health center for ambulatory care, a rudimentary satellite facility, and several automobiles with two-way radiotelephones for visits to the homes. The medical and nursing services were supplied by two field physicians, two nurses, one Navajo teacher, and four Navajo auxiliary health workers. The staff in residence received guidance from resident social scientists, and a steady flow of consultants in the various professions and disciplines was available from the parent university. Patients were usually seen in the central facility, but, when necessary, they were seen in their homes. Transportation to the government hospital 90 miles away, or to the mission hospital 55 miles away, had to be on an improvised basis over the corduroy dirt roads. Critically injured persons could be removed by light airplane in the daytime, weather permitting.

Over 90 percent of the population were examined in the central facility at some time during the study, and approximately two-thirds sought care at least once a year during those 6 years. Evidence exists that the health care delivered was of a consistently high standard; but since that evidence does not lend itself to a brief presentation, we can merely state our conviction that the results observed are representative of what happens when medical care from a large university medical center is made available to an impoverished rural society in the general circumstances of Many Farms.

The Society at the Start

The Navajo society at Many Farms was one of nonliterate, non-English-speaking people who lived in extended families in one-room, windowless, log and mud dwellings with dirt floors. These dwellings were separated from each other and from any supply of water by one or more miles of intermittently impassable dirt roads (McDermott et al. 1960). The water was pure at the source, but was easily contaminated through the communal dipper in the home. There was no refrigeration. The climate was one of harsh extremes of winter cold (averaging −4°C) and summer scorching (reaching highs of 43°C during the day and dropping 22° or more at night). Rainfall averaged 12 to 15 inches per year. Six or seven, and occasionally as many as 15, persons might sleep in a single, large, poorly ventilated room, usually on sheepskins or the dirt floor. A wood stove, sometimes made from a kerosene drum, supplied the heat and was used for cooking. The meals were not usually served on a table, but were eaten while sitting on the floor. There were no latrines or privies; horses wandered up to the hogan door and dogs roamed freely.

The economy consisted of a little dry farming, sheepherding, the weaving of wool rugs, some silver work, and occasional laboring jobs, usually farther than an overnight trip from the home. The average cash income for a family of four was estimated to be $586 per year, or $147 per capita per year (Sasaki and Basehart 1961). Of this income, 82 percent was earned and 19 percent was from various sources of welfare. There was a federally supported, tribally administered supplemental food program. Primary school children would learn to speak English, but it was not spoken in the home; not all children of school-age actually attended school.

Poor as these people were in a material sense, they did not show the apathy and lack of community feeling that Oscar Lewis describes as the characteristic of the "culture of poverty" (Lewis 1966). On the contrary, the Navajo culture was fairly well maintained, and included an indigenous curing system run by medicine men, who were highly respected. This gave the Navajos a kind of "regal poverty," in that they were well adapted to the harsh circumstances of the environment.

For the way of life, the disease pattern was predictable (Adair et al. 1957). Windowless, one-room homes, when the winters are bitter cold, favor airborne transmission of tubercle bacilli and other agents of respiratory disease. The scarcity of water, the chance of its contamination in the home, the absence of water at the sites of defecation, the serving of meals on the floor, and the potential of horse dung for breeding flies favor the spread of enteric diseases, skin disorders, and trachoma.

Clinical impressions of the disease pattern were largely derived from what had been seen at the reservation's six hospitals. The diseases just mentioned, as well as the severe burns and traumatic injuries of the sort common to primitive rural living were prominent, as were congestive heart failure, gall bladder disease, and arthritis. Infant mortality and the birth rate were thought to be considerably higher than the U.S. average. All observers agreed that the Navajos were a disease-ridden people whose disorders would be largely preventable within a modern society.

Previous Biomedical Influence

Within the Many Farms–Rough Rock community, there were no physicians in residence, nor, as far as is known, had there ever been. The principal medical influences were a quite rudimentary outpatient facility, which was 14 miles from the southern border of the area and was manned by an elderly physician, a mission hospital 55 miles away, and a government hospital some 90 miles away. At both of these hospitals, limited general surgery could be performed. About half of the births were at the hospitals or en route to them; the other half occurred unattended in the hogans. At various times in the past, solitary public health nurses based outside the community had tried to mount immunization programs in the one boarding school or the two day schools. The latter were held in overheated Quonset huts and similar makeshift structures, with outside temperatures in the winter frequently ranging from −23°C to −29°C. As these public health nurses would be responsible for as many as 10,000 people scattered over 4,000 or 5,000 square miles, the field nursing position was understandably vacant more months than it was filled. Most of the community had received smallpox immunization. Any other immunizations were haphazard, and no program of tuberculin tests had ever been carried out. Thus, the introduction of primary health care through the clinical physician system was a virtually complete innovation when it was introduced to the community on 19 May 1956 (Adair and Deuschle, 1970).

Observations

Although the innovation was made suddenly, its early influence was gradual. Accordingly, the results reported are for a period of five consecutive calendar years in the middle of the total 6-year study. Careful checking of the half-year phase-in and phase-out periods indicated that it is not misleading to concentrate on the middle 5 years. The phase-out itself was accomplished smoothly, and the community was not left without an adequate system of medical care.

The disease pattern was determined by: special examination of structured samples of the population; a review of all deaths and hospital records; demographic studies, including an annual census of the community, and rates of the incidence and prevalence of certain of the common conditions in the two-thirds of the population that sought care each year. Studies made in the later years of the project revealed no evidence of significant illness for which care had not been sought.

By actual rates of incidence, the five most common diseases in the population as a whole each year were diarrhea, otitis media, impetigo, pneumonia, and burns. The incidence of fractures and head injuries closely followed that of burns. There were nine instances of purulent meningitis in the entire 5-year period. In Table 10.1, which is arranged by episode, it may be seen how much of the professional time was occupied by pneumonia, diarrhea, and otitis media. In the second year (1958), these three, along with measles and impetigo, represented a total of 958 episodes among the 1362

Table 10.1. Major acute microbial diseases observed in 5 years.

	Year				
Episode	1957	1958	1959	1960	1961
Pneumonia	132	125	37*	105	98
Diarrhea	220	314	282	359	247
Otitis media	159	239	224	219	95
Measles	22	139	5	86	53
Impetigo	113	142	157	149	106

*A clear relationship existed between pneumonia and measles for the age group 13 months to 10 years. Had antimeasles vaccine been available then, a substantial portion of the childhood pneumonia *after* infancy presumably would have been prevented.

patients who sought care. Especially noteworthy, however, is the fact that except for otitis media in the last year (1961), there is no evidence of a significant decrease in the number of these episodes throughout the 5 years. By contrast, the incidence of otitis media during 1961 can be shown to be significantly lower ($P<.0001$) than the incidence during the previous 4 years.

Turning to three major chronic diseases: in a 50 percent sample of the Many Farms population, the prevalence of congenital hip disease, as determined roentgenographically, was about 200 times greater than it is in the general population (Rabin et al. 1965). Although there was no change during the 5-year observation period, there was evidence that both genetic and environmental factors are involved and that change could occur over a longer time period. At the start of the study, trachoma was present in 2.9 percent of the school children under age 10. While there were some indications that the situation might have improved very slightly during the 5-year period, there was no definite evidence of a decrease in incidence.

The prevalence of tuberculous pulmonary disease, determined roentgenographically in a 50 percent sample was 75 per 1000 (Omran and Deuschle 1965), two to three times that generally obtained in the U.S. population, and 15 times that found in a rural area of southern Scotland which was studied at approximately the same time (Cochran et al. 1957). A community of 2000 persons, is too small to reveal significant change in the incidence of tuberculous disease, yet is large enough to show change in the incidence of tuberculous disease, yet is large enough to show change in the incidence of tuberculous infection. One-third of the 5-year-old beginners in school were cutaneous reactors to tuberculin when the study was started; 5 years later, in 1961, only 3 of 55 beginners were positive. This constituted evidence that the transmission of tubercle bacilli from one host to another had declined within the community during the study period.

In the present analysis, that portion of the disease pattern that was treated by surgery is considered as an entity; about 25 persons per 1000 of the population received surgical treatment each year. Another 25 persons per 1000 were hospitalized each year for non-surgical reasons. The surgical conditions involved ranged from cholelithiasis to severe gunshot wounds to hemorrhage and shock complicating pregnancy. Of this total of 50 persons hospitalized per 1000, some 7 to 14 died each year (Table 10.2). This left 35 to 40 persons per 1000, or 3.5 percent of the total population, who presumably benefited each year from hospital care, whether medical or surgical.

Absent Diseases

The incidence of certain diseases that might be expected was either very low or absent altogether. Credible explanations are at hand for most such cases—for example, coronary heart disease

Table 10.2. Mortality in the Many Farms–Rough Rock community.

	Year					5-year experience*
	1957	1958	1959	1960	1961	
Population	1963	2044	2127	2221	2299	
Deaths	20	15	7	9	14	65 (total)
Infant deaths	11	7	2	7	7	34 (total)
Infant mortality†	115.8	70.0	21.3	66.7	76.1	70.0 (average)
Crude death rate‡	10.2	7.3	3.3	4.1	6.1	6.2 (average)

*The U.S. Public Health Service estimate of crude deaths averaged 7.9 for 5 years before 1957.
†Infant deaths per 1000 live births.
‡Deaths per 1000 population.

(Fulmer and Roberts 1963). The extreme decentralization of the society served as a "fire-break" against the spread of food- or waterborne disease, because the consequences of poor sanitation were largely confined to the individual camp. The absence of tetanus neonatorum is presumably due to the fact that, unlike some other cultures, the Navajos have no harmful practices concerning the umbilical stump. Also not included is the so-called "hidden component" of the pattern—namely, the illnesses recognized as such in the one culture and not in the other. Our observations on this "hidden component" have been presented elsewhere (Adair and Deuschle 1970); suffice it to say that these illnesses presented no real problems in management, largely because they were so well handled by the Navajo medicine men.

Deaths

Examination of mortality affords another measure of the disease pattern at the beginning and throughout the study (Figure 10.1; Table 10.3). Two findings are especially noteworthy: 34 (52 percent) of the 65 deaths occurred during the first year of life: and there was only one death beyond the age of 3 that could reasonably be called preventable by contemporary medical science. This polarized pattern of deaths was generally constant: during the fifth year of the study, 50 percent of the deaths occurred in infancy, as had been the case in the first year of this study. Of the 34 infant deaths at Many Farms, 20 were from the pneumonia-diarrhea complex. Thus, the most prevalent disease among the living was also the leading cause of death.

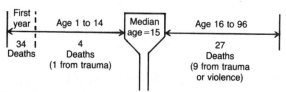

Fig. 10.1. Mortality in the Many Farms–Rough Rock community (by demographic pattern). Note that 52 percent of all deaths came from 3.7 percent of the population (that is, from infants in the first 12 months).

Table 10.3. Deaths in the Many Farms–Rough Rock community during 1957.

Age (years)	Deaths	
	Cause	Number
<1	Pneumonia-diarrhea	8
	Congenital heart	1
	Unknown	2
1–28	None	0
29	Severe trauma	1
46	Post-cholecystectomy	1
46	Myocardial infarction	1
49	Severe trauma	1
75	Anemia, unknown cause	1
81	Congestive heart failure, with pneumonia	1
89	Fractured neck of femur	1
90	Congestive heart failure, with pneumonia	1
91	Pneumonia	1

The lack of change in the disease pattern, as revealed by the causes of death, was thus in agreement with the lack of change seen in the most prevalent diseases among the living during the 5-year period (Table 10.1). However, an important effect of the application of technology might be overlooked if change in the incidence of disease were the principal criterion. The incidence of a microbial disease could remain unchanged, yet the individual episodes could be aborted or readily controlled by specific therapies. It was not possible to measure accurately the therapy-induced curtailment of otherwise self-limited illness. From judgments based on well-documented experience with the particular diseases in question, except for otitis, there was no evidence of any widespread effect.[4]

Change in Crude Death Rates

Theoretically, a measurement of the extent to which lives were saved by the new system would be provided by comparing the crude death rates for the 5-year study period with the rates in the same community for the preceding years. Such rates were indeed determined for the 5 years of the study (Table 10.1). Unfortunately, however, the only data with which they can be compared are not true rates, but estimates. What is more, they are estimates not for the population of the Many Farms–Rough Rock community, but for the Navajo Tribe as a whole (Loughlin and Dennison 1961). The reason for this inadequacy is that, in order to obtain mortality rates, it is necessary to know the size of the population, and no accurate census of the Navajo Tribe by regions or as a whole existed. Because there were no census data and because the recall of infant deaths long afterward is significantly inaccurate, no attempt was made to determine retrospectively the total number of deaths for the community.

The crude death rate for the Many Farms population, calculated from our own exact census data, averaged 6.2 per 1000 population for the 5 years of the study. These data and death rates by individual are presented in Table 10.2.[5] As may be seen, the Many Farms average and the rates in each of the last 4 of the 5 years were lower than the estimated crude death rates of 7.9 for the whole tribe in the 5 years immediately preceding the study. Our impression is that, in the pre-study period, the Many Farms health situation has been generally similar to that of the tribe as a whole. Similarly, it is believed that the estimated death rates were probably slightly lower than actual figures because of the known tendency to fail to report the deaths that occurred in the first few days after birth.

This comparison of hard data and estimates based on impressions admittedly leaves the door open for the possibility that the study years were associated with lowered death rate. Yet without well-established rates for the past, and with the necessity of having very large populations in order for small changes in crude death rates to be significant, it was not possible to establish a significant lowering of overall mortality as a result of the biomedical innovation. A priori, some lives were presumably saved, but there is certainly no clear-cut evidence to that effect.

Census

In evaluating the technological effectiveness of a health care system, however, it is not only essential to establish the nature of the diseases prevalent in the community, but also to establish the demographic profile of the community. In order to obtain demo-

Table 10.4. Births in the Many Farms–Rough Rock community.

	Year					5-year average
	1957	1958	1959	1960	1961	
Women (age 15–44)	363	378	390	417	429	395.4
Live births	95	100	94	105	92	97.2
Birth rate*	48.4	48.9	44.2	47.3	40.0	45.8

*Per 1000 population.

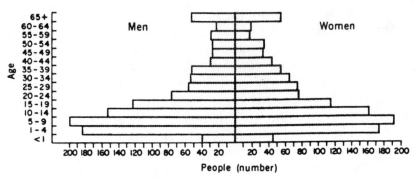

Fig. 10.2. Demographic profile (1961) of Many Farms–Rough Rock community.

graphic data about Many Farms, it was necessary to conduct a complete census of the population. This was done by constructing a map that included all households in the area and enumerated every resident therein, and by determining all births and deaths on a continuing basis. The total census was repeated each year.

As may be seen in Table 10.2, in the first full year (1957) there were 1963 persons in the study area—thus the observed value was close to the estimate of 2000. What had been grossly underestimated, however, was the rate at which the population was growing (Table 10.4). During the 5 years of the study, the population was actually observed to grow at a rate of 4 percent per year. Observations since the completion of the study have indicated that this extraordinarily high growth rate at Many Farms, and the demographic profile it produced (Figure 10.2), were indeed representative of the Navajo population as a whole.

The pool of women in the childbearing period (ages 15 to 44) each year ranged from 363 to 429, and the total live births each year ranged from 92 to 105. The government estimate of the birth rate for the tribe as a whole was 36 for the year 1956 (present U.S. rate is around 18). The birth rate at Many Farms was 48.4 in 1957 and averaged 45.8 for the 5 years. These sustained high fertility and birth rates resulted in a population with a median age 15. In any one year, the infants represented only 3.7 percent of the total population, yet they accounted for more than one-half of the total number of deaths and much of the other near-fatal illness (Figure 10.1).

Discussion

The 6-year period of this study coincided with a period of "tooling up" for the Public Health Service Indian program and for other tribal and governmental programs in Indian affairs. As a result, during the 8 or 9 years since that time, both Navajo health and certain other aspects of Navajo life, including the quality of life in the Many Farms–Rough Rock community, have undergone appreciable improvement. During the actual study period, however, there was virtually no change in the living conditions of the people in the Many Farms–Rough Rock community. In these static conditions, with no real change in either the home environment or the level of formal education, the wide application of biomedical science and technology through the clinical physician system resulted in:

1. A definite reduction in the transmission of tubercle bacilli.
2. A definite reduction in otitis media in the fifth year.
3. No reduction in the occurrence of active trachoma.
4. No reduction in the occurrence of the pneumonia-diarrhea complex, which remained the single greatest cause of illness and death.
5. The identification of those individuals who need hospital care (35 to 40 persons per 1000 each year)—that is, the establishment of a medical scan.
6. A possible slight reduction in crude mortality, despite an infant mortality that persisted at three times the national average.

This list of positive and negative accomplishments delineates the "technological substrate"—that is, the fitness of the system's technological component for meeting the disease situation as it actually existed in the community. Thus, an analysis of this list reveals the limits of contemporary biomedical capability in this particular set of circumstances. The first four entities all had a microbial component; two were influenced and two were not. The two that were favorably influenced (tuberculous infection, otitis media) were not in themselves contributors to the total mortality. For this reason, it seems likely that the apparent influence on crude death rate is largely attributable to the health care system's capability for making discriminating use of the hospital facilities. Expressed differently, it appears that items 5 and 6 (hospital referrals and crude death rate) bear a direct relationship to each other and are unrelated to the favorable events of items 1 and 2.

The first four conditions on the list have three features in common: they are all microbially linked; they are all especially prominent in various settings of poverty; and they are all either well controlled or actually absent from most of U.S. society. Presumably, therefore, the knowledge of how to control them on a wide scale exists. When this knowledge is analyzed in relation to Many Farms, however, it becomes clear that, depending on their specific biologic nature, diseases vary enormously in their susceptibility to medical management in slum conditions. For example, it has been convincingly demonstrated (Riley et al 1959; Hyge 1946) that tubercle bacilli can be transmitted through the air and can remain suspended in the air of an unventilated room for at least an hour or so. At Many Farms, the windowless, one-room dwellings, made of logs chinked against the bitter cold, were ideal transmission chambers. Once tubercle bacilli are introduced to a community with such housing, a self-perpetuating system is set up. The transmission is so widespread that even the small percentage of infected people who ultimately develop the disease represent a large number in absolute terms; and the probability of an encounter between emitter and potential recipients is considerably increased.

The transmission of tubercle bacilli is, thus, greatly facilitated by certain specific characteristics of slum housing. The particular nature of this transmission process, however, is such that it can be easily interrupted without changes in the housing namely, by exhaustive case-finding followed by self-administered drug therapy.

Before the primary health care system was introduced at Many Farms, the parents of a child with acute otitis understandably tended to try to "sweat it out" before embarking on the long trip necessary for obtaining care. Consequently, ruptured eardrums were commonplace. The advent of primary care would not be expected to alter the incidence of the initial (presumably viral) process, but it would be expected, through antimicrobial therapy, to reduce the incidence of the serious bacterial complication. Such a reduction occurred. Why it was not discernible before the fifth year of primary care is not clear. Possibly it resulted from the frequent practice of administering antimicrobial therapy for the undiagnosed febrile illnesses of children, thereby "curing" some cases of bacterial otitis before they had evolved sufficiently to be clinically recognizable. Such an effect could have been masked earlier by the fact that a substantial, but undefined, portion of the acute episodes were actually exacerbations of chronic otitis, rather than first attacks. With fewer new inputs, this backlog of chronic cases would gradually have grown smaller as the children grew older. The question merits further study because there is a real possibility that the otitis of children can be used as a key indicator of the availability of medical care.[6]

Trachoma, like otitis and tuberculosis, is caused by a group of microbes that are susceptible to antimicrobial drugs. The beginning of the pathogenic chain could be considered as the multiplication of the trachoma agents in the lesion, which is located in and around the eyes. Theoretically, this pathogenic chain could be severed, as was done with tubercle bacilli, by suppressing the microbe in the lesion with drugs, thus preventing it from being discharged into the environment. Indeed, this was the procedure at Many Farms; but, unlike the situation with tubercle bacilli, the treatment of the active cases of trachoma had little impact on the problem. The reason the chemotherapeutic approach is inadequate is that the transmission of the agents appears to take place by way of the contaminated fingers of those afflicted—usually quite small children. Thus, before the ocular process is brought under final control, the children's fingers are continually contaminated. To decontaminate their fingers (and the communal towels and vessels) would have necessitated a permanent change in such household habits at

Many Farms as hand and face washing, the use of soap, individual towels, and precautions in their handling. Experience gained after this study has indicated some promise for the chemotherapeutic approach, but only if it is carried out on everyone in the community simultaneously (Portney and Hoshiwara 1969).

As in the case of trachoma, there was no reduction in the occurrence of the pneumonia-diarrhea complex, which remained as the single greatest cause of illness and death throughout the 5-year period. The grouping of the pneumonias and diarrheas of early life into a single complex has no biologic justification. Nevertheless, the practice is useful, not only because the two entities frequently occur together, with the pneumonia triggering the diarrhea, but because in every aspect, from genesis to therapy, the nature of the problems presented by these two conditions is essentially the same. The critical feature of the complex is that the syndrome is endemic in the unsanitary home environment; thus recovery from one episode does not mean that another may not occur. It is not always realized that this complex is far and away the single greatest cause of death in economically underdeveloped societies.

The diarrhea, well named "weaning diarrhea" by Gordon and his associates (Gordon et al. 1963), has a nutritional component, the precise role of which is unclear. It is definite, however, that, while anti-microbial therapy may be helpful in some instances, it does not predictably and decisively alter the disease. Likewise, acute disease of the respiratory tract (including what has to be rather loosely termed "pneumonia") in this primarily infant age group is caused, in well over 90 percent of the cases, by agents other than the pathogenic bacteria known to be susceptible to the antimicrobial drugs (Coriell 1967). Thus, this major portion of the total technological substrate, or potential target of the biomedical technology available for delivery at Many Farms, was largely beyond the capability of that technology to influence in a decisive way.

The sequence of events that makes the home environment so hazardous to the infant has been discussed elsewhere (McDermott 1966). The remarkable self-correcting mechanisms that maintain physiologic stability at other ages are just in the process of being developed in early infancy, and in primitive home conditions the microbial challenge is virtually constant. In contrast, given the sanitary barriers provided by modern housing managed by educated parents, it is possible both to spread out many of these microbial challenges throughout childhood and adolescence and to artificially substitute warmth, special feeding, and fluid and electrolytes for the imperfect homeostasis when the infant is ill. Measures such as these form an essential part of the deliverable technology of modern pediatrics. This technology is hardly deliverable in a house without central heating or insulation against freezing temperatures, with no running water or even a nearby well, and with several other quite young children requiring the attention of a mother who had only a few grades of primary school education a decade or so ago.

The unique character of the relationship between the infant and its home environment may be seen from the observation at Many Farms that preschool children living in the same homes might fall ill, but fatal illness was extremely rare. In societies with a lower level of health, this phenomenon is less readily perceived because of the continued operation of factors (notably an inadequate supply of protein) that keep both the infant and the preschool child at risk of fatal illness. For example, in Peru in 1968, it was reported that 50 of every 100 deaths occurred in children under age 5, but that only 30 of these 50 deaths occurred during the first year of life. This contrast between the infant and the 2- or 3-year-old child living in the same sanitarily unprotected home environment merely underlines a highly significant fact: the effectiveness of contemporary medical technologies is far more dependent on the socioeconomic circumstances of the recipient in the case of the infant than it is in the case of older children.

Thus, the delivery of this carefully organized and well-received primary health care system to the Many Farms–Rough Rock community had relatively little influence on disease there. When both the disease and the demographic profile of Many Farms are examined together, the reason that the accomplishments were only modest becomes evident: it was the nature of the substrate (the particular diseases present in the living and the ages of those afflicted). The high fertility ensured that infants would comprise the major portion of the people that were sick at any one time, and modern medical technology has relatively little to offer infants who are located in an unprotected home environment. It should not be inferred that no attempts were made to change household practices. On the contrary, a variety of programs were conducted for that purpose, and considerable effort was expended in the instruction of mothers in the home. The influence of such programs was sharply limited, however, in the absence of any significant change in the physical environment of the home. The two conditions that did not require changes in household practices for their control—otitis media and the transfer of tubercle bacilli—were significantly influenced, whereas the two that did require such changes were not.

In using the concept of the substrate, emphasis is placed on "disease in the living," because causes of death are imperfect indicators of where medical effort must be expended on a day-to-day basis. The substrate determines the limits of biomedical technology in a community; it also determines how the physician must allocate his time. When a health care system is based on a geographically defined community, it is locked into a situation in which there is no "give" in the matching of technological capability to substrate. Not only was the physician's technology for infants severely compromised at Many Farms, but his technology for the adult population was also limited—because of the population's proportionately smaller size, its relative youth, and certain attributes of rural living (French 1967). With the demographic mix of Many Farms, any enlargement of medical coverage to bring in more adults would also have brought in more children in the same high ratio, and there were already enough young children to occupy the major portion of a physician's effort. The mismatches of technology to substrate that occur when a physician's services are allocated on a geographical basis can be managed when a group of physicians with different skills are available. In a rural, economically underdeveloped society, however, such options are not available, and the mismatch causes a waste of precious assets.

Two questions arise: If the technology was of such relatively limited effectiveness at Many Farms, why wasn't the infant mortality much higher, for example 150 or more, and why was the mortality among pre-school children concentrated within the first year of life rather than within the first 4 years, as it is in so many other economically underdeveloped areas of the world? The available information simply does not permit definite answers to these two questions. Nevertheless, it is fairly certain (despite the poor quality of the vital statistics) that in the two decades prior to the study, decades in which there were no significant field health services, the overall Navajo infant mortality had been steadily falling from around 150 to around 85 per 1000 live births (Young 1961). The principal identifiable change in that period is the improved services in the six hospitals that are distributed over the 23,000-square-mile area. In addition, an effective technology, available only in the hospital environment, did exist for important segments of the infant disease pattern. Thus, some potentially effective medical care existed; although it was relatively accessible to some people, it was as far away as 100 miles from others. In much the same way, the low mortality at Many Farms in the second and third years may, to some extent, have been an otherwise unmeasurable result of the primary health service that was innovated there, especially because that service could get the patients into slightly better condition before they were transported to the hospitals. A generally low mortality in the preschool group was present before the start of the primary health service, however. It is believed that most health professionals with field experience would attribute that low mortality primarily to the fact that the food supply of the community, including the supply of animal protein, appeared to be adequate.

Indeed, a whole combination of circumstances, fortuitous in part, created a situation at Many Farms such that many key health factors could be isolated almost as so many experimental variables, thus permitting inferences concerning the other factors. To a considerable degree, therefore, the situation at Many Farms, in terms of health development planning, was analogous to an "experiment of Nature."

The constant was the presence of unschooled families, with a crude birth rate of 45.8, crowded together in unsanitary premises and grouped in small foci that were scattered over a vast, semiarid land. The observed results could be regarded as characterizing the disease problems that would remain in a rural economically underdeveloped community with unimproved housing *after* there had been introduced an adequate supply of food, including high-quality protein; control of all protozoan and helminthic diseases such as malaria or hookworm, a protected water supply at some distance from the home; effective prevention of cigarette smoking and chemical contamination of the air; a system of primary medical care, with a clinical physician, nurses, and indigenous health care workers in residence.

The observed result of "what remained" was an extraordinarily youthful community (median age 15), increasing at an annual rate of 4 percent, with a health status characterized by an infant mortality three times the U.S. average, with the infant death representing one-half of all deaths and with other childhood deaths extremely rare; most noninfant deaths postponed until middle or old age; and the hemorrhagic complications of pregnancy and the results of trauma representing the principal health problems up to age 45. Once past the first birthday, the individual's prospects for continued health were quite good.

On an ascending scale from the primitive to the modern, the Many Farms pattern of community health is at a relatively high stage. In attaining this stage, the institution of a clinical physician system of primary health care in the community played some role, but clearly not a major one. An analysis of each of the measurable accomplishments of the innovation reveals that these accomplishments could also have been made through a system that did not have a physician to render individual medical care. Such positive achievements as blocking the transmission of tubercle bacilli, reducing otitis media, or starting antishock measures for hemorrhaging patients on the way to the hospital represented activities that did not actually require the presence of a physician. To be sure, the establishment of a medical scan for the community (identifying those individuals who need hospitalization) was presumably more discriminating when conducted by the physician, but the great bulk of patients referred to hospitals were in such obviously acute conditions that they would inevitably have been brought to the hospital, either through nurse referral or patient or family action.

Thus for Many Farms, a clinical physician system of primary health care was a poor choice, in terms of potential achievement through technology. Some form of the nonclinical or community medicine system, in which the physician did not care for individual patients, would have been more rational. Such a course would be a realistic option for development planners in areas of the world where there are very few physicians and where the economic-ecological situation is such that the attainment of the Many Farms community health pattern would be a tremendous achievement. It must be recognized that, at the Many Farms stage, the community's health would not impede its socioeconomic development; for example, programs to limit family size could be introduced with a reasonable prospect of continued success. However, to attempt to employ a health care system without a clinical physician in a society such as ours, in which physicians are numerous, although not plentiful, would be quite another matter.

It should be emphasized that everyone who participated in the choice of the system introduced at Many Farms was knowledgeable about Navajo health, as seen in the hospitals, and had a store of "conventional wisdom" about it, virtually all of which turned out to be true. All of them were fully confident that the system selected would have a major beneficial impact on the health status of the people. What was not perceived in advance was the extent to which the serious, technologically vulnerable conditions were already being treated in the hospitals outside the community, and just how much the demographic-disease pattern was skewed toward the diseases of infancy, which are dependent on conditions in the home. In short, the "conventional wisdom" lacked the quantitation essential for such a choice.

Although this article is concerned with technological performance, it should be noted that, in terms of individual and community expectations, the Many Farms experiment was a clear-cut success. The system was set up with full community participation, and there was a mechanism for effective, continued community control. Members of the community repeatedly expressed their satisfaction with the care they received, and the community was left with an operating system. Moreover, it can be safely predicted that, faced with a similar choice today, the community would opt for what was actually introduced there, rather than for a system with a much better technological "fit," if the latter meant no physician in continued residence. And this, the other side of the coin, is wholly understandable.

Popular expectations and misunderstandings of what an individual physician can do operate as a formidable constraint on the rational use of biomedical technology. Indeed, because of the nature of medicine, as a practical matter its technology has to be deployed irrationally. This is largely the consequence of our tradition of having both essentials of medical care—the technology and the human support—administered by the same person, the physician. As a result, the limits on the number of people to whom the physician can offer human support by way of personalized care also largely determine the people to whom he can deliver the technology. Yet important elements of that technology might be more widely useful if applied in some other way.

Thus one of the two essential parts of medicine can act as a significant constraint on the other. This is forming an issue with large implications; clearly, a systemtic analysis of both essentials and of who would make their most effective ministers is in order. Yet who can measure the value obtained by those Many Farms parents who could see obviously expert professionals hovering over their child, desperately ill with pneumonia caused by respiratory syncytial virus? They see someone making a fight. To point out that, in the particular circumstances, the penicillin the child is receiving happens to be valueless, in a technological sense, would seem a petty, if not callous, irrelevancy.[7]

11.

Collaborative Study by Physicians and Anthropologists:
Congenital Hip Disease

by Clifford R. Barnett, Ph.D., and
David L. Rabin, M.D., M.P.H.

In the preceding chapters the work of an anthropologist as a member of a medical team dedicated to research and service in a cross-cultural situation has been delineated. Such interdisciplinary research was, when we wrote this report for the first edition, in its infancy. When William Caudill reviewed the literature of medical anthropology in 1953, he reported that "detailed studies of the incidence and cultural context of chronic or other illnesses in nonliterate societies are practically impossible to find. (Caudill, 1953, p. 795). A review of the field 9 years later by Steven Polgar showed little change had occurred in the interim. (Polgar, 1962). Benjamin Paul recently noted that the largest category of medical anthropologists has been concerned with the analysis of "popular reactions to programs of health maintenance and health improvement," rather than the investigation of "cultural components in the etiology and incidence of illness. (Paul, 1963, p. 36).

Today in 1988, there is a developing field of interdisciplinary research; several journals report on such findings regularly.

The situation at Many Farms provided an unusual opportunity for collaborative research since an understanding of the cultural components of the disease was essential in investigating the epidemiology of congenital hip disease and evaluating the importance of biological and cultural factors.

It is fitting, therefore, to describe the nature of a working relationship between the medical group and the anthropologists in some detail—the needs that occasioned it and the benefits that accrued to the disciplines involved in the research on this disease. The way in which the research was carried out, and the role of the anthropologist working with the doctor and the nurse will be described in considerable detail in this chapter. The actual medical findings are given in brief, as they are published elsewhere. (Rabin, 1965).

Why did the physician feel the need for an anthropologist to help with the organization and execution of this research design? There were three principal needs that the anthropologist could meet. First, there was need for an individual familiar with specific materials on the Navajo relevant to the study of environmental, genetic, and attitudinal aspects of the disease. Second, there was need for an individual conversant with the techniques for eliciting information in the community through an interpreter and making observations under field conditions. These techniques included skill not only in the handling of the more usual qualitative data collected and analyzed by anthropologists, but familiarity with more structured and basically quantitative material. Finally, there was need for an individual who had a role in the community different from that of the physician. It was felt that data about Navajo attitudes towards the disease, their reluctance to accept surgical treatment for its complications, and observations of home treatment could best be obtained by someone other than the physician.

Even when the physician ventures into the field, he maintains his image as a healer and soon finds himself occupied with a medical problem which may preclude his attempt to interview. To refer the patient to the clinic, rather than treat him in these circumstances, would be unacceptable to the physician and would do little to maintain rapport with the patient as an informant. In the clinic the physician's role as a dispenser of medical care, aggravated by the pressures of the workload, would make it difficult for him to question the recipients of this care regarding their attitude towards it or, as was so pertinent in this research project, to obtain reliable information regarding the faithfulness with which they carried out prescribed therapy for congenital hip disease.

Although the anthropologist was associated with the clinic, he was divorced from the actual dispensing of medical care, and therefore it was easier for him to elicit subjective comments.

Even when the physician becomes familiar with the customs of the people among whom he works, he finds that obtaining the specific information he needs for his studies is accomplished only with great difficulty and the expenditure of excessive time. For example, in order to obtain the details of genetic relationships among Navajo, it is necessary to unravel a complex web of clan membership and tribal custom which slows the acquisition of the particular facts the physician wants. When the physician obtains the specific information he needs, he discards much general information which is of value to the anthropologist, e.g., marriage customs and clan relationships.

The anthropologist had several objectives in undertaking the study of Navajo attitudes toward congenital hip disease and its treatment. Because one objective of the research was to determine the course of the untreated disease, it would be necessary to confirm the general belief that the Navajo were resistant to surgical treatment of the condition by physicians and ascertain the nature of the native treatment, if any. This objective was consistent with the basic research goals of the entire Many Farms Project to uncover the nature of Navajo medical problems and assess the barriers which impeded the delivery of optimal modern medical care. Another objective was to study the genetic relationships of the disease. These genetic studies also required an understanding of the disease as a factor in natural selection: Did the affected individuals marry later, have fewer children, or die early in life?

The roles of the anthropologist, the physician, and the nurse, as well as interaction among them had been defined by the relationships that had grown up among the members of the team in the years prior to the investigation described in this chapter. It would not have been possible for this team to carry on their investigation without the accumulation of basic medical, demographic, and cultural information that had been built up between 1956 and 1959. Nor could this research have preceded the establishment of the camp file record system and the presence of trained health visitors who could go to the field and explain the need for x-rays and request individuals to come to the clinic for them. All of these features of the clinic service were basic to the success of the research on congenital hip disease.

Preliminary work in obtaining genealogies and an understanding of Navajo attitudes towards the disease was carried out in 1958 by a resident anthropologist (Cara Richards Dobyns) and a fourth-year medical student. The study of the natural history of the disease began in 1960, when the epidemiologic study to determine accurately the prevalence of the disease in the community and to learn of differences characterizing the affected and unaffected populations was designed by the physician. To do this study it was necessary to have the help of physicians in close clinical contact with the Navajo, anthropologists familiar with social organization and the cultural patterns of the Navajo, as well as geneticists, orthopedists and radiologists remote from the project. Detection of affected individuals was to be accomplished by taking pelvic x-rays of a defined pediatric and adult population of Navajos residing in the Many Farms Clinic Area. The resident nurse organized the program of obtaining x-rays on the selected population with the help of the health visitors. In 1961, when the method of case detection was well under way, the anthropologist joined the Many Farms Project and began to work with the recognized cases and to gather the basic genetic and environmental information from the community. All x-rays were sent to a pediatric orthopedist and to a pediatric radiologist at the Hospital for Special Surgery, New York City, to be read without benefit of history. They returned their readings to Many Farms where follow-up of affected individuals was initiated.

Although no accurate rates had been published for the Navajo, the physicians at Many Farms knew that the Navajo had a high prevalence of congenital hip disease. They were also aware of a survey of the San Carlos Apache, an Indian group closely related to the Navajo, that revealed a case rate for congenital hip disease of 230/10,000 (Kraus and Schwartzmann, 1957) as compared to a case rate of 13/10,000 in a study series in New York City. During the first 3 years of clinic operation, without any special attention to case finding for congenital hip disease, the project established a provisional case rate of 110/10,000 for the Many Farms Navajo population. It was also appropriate that the disease be studied among the Navajo because of their rejection of surgical therapy for the complications resulting from the disorder. To understand the situation one must know something about the disease and its treatment. Congenital hip disease is present at birth and is characterized by an abnormal relationship between the hip socket (acetabulum) and the long bone of the leg (femur). The hip socket in individuals with this disorder is underdeveloped and thus does not securely grasp the head of the femur. As a consequence, the femur may move completely out of the socket and become dislocated, or it may be seated insecurely within the socket and predispose the joint to excessive trauma. In the latter case, some time between the ages of 30 to 50, the individual may develop a painful refractory traumatic osteoarthritis in the affected joint. The dislocated hip causes the individual to walk with a limp and, similarly, the strain eventually leads to a severe arthritis for which little can be done, save to alleviate the pain.

Because of the severe disability occasioned by this disorder, treatment has been devised to prevent the late complications of the disease. In recent years, the disease has been diagnosed at a progressively younger age, at which time it is evident only by x-ray and special physical examination. During the first months of life, the use of multiple diapers between the legs or some other device, such as a Frejka apron, to keep the legs in an abducted or frog-leg position, has been sufficient to promote normal development of the joint. As the child grows older, more rigid methods of assuring an abduction position are necessary and a plastic, metal, or plaster splint is used. If the deformity has been detected when the child first begins to walk, at which time the first obvious clinical signs become apparent to the family, the treatment usually is manipulation under anesthesia, followed by prolonged casting. By the time the child is several years of age, the only treatment possible has been open surgical intervention. The joint may be fused or, using a more recent procedure, the hip sockets may be reconstructed. Either of these procedures would necessitate a prolonged postoperative period of casting and immobilization.

Conservative treatment of the disease is dependent upon early diagnosis, but the diagnostic criteria in the very young has been a matter of medical controversy. Congenital hip disease is distributed over a wide geographic area and occurs with varying frequencies in different countries—even among people of similar racial background, living within the same country. In some of the high incidence areas people are known to swaddle their children or place them on cradle boards, as do the Navajo. This environmental factor, along with others such as type of birth and birth order, has been correlated with the occurrence of the disease. (Record and Edwards, 1958).

There was also medical controversy concerning the natural progression of the disease. In adulthood, it was only through inference that some arthritic disorders were thought to be late consequences of a congenitally abnormal hip. The natural progression of the disorder in children was not known. Generally, children thought to be abnormal by any of the existing criteria were treated, and, therefore, the frequency with which an abnormal hip in an untreated child goes on to dislocate cannot be predicted. Improvement of an untreated abnormal hip joint had been known to occur, but it had been considered of such rarity that its documentation was justification for a case report. (Drehmann, 1939, pp. 410–429).

The Navajo were a good study population since they had a high prevalence of the disease and had received little medical care in the past, when opportunities for diagnosis and treatment of the disease in the very young had not existed. The fusion operation was performed on some Navajos in the early 1950s, one of whom resided in the Many Farms area; it produced a strong, but non-flexible hip joint. This type of joint was acceptable in our society, but for the Navajo it created a severe handicap: He could not sit on the ground with his family during meal times in the hogan; he could not ride horseback; nor could he walk easily over uneven ground. Navajos in the Many Farms district were most familiar with the fusion operation. The hip reconstruction procedure is relatively free of these difficulties and creates a functioning ball and socket joint. Unfortunately, however, the first child in the Many Farms area to be treated this way had an unsatisfactory result. Furthermore, either of these procedures require that the Navajo child be separated from his family for a period of several months, hundreds of miles away, perhaps among people who do not speak his language.

In Western culture, the social stigma attending skeletal deformity, and the knowledge that an abnormality will be painful and untreatable in the future, make these extensive surgical treatments acceptable. The Navajo, however, view the disease and its treatment somewhat differently. Our preliminary investigations revealed that the individual who limps from this disease does not suffer any social stigma and, most importantly, he is a fully participating and functioning member of the group. The fusion operation for the Navajo replaced an insignificant abnormality with a severe disability and a promise that the distant occurrence of a vaguely conceived disorder, traumatic arthritis, had been prevented. Such preliminary information gathered in the community indicated that in studying this disease we would be touching upon a sensitive area regarding treatment in the older child with dislocation. Too, the individual who limps because of a dislocated hip has an obvious physical symptom of which he is aware. Conservative treatment, however, must be instituted before the child is weight bearing. The child, therefore, has no observable symptoms and the parents then must first be convinced that their child is abnormal before they will consider the need for treatment to prevent a condition which *may* develop some time in the future.

It was realized that the entire population could not be x-rayed given the nature of the population and transportation problems in the area. Therefore, two groups were selected for x-rays. The first of these groups consisted of all children born between January 1, 1955 and December 31, 1961. X-rays of this group would reveal the prevalence of this disease among this age group. In addition, because many of the children would be born during the life of the project, information regarding birth practices, use of the cradle board, and a follow-up of natural history and possible treatment of affected individuals could be obtained. The second major prevalence group consisted of adults born between 1910 and 1930. These people were selected because at time of x-ray they would be between ages 30 and 50, and they could be expected to show the arthritic sequelae of the disease and provide insight concerning the prevalence of the disease in a previous time period.

A third population group selected for x-ray examination consisted of the siblings, parents, grandparents, and children of affected individuals. This group was studied in order to investigate hereditary transmission of the disease. It was preferable to obtain x-rays rather than rely upon histories for the genetic study, because many children of pre-toddler age did not have observable symptoms of the disease. Similarly, some of the adults with the disease could be asymptomatic if the maldevelopment of the hip socket and femoral head did not produce complete dislocation.

When the study was initiated, the reaction of the health visitors seemed to confirm the general literature on the Navajo indicating that congenital hip disease was a sensitive area. (See Hrdlicka, 1908, p. 178; Reichard, 1928, p. 135; Leighton and Leighton, 1944, p. 61.) The health visitors and the Navajo interpreter working on the project stated that they did not want to talk about the disease with people in the community. Careful and discreet inquiry revealed that the central concern was over treatment and treatment failure, not discussion of the disease itself. It is perhaps significant that the health visitor who was most adamant about not interviewing in the community had a brother who was unsuccessfully treated for a dislocated hip a number of years ago with the hip fusion operation.

It was decided that the Many Farms Clinic would not determine treatment for any cases diagnosed because of the specialized nature of the medical problems and awareness of the antipathy in the community to surgical treatment. Such cases were transported to a crippled children's clinic run by an orthopedic consultant of the Public Health Service who examined the children and prescribed treatment. This treatment was then dispensed through the Many Farms Clinic where the children were followed by serial x-rays.

In this manner, the Frejka apron, previously mentioned, was prescribed for 5 of the 18 children with hip abnormalities short of outright dislocation. Upon subsequent x-ray examination of these children, definite improvement was observed, which was attributed to use of the apron. However, when the physicians dispensed the apron, they were aware that some parents were disinterested or apathetic to instruction about use of the apron for the child. The natural question asked by the nurse and the physician was, "Why do some people resist such conservative and successful treatment?"

The anthropologist on the other hand asked "Why would any of the people accept even the conservative treatment?" Use of a therapeutic apron, which keeps the child's legs in a frog's leg position, is incompatible with use of the traditional cradle board. The anthropologist observed that the cradle board was in wide use in the community and a survey carried out by a fourth year medical student showed that 85 percent of the children born in 1960 and 1961 at Many Farms were raised on such a board. Mothers are loathe to give up the cradle board. Its use is sanctioned not only by custom, but is of great practical benefit in a hogan which ordinarily does not have a crib, and when transporting babies on horseback, or in a wagon.

A second finding which seemed to militate against use of the prescribed apron has been referred to earlier. The Navajo do not consider the disease to be a social, personal, or economic handicap. The strength of this attitude and its relationship to actual behavior was shown by analysis of our demographic material; e.g., there was no significant difference in the median age at marriage for normal women and those born with abnormal hips.

With these difficulties in mind, follow-up interviews and observations were made in the hogan by the anthropologist. These revealed that even in the cases which had shown great improvement, the prescribed treatment had not been followed. This information was basic to one of our major findings: that of the 13 cases uncovered and followed with abnormalities short of dislocation in the group born between 1955 and 1961, 12 showed marked improvement. Four of the 12 progressed to complete normalcy. Further inquiry revealed that an apron had been prescribed for five of these patients, and only two had used them to any extent at all; even they had used the apron erratically.

The anthropologist was also concerned with the genetic portion of the study. It was his thought that since clans regulate marriage, a shortcut to uncovering a simple pattern of genetic transmission would be to first analyze the clan affiliation of affected individuals. A clan tabulation was made, on the basis of the social demography already compiled. It was found that the clan affiliation of the affected children did not differ from the clan membership of the normal population. Therefore, there was no correlation between the occurrence of the disease and clans. If such a correlation had been found, the environmental factors associated with particular clans would have required investigation. For example, the existence of separate clan subcultural practices with regard to the birth process and care of the infant would have been more thoroughly investigated.

The anthropologist must also be willing to investigate points of fact already well established in the *general* literature on a people because any medical investigation requires that a *field check* be made to determine the extent of local variation, if any, or, in some cases, to relate environmental factors to a specific individual with a known medical condition. It is well reported, for example, that

Navajo children generally are raised on cradle boards. Testing this fact was pertinent to assessing whether parents were keeping their children off the board and in a Frejka apron. The cradle board also keeps the child's legs in an abducted position which is the opposite of that thought necessary for treatment of the abnormal hip, and therefore its use was thought to be related to expression of the disease. Thus, the aforementioned survey of cradle board usage at Many Farms was carried out, along with a similar survey at Fort Defiance, an urban Navajo community where it was expected there would be less use made of the cradle board. In addition, determination of its use in individual cases by parents of abnormal children permitted us to show that progressive improvement occurred in abnormal children despite the fact that they were on the cradle board.

In summary, the study of congenital hip disease among the Navajo could not have been done without combining the complementary skills and orientation of the anthropologist and the physician. For the physician, the study has resulted in accurate documentation of the high prevalence of the disease among the Navajo; it has shown clearly that there is an interplay between genetics and environment in the causation of the disorder; it has elucidated the natural history of the disease, which has important implications for treatment and for the future study of the disease. For the anthropologist, additional social demographic data has been obtained, such as marriage frequencies between clans; residence patterns before and after marriage; too, marriage and kin relationships over six generations were traced and information regarding birth practices was gathered. These data constitute the material for solid ethnographic studies as well as the raw material for analysis of social structure and culture change. It is rare that the anthropologist on his own has the resources to gather such information on every individual in a community of 2,300 people.

The reasons for the success of collaboration on this project lie principally in the structure within which the research was carried out, but they also relate to the previous experience of the individuals involved. The physician had a favorable academic experience with anthropology and joined the project because of its sociomedical orientation. The anthropologist had extensive experience in interdisciplinary projects and was familiar and comfortable with quantitative data. More importantly, however, many of the elements enumerated in Chapter 9, which threaten the synthesis of the two disciplines, were not present in this project. The research situation was well defined in terms of the research orientation and the type of data which had to be collected. The roles of both physician and anthropologist were clearly delineated in regard to their respective areas of research responsibility. Much of the material collected was expressed quantitatively in such a way that both investigators could contribute to the evaluation and interpretation of findings as the analysis progressed. Lastly, there was feedback of the qualitative material (such as reactions to treatment), which was of significant clinical interest to the medical staff in their understanding of the disease process in their patients.

12.

The Culture of the Innovator

The reason the United States Public Health Service has written this contract with Cornell University is to explore things just of this nature (health visitors). Not to do so undercuts the whole reason for the program. In that case we might as well carry on the work ourselves without a pilot study.

These were the words of Dr. Shaw, Chief of the Division of Indian Health of the United States Public Health Service, when he assembled his field staff to meet with the Cornell University medical staff a few months after the research contract was signed.

The contract with the Department of Health, Education, and Welfare represented a formal agreement between the University and the government, stipulating that the University would have the responsibility for developing, on a pilot study basis, health information and appropriate medical care through research for a group of Navajo Indians living in a geographically defined area and for a specified period of time.[1] In effect, the government was turning over its sovereignty in health in that area to the University.

In this respect, the contract differed from former ones in which University participation was limited to a consulting role; or from a contract which specified that information for the government was to be developed by a survey team working in collaboration with government personnel who still assumed responsibility for medical service. For example, the University of Pennsylvania had carried on a tuberculosis survey in the Pueblo communities of the Rio Grande Valley, and the University of California had contracted for the development of a health education program on the Navajo Reservation. In each case, research was done with University investigators incorporated within the administrative hierarchy of the United States Public Health Service. This, too, was the nature of the research at the Tuberculosis Sanatorium at Fort Defiance (Chapter 3).

The University, as perceived by the government and formalized in the contract, would need a high degree of independence in order that it might initiate studies in health and experimental approaches to improving medical care under Reservation conditions. At the same time the government, through the contract, was assured a high level of medical care for the Indian group who would be the recipients of the program. It was written into the contract that the University would provide the same general health services which were being administered by the government. In fact, reports of vital statistics, morbidity, and so on were to be completed and submitted through routine government channels. It was recognized that the University, by virtue of its extensive research experience and its technical facilities, would provide the kind of research environment required to develop solutions to the long-standing health problems of the Navajo people, which were recognized to be in the area of public health and field health services.

Indeed, there was a chronic shortage of personnel in government to tackle the formidable task of working out such services. It was believed that the University would find it much more feasible to attract bright young medical personnel to the challenge of a study program, field conditions notwithstanding. Thus, the advantages of a research group from a University were readily discernible. A more subtle advantage, but one of great importance, was related to the relationship of the Navajo to the University rather than to the government. The Navajo had held government programs in great suspicion. If the government had entered into an experimental field program, the Navajo would probably have reacted in an indifferent, if not hostile manner. On the other hand, the University, especially Cornell, enjoyed a splendid reputation among the Navajo immediately following the success of the work in tuberculosis at Fort Defiance and could attempt something new without, to the same degree, being put on trial. In effect, the University's reputation was such that it could plan a vigorous study program without the criticism that might accompany government programs. The Federal Agency could also disavow the mistakes made by the University in a way it could not if it were directly responsible for the program, and it could also pick up those features that proved practical and helpful after adequate testing by Cornell. So the leaders in Washington realized that it would be easier for an organization outside of government to experiment with new means of approaching Navajo health needs than it would be to bring about change in their own organization. The University organization was much more flexible and could experiment with designing new job categories which were thought essential to the task required for such a field program, whereas the government was hampered by many Civil Service personnel regulations, accounting procedures, and administrative strictures.

Turning now from the University's role as perceived by the government, let us see how the University itself viewed the contract. On the positive side, by assuming administrative responsibility, the University would be able to cut through the tremendous amount of red tape that goes with Government Civil Service personnel procedures. This made for easier relations with our own staff. We could select men and women according to our own needs and according to their skills. If it seemed wise to select as a health visitor trainee a Navajo who had just recovered from tuberculosis, we could do so and ignore government regulations; if we thought that a candidate for training as a laboratory technician had that ability, we were able to select on a lower level of education than the Civil Service regulations specified. In short, personnel relations could be handled in a much more informal and expedient way throughout, as the administrator had direct control of the situation.

Likewise, a tremendous amount of time would be saved by having the responsibility for all property and housekeeping functions transferred to the University. Acting with the guidance of the Treasurer of the University, the project directors were able to purchase a prefabricated steel building from a local company and see it completely erected, equipped, and functioning as a clinic in a period of 7 months after the time the first meeting took place with the community in September 1955 (Chapter 4). The Navajo leaders were impressed. If it had been necessary to carry out this action through government channels, it would also have required a much larger staff to administer. It is highly unlikely that a field unit of this size could have functioned at all without completely bogging down in red tape, had it not had these administrative responsibilities.

The greatest advantage of all in having this degree of autonomy, from the University's point of view, was that it gave the directors virtually complete independence in research. The University group, for example, could assume the responsibility for an ambulatory tuberculosis chemotherapy program, administered on a home basis, whereas in 1955 the United States Public Health Service had to assume a more conservative attitude due to public and bureaucratic pressures.

Once autonomy for the University researchers was established by this contract, one of the first actions of the Cornell group was to design and develop the health visitor program. In effect, new means of communication were needed for effective work in rural health. As we have seen, this program was a success from the point of view of the Navajo and the University. As long as the work maintained a research orientation, all was well. But when the University attempted to implement the findings of its pilot program by encouraging the government to take over the health visitors and use them in the way they had been trained to work at Many Farms, it ran into serious resistance and ultimate defeat. Finally, only one of the total group of eight was used in anything like his full capacity. Others were used in various ways on clinic and hospital staffs, but not in the role for which they had been trained.[2]

Here we find in microcosm a situation that is widespread in technologic aid: Programs that are welcomed in less developed countries are often defeated due to conflicts within the society of the donor. The anthropologist, in his emphasis on cultural differences between the developed and less developed societies, has tended to ignore these subcultural differences on our own domestic scene which may be critical in the success or failure of a program.

By and large, the innovations described in the foregoing chapters were welcomed by the Indians; the health visitor program, the modification of the customary government modes of running a clinic with the development of such new techniques as the camp file system, and the supportive attitude of the physicians and nurses toward traditional Navajo curing practices, were all perceived by this group of Navajo as being to their advantage. From the point of view of the community, we had indeed built a "Hospital Without Walls."

Gaining acceptance for scientific medicine by such means, as well as for other programs in technologic aid, may well be the easier part of the total innovative process. The designing of services which properly fit the needs of a society as different from ours as that of the Navajo requires a modification in our own institutions and in the customary procedures of our own professionals. That is the more difficult part of the job. Innovation requires changes in both the donor and the recipient societies. Too often, anthropologists have looked only at resistances set up in the transfer process from the one society to another, yet it may be safely said that as many programs have come to a disastrous end due to resistances set up in the bureaucracy at home. Stated figuratively, while we had been successful in removing the walls that impede good communication between cultures, those walls that prevent good communication between subcultural groups in our own society were still standing.

Innovation, new technology, carries with it new roles which are often prestigious in the developing society. There the teacher or technologist trained to pass on new ideas and techniques of the more advanced country will be looked up to for his new knowledge; his job has a proper "fit" in the total acculturation and modernization process. But, looking now to the advanced country itself, programs which call for modification of bureaucratic behavior found among professions both in and out of government, call for a modification that is a threat to the establishment. Such new jobs do not carry prestige, but are often thought of as denigrating—a step backwards rather than a step forward.

Examination of why there was resistance to the health visitor program among the government public health nurses will serve to illustrate this important aspect of the total innovative process. At a meeting in April 1959, called at the request of the Washington office of the Division of Indian Health, members of the Cornell staff met with middle echelon members of the government staff in Albuquerque. The public health nurse on our staff was vigorously opposed by the nurse in supervisory charge of public health nursing on the Navajo Reservation. The following emotional exchange ensued:

> *Government Nurse Administrator:* I would like to cite an incident for you. Just to show you that things are different when you are working for the government. A licensed practical nurse in our division, an excellent practical nurse, believe me, gave a medication and misread the label. She was severely reprimanded. But such cases as this aren't left in our hands. In government they are reviewed on the departmental level, as this was. It isn't that we are being 'chintzy' about not letting your health visitors do what they have been so well trained to do. We have been scorched and we don't intend to be burned. Thank goodness more of our girls are carrying insurance. I don't think that we could even keep them on the job if they had health visitors working out in the hogans independently. I just don't think that they would take that kind of responsibility. In the Government service we have to fix responsibility very carefully.

> *University Nurse:* Well, as far as that goes, their service doesn't depend on their giving shots and medications—they are useful in lots of other ways.

> *G.N.A.:* Well, it comes right down to this. I will not be able to grant them that authority, not on the level of my responsibility for the public health nursing program. If they are to give medications and work out in the hogans alone that will have to be a medical determination, that will be up to the government doctor in charge. I should think that they would be valuable as interpreters in the clinic.

> *U.N.:* They are, very; but I should hate to see them used only in the clinic.

> *G.N.A.:* I can't recommend that they be put on a home visit basis working by themselves, even with supervision.

> *University Anthropologist:* If that were to be the case, who would have to make the decision?

> *G.N.A.:* That would be up to the government doctor in charge and the medical staff. But I will recommend that they are to be used in the clinic to relieve the case load and so the nurse isn't a handmaiden to the doctor.

> *U.A.:* How, exactly, would you fit them into the clinic? What would

their relation be to the blue girls* and the practical nurses who, I understand, will soon be placed in your permanent and field clinics?

G.N.A.: That will have to be carefully specified. There may be some overlap. But that is to be expected at first, but will be ironed out. After all, there is a place for all of the Navajos we can train on these different levels. They are all valuable as record keepers and interpreters for the nursing staff. The blue girls are illiterate and they, the health visitors, would be closer to the people than some of the practical nurses. There is going to have to be some give and take. We can't just fit all of your program into ours. We have thousands of things to consider that you don't; salary levels, tenure, overlap of functions, compatibility of personnel, overall program determinations. Believe me, it isn't easy. In government we have lots of things to consider. Do your health visitors have government drivers' licenses?

U.N.: No.

Government Personnel Officer: Well, that rules out their making solo trips out to the hogan. If the University of California people can't drive government cars by a ruling handed down from Washington, then there is no possible chance that these Navajos could drive government cars.

This exchange illustrates important differences in the values of the government civil servant and the University research group. The government worker values above all else the structure and the functioning of his own social organization, whereby adhering to regulations and the carrying out of programs through existing means bring rewards in terms of promotion and an increase in prestige. The introduction of a subprofessional would be a threat to the *status quo* of public health nursing as careful supervision, a basic tenet of the profession, would call for working close to the community level. Thus, what the University researcher saw as advantages to the nurse—covering four times the usual area through supervising Navajo who would make many of the home visits—was construed as a threat rather than as a reward. Rather than risk the delegation of responsibility outside of their own organization, they would prefer to make such home visits themselves. The efficient inner working of the nursing service took precedence

---

*Blue girls are equivalent to nurse aides.

over what the University group saw as the ultimate need—training Navajo to participate in rural health service. Only through such participation would understanding grow and community health needs be fulfilled. These values are not, of course, restricted to the nursing profession, but pertain to the upward mobility of middle class society generally.

The program which was favored by the government nurses was one in which carefully screened high school graduates were trained far from the home environment in a government hospital in Albuquerque, as practical nurses. Following that, they would be introduced to rural health needs under careful supervision. Such a plan, of course, was in keeping with the usual upgrading of training in government, but diametrically opposite to the rationale of the Many Farms experiment.

Resistance to the health visitor program was encountered for one other important reason: The project administrators did not work down through the power structure of the nursing profession in the way they did in gaining the acceptance of the Navajo on the community level. The top levels of the nursing profession at Cornell and in Washington were not brought into the initial planning of the health visitor program to the degree that the medical profession itself was consulted. While this initial error was corrected at Cornell shortly after the contract was signed, and close working relations were established, this was not the case in Washington. As a result, top leadership in nursing circles there put their efforts into the practical nursing program and never did develop a vested interest in the health visitor program.

Innovation is not likely to take place by direct diffusion to the middle and lower echelons of government from an outside agency, no matter how great the need. The lesson to be learned from the above example is that in the medical field innovations may be more readily accepted by the recipient society which is less complex socially and economically than by the government of the donor society, wherein any change must overcome numerous vested interests of the professions and bureaucratic organization.

Consequently, when a contract organization, such as Cornell, is performing a demonstration program for the government, there is a need for close liaison throughout the life of the project on all echelons. Otherwise the full benefits of the demonstration will not be taken over by the government at the termination of the contract.

Stated in another way, there is a higher level of motivation on the part of the acculturated Navajo to learn from us than we have to learn from him. The attitude of the government nurses to the health visitor program is not only an illustration of bureaucratic resistance to social change in their own organization, but also one of reluctance on the part of the members of the donor society to meet the peoples of the other society in their own communities where language, behavior, and custom are strange and different. A program such as that of Cornell's involved a greater degree of participation in the community than was customary in government circles. This program was accepted in principle by the top leaders in Washington, but was resisted by the nurses who preferred to train nursing assistants in their own cultural milieu, that is, the hospital. Basic to this reluctance is the matter of culture shock which affects everyone working in a society other than his own. Lack of guidelines for behavior, difficulty in verbal communication, even through interpreters, inability to read customary cues offered by gesture and facial expression, together with other factors, all tend to produce discomfort. Such situations are avoided not only by nurses, but by all members of technical aid teams, who would rather build services in their own environment with the customary surroundings of the clinic, classroom, or administrator's office. This is a worldwide tendency; once people have been trained in new technology in urban areas, they are loath to return to rural regions, no matter if it is village Indian, rural Africa, or a remote spot on the Navajo Reservation.

Additionally, the innovation process usually involves working relations between professional people not only trained in different disciplines, but who probably have never before worked together. At Many Farms, the medical team and the social scientists each had their own subculture, and just because the doctor, nurse, or anthropologist had the same national background and spoke the same language, it should not be assumed that there would be no communication problems. The difficulties in communication resulting from such subcultural differences may be appreciated by examining the varied roles of the staff members on the project.

The Resident Staff

Physicians

All of the physicians who were full-time in residence were young: one had just finished his internship, and the others had a year or more of residency training. The most advanced were ready to qualify for writing their specialty board examinations.

Three of the seven doctors who worked during the course of the project were under the doctor draft, serving with the United States Public Health Service, and had been assigned to the Cornell Project by the Indian Division of that service. But all of the doctors were recruited for the research team by Cornell and carefully selected as to training and qualification.

Two of the seven were attracted to the project as they had a particular personal interest in gaining research and service training for medical work in an underdeveloped area. Only one of the group had actually had medical experience overseas. All of the doctors were attracted to working with a university research team where they would receive some guidance in developing research techniques and undertaking independent investigations which they would not gain working for a government organization on a straight service operation. On the whole, the physicians were uniformly adept in providing good medical care, but interest, training, and experience varied with respect to research abilities and skills.

None of the physicians (with one exception) had had any formal experience in medical administration beyond what they might have picked up on residency or internship training, where they were part of a well organized ongoing hospital organization with well defined responsibilities with respect to nurses, laboratory technicians, and others on the staff.

None had had experience in working with public health nurses, or in dealing with the general administration and housekeeping functions that faced them at Many Farms. With the exception of the one physician, who had had experience overseas, none had had previous medical experience or indeed professional experience of any kind with peoples of another culture in their own environment.

As young doctors just out of their internship or residency training, they had not developed a sophisticated public health attitude or approach to medical care, but were still operating on a hospital basis of providing the best possible care to individual patients. "I am interested in treating patients, not communities," said one doctor.

While all of them were dedicated to rendering as good a medical service to the Navajo as possible, their prior training in university medical work in an urban setting oriented them to unusual and serious medical and patient care programs. By virtue of such training they had less interest in preventive aspects of medicine or day-to-day care of minor health problems. As a result of exposure to the medical needs of the Navajo, a reorientation gradually took place, whereby some of the physicians gained further perspective and learned to view health problems in the context of the social environment.

The physicians, trained as they had been in university hospitals, were accustomed to a different type of social organization from the one that they found in the research team at Many Farms. In the hospital setting, the doctors were accustomed to a highly disciplined organization in many respects like military organization, in which the ranking physician is the head of a graded authority system. Such a system is functional to medical practice, where life and death of a patient population must be handled daily and where hospitalized patient care demands quick decisions from the doctor who has ultimate responsibility for the patient. Nurses, nurse's aides, laboratory personnel, and hospital administrative officers all work within this hierarchy and each has his own well-defined responsibility and his own graded degrees of authority.

As a result of such organization, the young doctors are well trained in both following orders and in passing them on to their subordinates. Vertical communications are good and decisions pass from the top to the bottom in an efficient manner, again not unlike a military organization. The young physician is taught to make his own decisions after carefully weighing all the evidence at his command. In fact, training for responsible decision making is a central theme that runs through the professional education of the doctor. Starting with his first experience in his third year as an undergraduate, with increasing responsibility through internship and residency, he is carefully trained to recognize when he is acting within the competence of his training, and when he is not. When not, he seeks the guidance of a more experience man. But responsibility for the patient's care demands that the final decision be his alone. Only by a formal referral system does he relinquish this responsibility, along with the patient, to another physician.

However, medical research demands a restructuring of the traditional roles of the young doctor and the more experienced research director. In the usual situation as mentioned above, the doctor in charge of the particular case had to make final decisions. But in a medical research project final decisions as to policy must be made by the superiors in the research organization. This at first is difficult for both parties, but is resolved by the doctor in charge of research by keeping his distance from supervising the younger man in his role as a clinician when patients are present.

All of this is obvious and commonplace, part of the world of the physician in 20th century urban society. Furthermore, the structure, the beliefs, behavior, and values of such a subculture are not challenged by those who compose such a society. But when members of other subcultural groups, public health nurses and social scientists are brought together with physicians on a research team, problems of administration arise as a result of those differences.

The Public Health Nurse

The public health nurse, on the other hand, has a very different orientation. She represents a self-selected group of nurses who for a variety of reasons have obtained more satisfaction out of nursing in the home and field than in a hospital or clinic. Out of the four resident nurses on the program, two had had previous experience with Navajo, and two had had experience in the New York City area. All four, by virtue of their training, were taught to look at health in its social context and were more interested in preventive aspects of medicine, including educational work in the community.

Insofar as they had to get the cooperation of whole families, as well as community support in many of their programs, such as well child clinics, immunization programs, school health programs, and so on, they had a familiarity with the community and a rapport which made their work sympathetic to the anthropology staff at the outset.

When nurses have not worked regularly in a clinic or hospital for some years and have become accustomed to receiving orders from their own superiors in nursing and to making decisions on their own with a considerable degree of autonomy, then a period of adjustment must take place before they can work effectively in a clinical setting.

The Social Scientists

The social scientists in residence at Many Farms, like the doctors, have been young members of their profession; except for one (the sociologist) all of them have been in the process of gaining a Ph.D. or had that degree just behind them.

The professional society that they had known is the graduate school of an American university. There they were part of a very loosely structured society which is at the opposite extreme from the medical society with its well defined levels of authority and responsibility.

The education of the social scientist in graduate school is not unlike that of the medical student during his preclinical years. He is held responsible for mastering certain areas of study and demonstrating through examination a proficiency in such fields. But from that point on, the training for each profession differs significantly. Gradually the young physician learns to assume greater degrees of responsibility for the patient, under careful guidance.

The anthropologist has no tradition of training comparable to that of the medical student in his clinical years. Only in exceptional circumstances does even the seasoned anthropologist assume responsibility for decisions affecting communities of men, and such anthropologists have in nearly all cases left academic work for government administration. For most anthropologists professional responsibility is defined by the role of teacher or researcher.

In contrast to the doctor in training, the young anthropologist, following the classic tradition, is trained to pursue his field investigation of a primitive society (or in more recent years possibly a community in Western society) with a minimum of guidance from his professional superior at the university.

He may work under close supervision in classroom training, and again in the analysis of his field data. But there is no tradition in the field of anthropology comparable to the "bedside" teaching which every medical student receives in the university hospital, where the instructor and the student are able to make simultaneous observations of the patient.[3] Unlike the doctor in clinical practice, or in public health, the anthropologist in the academic tradition does not involve himself in decisions that affect the individual or the community. Only in recent years relatively few anthropologists qua anthropologists (and not as government administrators) have engaged in "participant intervention" whereby change has been effected on the community level analogous to change in the individual's health due to the practice of the physician.

Furthermore, the anthropologist fresh from graduate school is not likely to be trained to work on a team. In most cases he has worked on a field problem by himself. Group research may be part of the experience of the older anthropologist, or sociologist, but even with such experience behind him, the social scientist as a professional has not had the experience of working in an organization with graded degrees of authority, responsibility, status, and prestige which he meets when joining a medical team.

As a result, the social scientist is not accustomed to working in an organization structured along vertical planes in which there is a graded series of rank within the medical field proper, and an ordering between doctors, nurses, the supporting personnel in laboratories, and subprofessional ranks. Nor is he accustomed to the nature of decision making in such a vertically arranged society, or with the way in which information is passed up and down through the system. By the same token, even the experienced anthropologist is less adept in directing the work of his subordinate; and the younger professional is not accustomed to close supervision.

The older anthropologist, or sociologist, who has had experience in interdisciplinary research, with, say, demographers, social psychologists, and economists, tends to regard communications resulting from exchange of information between any two professionals as horizontally structured. Decision making is in this context and is dependent on group action and resolving of differences and conflicts through meetings and conferences. Whereas the doctor on a medical team is likely to follow the habits he has learned in the hospital and confers only when necessary, and then with his medical superior, or subordinate, with nurses, and laboratory personnel separately. The teaching physician must be careful not to embarrass his student before a seasoned nurse, for the young doctor must learn to give her orders with confidence.

Methodology

The clinician and the field anthropologist are again at opposite poles with respect to research methods. The doctor follows well defined and carefully worked out methods of history taking, examination, and laboratory work-up. These are well standardized, may be carefully measured by various instruments and procedures, and do not vary significantly from one physician to the next, although the way in which they are performed and the way in which the doctor relates to the patient may vary considerably.

On the other hand, the anthropologists vary considerably in the way they approach a community. Although every anthropologist will include much the same type of material in a description of a community, i.e., social organization, economics, religion, technology, and so on, the ways of obtaining such information are not standardized as in medical methodology. Much of the data he collects cannot be subjected to meaningful quantification, much of it being dependent on lengthy description for its exposition and subjective judgment.

While the ideal objective of the anthropologist may be the description of the whole culture, just as the clinician may be concerned with the whole patient, and the public health oriented doctor with the total pattern of diseases and epidemiologic studies of each in a community, the nature of medicine allows for a building up of knowledge as each patient contributes to the medical segmental study.

Much of anthropology does not come in such discrete additive units, and the more cumbersome nature of its recording methods necessitates a longer time before results can be fed back to the medical team. This too contributes to misunderstanding and difficulty in smooth planning between the two professions.

When the anthropologist uses the paper-pencil surveys of the type identified with sociology, or when they are used by the sociologists, the research role may be more easily understood by the clinician; additionally, when the material is structured so that it may be subjected to quantitative analysis, the feedback to the medical team is more efficient.

Likewise, the role of the anthropologist may be readily understood when he is doing work of a restricted, and even technical sort. For example, one of the resident anthropologists at Many Farms made a study under the direction of the physicians and a nutritionist on Navajo diet. Here the anthropologist was working within a medical frame of reference and was essentially applying knowledge to immediate medical need. But the anthropologist who is working on problems more germane to his own field, and which do not necessarily have any immediate application to medicine has a much more difficult time in defining his role and communications with the medical team become more difficult.

For example, when the anthropologist was applying his knowledge of Navajo culture to answer such questions posed by the doctor as: How do we gain entry into the community? How should we train interpreters? What is the Navajo attitude towards congenital hip disease? Communications were at the maximum, but they were at a minimum when the anthropologist investigated a problem basic to his own field, such as changing patterns of social organization as affected by economic change, which eventually might lead to more important data basic to cross-cultural medical practice. This, of course, is true in any group research endeavor; where knowledge has immediate application there is closer cooperation than when basic research is involved.

Conflicts Resulting from Organizational (Structural) Differences

The anthropologists from the very start of the research project asked the medical officer in charge to call staff meetings, so that research problems of common interest could be discussed. From their point of view, this was the natural way of arriving at decisions. Also, because of the nature of the vertical flow of information in the medical staff, a new policy might be set by the New York staff, or by the medical officer in charge, or a new research project set up and the anthropologist not consulted. He was not deliberately overlooked, but simply because the doctor was not accustomed to consult him unless his thinking was crucial in the matter. Later the anthropologist might learn of an untoward reaction in the community to this policy and feel miffed that he had not been brought in on the decision.

As indicated earlier, the young physician did not see any need for staff meetings in the first place, as the usual method of consulting with staff members individually seemed the logical way of handling administrative and research matters.

As one would expect, there was a strong identification between the anthropologists and the Navajo. Insofar as their training to date had been in the analysis of the behavior of nonliterate societies, and they had had only personal experiences with doctors, they were not in a position to be as free of bias as would be desirable in a research situation.

As a result of this identification with the Navajo patients, reinforced by their own "outgroup" image of themselves, several of the anthropologists became repeatedly embroiled in arguments with the physicians as to certain policies and procedures, and argued that for cultural reasons a particular policy would not be accepted. For example, disrobing of the patients. While there was, to be sure, a good deal in the anthropologic literature on Navajo patterns of modesty, the values of bodily modesty gave way to the even greater value of careful medical attention.

Likewise, the anthropologists became incensed when patients were kept in the waiting room a long time, or when a referral went astray. It is not that sloppy medicine should be condoned, but it would have been helpful had the anthropologists had a broader perspective and realized that these were problems that were sometimes unavoidable in medical practice, and not to be judged only in terms of cultural reactions.

This identification with the patient by several of the anthropologists was aided and abetted by the public health nurses. As mentioned above, their interest in preventive medicine, their accustomed freedom in working away from the strict discipline and routines were all frustrating to them on the research team. But in most cases the anthropologists tended to sympathize with the nurses, and vice versa.

The structure of the medical team has been described; the efficiency of medical communication between members of the team has been discussed. Communication up and down through this vertical structure was also utilized in effectively educating the political leaders of the Navajo. At Many Farms this same vertical structure obtained, and there was efficient communication between the Cornell physicians directing the project in New York and the field medical officer in charge, and from him to his patient via the health visitor. Likewise, there was a comparable structure in the nursing group.

In contrast to the situation at Fort Defiance and in clinical medicine generally, the goals established for work at Many Farms called for work in both curative medicine in the clinic and preventive medicine carried on by the same set of nurses. When the nurse was training the health visitors for their job in the clinic, and when they themselves were drawn into this sphere of nursing, the relations between the doctors and the nurses went more smoothly. But insofar as the public health nurses had taken over other values in their own professional training, which suited them well for work in the home and community, they were placed at a disadvantage in attempting to combine both types of medicine. As a result, the relatively smooth operation of the medical team characteristic of a hospital service was often disrupted at Many Farms when the nursing staff pulled off in one direction and the doctors in another, due to the dual nature of the work.

Thus the primary orientation of both the public health nurses and the social scientists to the community and to preventive medical services designed in terms of community need tended to divorce these two professions from that of the young physician whose primary interests were often focused on curative aspects of medicine. As a result of the basic values underlying these professional interests, communication between the members of the team were skewed and often blocked to the disadvantage of the smooth functioning of the project. It was only when the medical officer in charge had a comprehensive view of the total service he was charged to render, and also the managerial skills called for in resolving the conflicts in his staff, that these difficulties were partially surmounted.

Finally, any comprehensive medical services rendered in a cultural setting call for antecedents in the training process whereby shared values, goals, skills, and knowledge can be intermeshed in a way that was impossible when the project administrators were forced to rely upon conventionally trained young physicians and nurses. In fact, if a training experience of working together in teams were made an integral part of their education for public health work, an increase in mutual understanding and sharing of values and goals would be included at an early stage in their development. That is, if nurses in training, doctors in training, and young social scientists were all exposed early in their careers to such comprehensive medical service as that offered at Many Farms, then the socialization of public health nurses to one type of professional endeavor, and physicians to another, would not take place, or at least would be minimized. Likewise, social scientists, if brought into training earlier in their careers in the medical setting, would not have such serious problems of adjustment to working on medical teams. All of this, of course, would call for a modification of the conventional medical, nursing, and social science-in-medicine curricula for those who plan to make their careers in community medicine—a revision which is now being experimented with at some medical colleges.[4]

The Outpost Community

A small group of people living in isolation from their own society is faced with many problems which do not confront communities elsewhere. When the community is made up of researchers, each with his own professional subculture, the problems of such group living become all the more difficult and it is almost impossible to maintain morale over a long period of time.

This phenomenon of living in isolation from one's own culture has recently been noted by Americans who have observed communities engaged in technical assistance programs. Much of what has been said there can be said about community life at Many Farms, but with one important difference. Americans overseas frequently live in cities where the level of technology and literacy make for a different type of life than is true of the "backwoods" community both abroad and in remote areas of the American Southwest.

In fact, the affluent life of the American in Teheran, Bangkok, Rangoon, and New Delhi is often one of the primary difficulties and makes for problems in working on the "grass roots" level. While Many Farms did not offer the cosmopolitan life enjoyed in such cities, it did share the phenomenon of "culture shock" with other communities of overseas Americans. As a rural outpost the residents were more directly subjected to such shock than would have been the case in a city environment.

Culture shock has been described by the anthropologist Kalervo Oberg:

> Culture shock is precipitated by the anxiety that results from losing all our familiar signs and symbols of social intercourse. These signs or cues include the thousand and one ways in which we orient ourselves to the situations of daily life: when to shake hands and what to say when we meet people, when and how to give tips, how to give orders to servants, how to make purchases, when to accept and when to refuse invitations, when to take statements seriously and when not. Now these cues which may be words, gestures, facial expressions, customs, or norms are acquired by all of us in the course of growing up and are as much a part of our culture as the language we speak or the beliefs we accept. All of us depend for our peace of mind and our efficiency on hundreds of these cues, most of which we do not carry on the level of conscious awareness.

> Now when an individual enters a strange culture, all or most of these familiar cues are removed. He or she is like a fish out of water. No matter how broadminded or full of good will you may be, a series of props have been knocked out from under you, followed by a feeling of frustration and anxiety. (Cleveland et al., 1960, p. 27.)

Every anthropologist has suffered this shock in "going to the field," but as time passes the shock lessens as he gains skills in recognizing cues, and as he learns at least enough of the language to maintain a check on his interpreter. If he is alone in the field and completely surrounded by the other culture, this process of becoming acclimated to the behavior of another people takes a varying length of time, from a minimum of a few months to many. The ultimate outcome of such an experience may be that such an individual may "go native," in which case he becomes completely absorbed in the other society and totally accepts their values and way of life. The anthropologist has to guard against this, which he does by periodic emergence and rejoining his own society. If he does go native, he loses his objectivity and his scientific "set" which makes him useless as an anthropologist.

Nor is the anthropologist the only one who can experience this phenomenon. Anyone who allows himself to be completely isolated to the same degree lives through this culture transference. The missionary, the trader, the isolated district officer have all had the same experience, and they too must guard against losing their own professional identity. But for the outpost community this complete break through the culture barrier is not possible to anything like the degree that is the case for isolated individuals.

The individual reacts to culture shock by a long series of accommodations through imitative behavior in part. Thus he learns the language, picks up the gestures unconsciously, and may even accept native values. Natives sometimes find him "queer," but like his company and respect him because he respects them, eats their food, lives in their village—rather than at the government compound or research station. But the outpost community reacts to culture shock in just the opposite way, by reinforcing its values and its own way of life. Both types of reactions have biologic value; for the individual living in a native community, procuring food, housing, sexual needs, and recreation may all be obtained by other cultural means and survival dictates the adoption of new ways of doing so.

But the group's social *raison d'être* is maintaining the cultural values of its members and perpetuating them for the next generation.

In the face of an uneasy situation, the American reacts as a member of even a small group of only a few families in the way he was conditioned to react by his own culture. Again, these are basic designs for physical and psychologic survival.

The members of the outpost community tend to become very dependent on one another, and living as they do, individuals cooperate in all sorts of ways familiar to the frontier, but lost in city life. Mutual aid in shopping, baby sitting, exchange of meals and group recreation all manifest the close solidarity of the society of outsiders in isolation.

Inherently the total situation of isolation from the larger society—coping with cultural differences and with professional disputes among the members of the staff—proves to be anything but conducive to group mental health. All of this is aggravated by the fact that it is difficult to get away from the job when the occupational community and the social community are one and the same. The result is that when the research is suffering from disagreements between staff members, these conflicts and resulting hostilities have no natural outlet but remain within a closed social system. If one or two individuals become upset, they upset the whole equilibrium of the community.

The best way to prevent such a build-up of tensions is by frequent period of recreation and relaxation, with as many trips away on weekends as financially feasible. Although members of the project were warned that they would suffer from "cabin fever" if they did not heed these precautions, administratively it was difficult to do much more than give such advice. In retrospect, it might have been well to have provided funds for such trips away from the project. As it was, the administration could not legislate such matters as, after all, the project site was each family's home and such trips were an added expense to the family budget. This was not a problem with the Navajo staff, as all of them (with few exceptions) returned each weekend to their homes on the Reservation.

If there is an integral relationship between the pattern of a society and the nature of its diseases, as has been advanced by many observers, then it is of interest to note the pattern of disease within this small outpost community of researchers isolated within a tribal society.

Anxiety, tension, worry, sometimes augmented by overwork and lack of relaxation resulted in mental stress; a number of the staff had to resort to psychiatric aid to regain their equilibrium. Such tension was probably a contributing factor for a member of the residence staff breaking down with a severe peptic ulcer. Other manifestations of ill health also resulted from prolonged exposure to the stresses of the job.

The Anthropologist's Dilemma

Living in our society in such an outpost community presented many problems for the anthropologist who was concerned not only with the effect of the new technology on the native society, but he was also interested in the social unit extending this new technology.

The anthropologist is trained to observe interacting individuals and interacting social systems. In his more classic role this may be observations and analysis of persons in different strata of the power system of a given society; or one occupational group's relation to another, as in studies of caste relations in India. He does not study, as a member of a medical team, the behavior of a Navajo patient as such, but the behavior of that patient interacting with the doctor or the nurse administering superior medical technology.

This poses a complex problem in research administration, for it necessitates the anthropologist playing an almost impossible set of roles. First of all, if he is new to the culture and society of physicians, he will, if well trained, be very much interested in the behavioral characteristics of the physician and nurse, assistants, and other members of the field medical team. He looks upon this medical team as part of his data for analysis in understanding the whole process of technical change in which there are three essential ingredients: the purveyors of the new technology, the technology itself, and the recipients of the new technology.

In order to gain any understanding of the process of medical service and research in an underdeveloped area, he must immerse himself in this new society, which after years of research and study of primitive societies he may find most fascinating and challenging. Yet he is also conscious of the need to study the native community and how it is reacting to the medical service. Simultaneously observing both medical team and the community poses difficult problems. If he lives with the medical team of which he is part, the anthropologist never comes sufficiently close to native life to gain the insight that he would if he were surrounded by the native society. He is apt to be caught up in the overwhelmingly strong pull of his own social group. Learning a language as difficult as Navajo, subjecting himself to all the anxieties of living with a people so different, can be a painful experience. It feels much more comfortable to remain in close contact with the medical team.

As a result, the anthropologist has difficulty crossing and recrossing the culture barrier and repeatedly experiences, over a long period of time, the anxiety that anthropologists feel in first breaking through to another culture. Ideally, this problem may best be resolved by having two anthropologists resident on such a field team, one assigned to living with Navajos in their hogans for several months, and the other stationed at the clinic for a comparable length of time. In order for each to experience the total situation, it may be expedient for them to shift from the one locale to the other. However, his ambivalence would be minimized if, as suggested earlier, the social scientist had had prior experience during his earlier training in work with a medical team.

Conclusion

In the Introduction to the First Edition, certain propositions are set forth as being basic to the success of the innovation process. The question was asked: Could a modern urban-based medical college follow these propositions and adapt its skills and technology to meet the needs of such a tribal society as that of the Navajo Indians?

If we review these propositions once more, it will become evident that certain of these were followed and others ignored.

Those propositions dealing with the culture of the recipient society were, by and large, well followed. The respect the medical team showed towards the Navajo and their religion, with its central concern for the health of the individual, was of the utmost importance in the success of the project. This respect was conveyed by involving the Navajo themselves in the administration of the clinic and by frequent consultations with their leaders in policy matters concerning this medical service. Also, a careful work-up was given to each patient in the clinic and great attention was paid to accurate medical interpretation. All of this was perceived by the community as being vastly different from the medical service they had been used to receiving from many physicians and nurses in the government service of a previous era and, in fact, which still persisted in some regions of the Reservation.

The establishment of the clinic at Many Farms met a felt need of the community for a better health service. But that better service could not be determined on an *a priori* basis; experimentation was essential. The Navajo value system is receptive to new technology which is proven to be to their advantage, and this outlook places a premium on trial and error. The fact that at the outset the Cornell team was associated with a successful experiment—namely, the technologic breakthrough in the treatment of tuberculosis—had much to do with the confidence of the community in this particular medical team, and their receptive attitude to the experimentation essential to the design of new modes of health service.

We have seen that the development of the health visitor program proved to be a vital link between the community and the clinic and was a demonstration of the validity of several of these propositions—that is, Proposition 3, having to do with participation, and Proposition 8, dealing with communication. But it should be emphasized that the health visitor program is also an illustration of Proposition 6. We effectively used acculturated individuals in the transmission of new ideas, techniques, beliefs, and so on to the more conservative members of the recipient society. They were not only bilingual and thus able to learn medical concepts basic to accurate communication, but they were to a significant degree bicultural, at least when compared to the conservative elders in their own society. This bicultural role enabled them to understand the ways of their own society and participate in it, but they also had an understanding of the donor society and participated with members of that society in the running of the clinic. Much has been said about the health visitors and mediation. It is this bicultural role that makes such mediation possible and thereby intercultural understanding and innovation are advanced.

We have followed in great detail the way in which the medical team identified and worked through both the political and the prestige structure of the Tribe, and of how the Navajo leaders participated in the setting up of the clinic at Many Farms. We have also seen that over a period of years a change in the attitude of the Navajo toward our physicians, and our physicians toward Navajo medicine, made possible the work of Cornell University

Medical College. The time was ripe for the experiment in innovation which followed.

The primary failure should be attributed to ignoring the second of the listed propositions. As pointed out in Chapter 12, we did not pay sufficient attention to the beliefs, values, and structuring of our own society. Success in mapping a cross-cultural program in public health and gaining the support and participation of a people such as the Navajo may be the easier part of the job.

Ultimately, if there is to be a successful introduction to less developed areas of Western technology, of which medicine is but one part, we must find more effective ways of bridging gaps within our own bureaucracy. It is only then that we will truly have a hospital without walls.

Social scientists and the medical professions must each be educated to the other's field in order to work effectively in a program such as the one described in this volume. Finally, more effective working relations must be obtained between the Federal medical planners and the University investigators if demonstrations such as this are to achieve their full potential as innovations.

Afterword

The People's Health has been out of print for many years. It is the authors' hope that with the publication of this revised and expanded edition the book will be used not only at the Navajo Community College, where there are nurses in training, but at other institutions as well where doctors, nurses, and public health administrators are involved in extending modern medicine to people of other cultures.

In closing it is important to note that in the years since the closing of the Many Farms Clinic the Navajo people have made considerable progress in taking over the administration of their own public health programming, especially in the areas of health education and prevention. The Division of Indian Health Services was established in 1977 by the Tribal Council. This was in accord with the Tribe's assumption of much of the responsibility for running many service programs formerly administered by the Federal Government.

Notes

Chapter 1

1. Case history reconstructed from medical chart at Many Farms Clinic by William F. Nydegger.

2. For a brief account of the physical environment, economy, social and political organization of the Navajo, see Appendix I.

3. Much of this material is either derived or quoted from Ladd (1957). The reader interested in greater detail is referred to the writings of Kluckhohn, Riechard, and Wyman. See References.

4. This medicine man spoke no English; the interview from which this was taken was conducted through a skilled Navajo interpreter.

Chapter 2

1. *Health Services for the American Indian*, U.S. Department of Health, Education, and Welfare, Public Health Service, 1956, p. 1.

2. *Ibid.*, p. 1.

3. Trachoma is an infectious granular conjunctivitis caused by a bacterial organism from the family Chlamydiaceae and order of Rickettsiales.

4. Hearings before a Subcommittee on Interior and Insular Affairs, United States Senate, 83rd Congress, Second Session, May 28 and 29, 1954.

Chapter 3

1. Letter from Dr. Walsh McDermott to Paul Sears, 1954.

2. *The Way of the Navaho*, produced by Columbia Broadcasting System, Television, as one part of the Adventure Series in collaboration with the American Museum of Natural History, 1954.

3. This project was sponsored by American Indian Development, a private organization.

4. Dr. Viola Pfrommer, a health educator with wide experience in cross-cultural work, and Mr. D'Arcy McNickle, an administrator formerly with the Bureau of Indian Affairs and Director of the Crown Point Project, played an important part not only in developing an understanding of modern medicine in that community, but also in being instrumental in the calling of annual conferences which did so much to further more effective communications between the Navajo patients and the staffs in the off-reservation contract sanatoria. Mr. Al Buckingham, health educator on the University of California Project at Window Rock, also played a leading role in the organization of these meetings.

5. Fourth Annual Report, American Indian Development, 1955. Mimeographed.

6. That is, miliary tuberculosis.

7. For many years Mr. Young sat in on the meetings of the Tribal Council and was the only non-Navajo who knew what was said in both languages. The growth and stability of the Council owes much to his dedication, and that of the late Allan Harper, General Superintendent.

8. Dr. René Dubos of the Rockefeller Institute and Dr. David Barr, Professor of Medicine, Cornell University Medical College, accompanied Drs. McDermott and Muschenheim on this field survey sponsored by the National Tuberculosis Foundation.

Chapter 5

1. In speaking of pneumonia and sputum, and in the recognition of medical symptoms, Frank, of course, looks back as an educated health visitor on his own earlier life when he regarded disease very differently.

2. These are from "A Syllabus for Teachers in Navajo Health," organized by Bernice Loughlin and financed by a grant from the Navajo Tribal Council. Copies have been distributed to health officials at Window Rock for use in their training program.

3. This study was divided into the following sections: (1) the *Community View;* home interviews were conducted by a random sample (15 percent) of each health visitor's family "caseload"; (2) the *Health Visitors' View;* self-appraisal of job performance conducted by structured interviews; (3) the *Doctor's View,* and (4) the *Nurses' View;* written response to a short questionnaire. Additionally, the anthropologist accompanied each health visitor on two home visits in order to observe interaction between them and the patients. Similar observations were also made in the clinic. This discussion is based, for the most part, on the findings of that study.

Chapter 6

1. All quotations from page 112 through 118 are from a progress report written by Donald Rieder, Resident Anthropologist.
2. The exact number of Navajo clans still extant is not known but is estimated to be between 40 and 50.

Chapter 7

1. In order to assist the doctors and nurses in Government service in building up a vocabulary for rapport purposes, a list of useful phrases, verbs, and numerals was prepared by Dr. Herbert Landar towards the end of the project. This short list was designed to be posted in a readily accessible place, on a clip board or on the wall of examining rooms. (See Appendix III.)
2. In retrospect, the authors recognize that this technical description of coronary heart disease was not well designed. However, because we were simply testing how this passage was actually translated by the Navajo interpreters, the succeeding comments on this material are still valid.
3. An orthography was devised for the Navajo language by a group of language specialists in the 1940s. However, the written language is known to only a very few Navajo.

Chapter 9

1. We are indebted to Dr. William C. Nydegger, resident anthropologist at Many Farms, 1959–1961, who gathered baseline data on the diagnosticians and singers. His findings were checked and updated by the author in 1961–1962.

Chapter 10

1. This chapter originally appeared in *Science*, 1972.
2. Primary health care is readily accessible and continuously available health care that is delivered to an individual and is frequently expressed in terms of a defined population.
3. This is not to say that the desire to develop knowledge of benefits to others was unimportant as a motivating force. On the contrary, the tribal leaders repeatedly expressed their pride in the fact that a study supported by them, and of immediate benefit to only a small portion of their people, would ultimately benefit not only the remainder of the Navajo people, but people elsewhere in the world.
4. To be sure, there were individual instances of a child or an adult with a technologically curable bacterial meningitis (nine meningitis cases with three deaths) or an adult with a bacterial pneumonia. All such cases taken together, however, represent a very small group because of the size and demographic characteristics of the population and would have been treated in hospital in any case.
5. The higher rate for 1957 is attributable to five deaths from influenza in November of that year.
6. The possible use of otitis media as an "indicator" disease by which to measure the availability and effectiveness of health services in various socioeconomic groups is under study by the National Academy of Sciences Institute of Medicine, David Kessner, study director.
7. The Navajo–Cornell Field Health Research Project was conducted by the Department of Public Health, New York Hospital–Cornell University Medical Center, New York. It received financial support from the Navajo Tribe; the Division of Indian Health; research grant RG-5209, Division of General Medical Sciences, National Institutes of Health, United States Public Health Service, The Russell Sage Foundation; and the Max C. Fleischmann Foundation.

Chapter 12

1. The research covered by the original contract was to last for 5 years; a 2-year extension was provided in 1960.
2. In 1964, 2 years after the termination of Cornell's work at Many Farms, Dr. Jerrold E. Levy, an anthropologist on the United States Public Health Service staff at Window Rock, wrote: "Public Health Nursing Aides were recruited from the graduates of the Cornell Health Visitor training program. Unfortunately, their current position descriptions do not permit them to practice many of the skills they have been taught and thus preclude opportunities for advancement." (Interpreter Training Program, U.S.P.H.S., Division of Indian Health, Window Rock, Arizona, 1964.)

3. There are certain notable exceptions to this generalization. During the 1930s the Laboratory of Anthropology in Santa Fe, New Mexico, supported field training for anthropologists. Ralph Linton, Leslie White, Al Lesser, Ruth Benedict, and others took students to the field and gave them close supervision in field methodology. In recent years, a program financed by the National Science Foundation has enabled a few university departments of anthropology to conduct field training for graduate students.

4. The University of Kentucky Medical College and Stanford University Medical College are two outstanding examples of reorganization of the medical curriculum, whereby a closer relationship between the behavioral sciences and the medical sciences has been brought about.

Appendix I

Navajo Culture and Environment

A Changing Land and a Changing Economy

The Navajo Indians live on the southern edge of the Colorado Plateau which ranges in elevation from 4,500 to 10,000 feet. This arid highland, cut by deep canyons and divided by mesas and mountains, extends across the eastern half of northern Arizona, over into northwestern New Mexico. To the north, the Navajo Reservation reaches into the rugged canyon country of southern Utah.

Today, as you ride across this land, you see the results of long periods of erosion which go back into geologic time. Natural forces have been augmented by human and animal agency in the last 200 years: sheep, goats, cattle, and horses introduced to the Southwest by the frontiersmen, first Hispano then Anglo, have denuded the plateau, which is always in a delicate balance in this land of severe drought.

During the second half of the 19th century, the Navajo Reservation was set aside by executive order and subsequently increased in size until it spread over 16,000,000 acres—an area as large as West Virginia. The establishment of trading posts in the early 1870s provided a link between Navajo sheep husbandry and the frontier economy of the white man. In an earlier time, sheep, cattle, and horses were stolen from settlers in adjacent towns. The flocks, highly valued by the Navajo, increased by the million. By 1935, little ground cover was left as overusage had accelerated the natural forces of erosion and caused arroyos which carried off the flood waters and scarred the land.

Livestock reduction was enforced on the Navajo Reservation as part of the larger Federal soil conservation movement. But it was enforced too rapidly and at great human sacrifice. Agents of the Indian Bureau, who only a few years before had encouraged the Navajo to build up their flocks, now told them they had overstocked their range. The program was put through in the face of considerable resistance and set back the slow beginnings of a consolidated Tribal Government and marred Navajo–Federal Government relations. The administrators, in their zeal to get the job done, failed to work through the people they were administering; it was a program imposed from on top. This sudden reduction of livestock, which was virtually the only source of livelihood, was, in effect, a traumatic experience for the people, one which they still speak of with great bitterness.

In addition to these changes in animal husbandry, there have been technologic changes which have affected the Navajo and his economy. The subsurface wealth of the land had begun to be developed some years before, when the first oil leases in the Shiprock area were let out to private industry. Two decades later, vast helium deposits were opened for a nation at war, and soon after, the largest natural gas dome on the continent was discovered and developed to the northwest of the Reservation. Pipe lines were laid across the Indian lands by Navajo labor. Then, only a few years after the war, uranium-bearing ores were discovered on the Colorado Plateau and some of the richest deposits were found to be on Indian lands. In the meanwhile, an old sawmill on the Forest Defiance Plateau had been greatly enlarged and modernized. After the war, millions of feet of ponderosa pine were cut and processed each year.

The income from timber and from oil, gas and uranium leases goes into a Tribal fund. Today the Tribe has considerable wealth with an annual income of more than 20 million dollars. The leaders of the Tribe have wisely resisted making a *per capita* distribution of this wealth. They have realized that this income divided among more than 85,000 tribesmen would bring immediate relief to many hundreds of needy families, but if that were done there would be fewer funds for the further exploitation of Tribal lands, nor would the Tribal Government be able to continue the scholarship fund which each year enables many young Navajo to obtain a college education.

The Tribal resources have attracted the interest of outsiders, but of even greater political significance is the fact that in recent years Indians have gained the right to vote in State and National elections, a right denied them prior to 1948 by the state constitutions of Arizona and New Mexico. Now, for the first time, the politicians in Phoenix and Santa Fe are paying attention to the wishes of the Navajo people.

There is still another economic change which has affected the way of life of the Navajo people even more than those changes listed above—the entry of the Navajo into the wage economy of the West. Prior to 1940, the individual Navajo had little or no cash; his economy was based on a barter system with credit extended by the traders between wool season in the spring and lamb marketing in the fall.

The war years started an irreversible trend: Navajo labor became prized by the railroads and produce growers of the West as the Spanish Americans and others left the Southwest for employment in war plants on the Pacific coast. The Navajo now became the gandydancers of the Santa Fe and Southern Pacific Railways, taking the place of immigrant labor who had walked the tracks before them. Indian men and women, along with their children, became the stoop-labor without whose help the produce growers could not harvest their carrots, potatoes, and sugar beets. Industry too attracted Navajo men. Many went to the shipyards in California, others to the copper mines in southern Arizona, or the Army munition depots close to the Reservation border. The trend once started continued; in 1948 it was estimated that 13,000 Navajo were living off the Reservation during the greater part of the year.

It is not that the Navajo prefer to live off the Reservation and work for wages, it is simply a fact that the land resources of the Reservation will no longer support their total number. Most of those who go off to work come back at frequent intervals, to see their families, plant and harvest their corn fields, or take part in religious ceremonies.

Today, evidence of this change in economic life may be seen all around. Autos have in large part replaced wagons, except in the most remote regions. Each week the Navajo on the southern reservation and those living adjacent to Farmington, New Mexico, go to town to market, rather than trade in the local trading post. Radios, store-bought furniture, packaged foods, and many other items have become important to the Navajo people.

Social Organization

Changes in the social organization have not been as rapid as those in economics and technology. To this day the people are organized into a series of some 50 matrilineal clans. These clans primarily function to control marriage. That is, if a man in Red House clan marries a woman in Bitter Water clan, the children of this union belong to Bitter Water, the clan of the mother. Marriage within the clan is incestuous from the Navajo point of view.

When a man marries, he goes to live with his wife's family, but he and his bride set up their own household in a separate hogan, often close to that of the wife's mother and her sisters, who live in the same immediate area with their husbands who, like this woman's husband, are members of other clans. This matrilocal pattern, which at one time was almost universal, has given way to considerable patrilocal and independent residence where man and wife live separately from either family.

So we find that the father and his children are in separate clan groupings. This does not mean that he is not responsible for their upbringing, as fathers are in our own culture, but it does mean that he has a dual responsibility; he must provide economically for his wife, but he must also pay close attention to his sisters' children, who by matrilineal rule are members of his own social group. He is not responsible for their economic support, but he is expected to guide them in becoming "good" Navajo who will behave according to the ways of the ancestors. As such, the mother's brother is not only a teacher, but a disciplinarian.

In Navajo society, a woman's responsibilities and obligations are all within her own clan—which, we must remember, is also the clan of her children. But for the adult male, life is not so simple. He not only has responsibilities in the upbringing of his sisters' children, but he must return frequently to the hogan where he was raised, to help plant and harvest the corn of his own clansmen and lend a hand on occasion with his mother's sheep. Today, the Navajo who works for wages in Denver or Los Angeles continues to have this additional economic obligation.

The fundamental unit in Navajo society is the nuclear family. That consists of the father, the mother, and their offspring. But beyond that there is the extended family, relatives of both spouses, which includes their parents, siblings, nephews, and nieces. This extended family is still important in Navajo society and gives growing children a security often lacking in modern Western society. The child is not totally dependent on his own parents. There are mother surrogates, the maternal aunts who live close by and who in Navajo kinship are called by the same term as the biologic mother. So the Navajo child grows up in an environment where his dependencies are not all focused on his own parents but fan out among numerous adults, all related through the kinship system. Also, it is evident that there are many cousins for playmates; in fact, the offspring of sisters are so close to one another, sociologically speaking, that they call each other brothers and sisters.

As a result of the increased travel to wage work off Reservation, we see certain strains within the Navajo family. These strains are especially evident in areas where the process of acculturation is most advanced—which coincide with the areas of greatest economic opportunity. Not only are adult males away much of the year, but the stepped-up educational program, which has placed many children in boarding school, has worked a hardship on the Navajo woman. She is left high and dry without her customary family responsibilities, once her children have entered first grade. In areas of advanced acculturation, there is tremendous strain, often resulting in broken families. Children have been orphaned— the extended family no longer feels that it has a responsibility towards the children if the mother, in time of psychologic stress, abandons them, and in some regions delinquency, murder, and rape have increased. Whereas 50 years ago the enforcement of native law and custom was handled by the clan or community, now frequently enforcement has been relegated to outsiders.

Housing

The Navajo nuclear family lives in a simple hemispherical one-room house built of pine timbers dressed and notched to fit together. This structure, called a hogan, has many variations depending on the availability of wood. Usually it has six to eight sides, a dirt floor, and the door always faces the east, the point of the compass associated with goodness, blessing, and plenty. There is a smoke-hole in the middle of the cribbed ceiling, and traditionally there are no windows. A gasoline drum with a hole in the front and stove pipe extending up to the smokehole makes a combination heater and cookstove. Often today the women have additional small wood ranges.

Furniture is sparse. In the old-fashioned hogan there was almost none, but in most houses today there is one double bed and a few chairs. The family eats sitting around a piece of oilcloth spread out on the floor, or on a low wooden platform. At an earlier period in Navajo history, even today in remote areas, the whole family slept on sheep pelts stretched upon the hogan floor and folded across racks in the daytime. Suitcases piled one on top of the other provide storage space. A water cask is always present, and a wash basin usually stands near the door.

In the summer the family is likely to move out to the summer hogan, or shade, a brush structure which may be made in the shape of a hogan or with a flat brush roof and timbers resting against a pole framework. The Navajo dislike extreme heat and feel much more comfortable in the summer living in such branchwork enclosures.

There is much variation in housing today. Many families live in log cabins with windows or in shacks built of roofing tin, assorted boards, and even packing crates. Such housing is not as satisfactory as the hogan which is, when well constructed and banked with a heavy earth cover, a remarkably weather-proof structure, and one which is easily heated.

Unlike in Euro-American society, housing has never been a status symbol. Navajo families with considerable property, even those with steady jobs or land leased out to an oil company, are likely to live in the same type of houses as do the poor. The hard packed dirt floor is easier to sweep clean of food and refuse than plank floors with cracks between.

The government, ever since the organization of the Indian Service in the last century, has attempted to change the mode of housing. Each attempt has met with failure because they have *projected our values* with regard to housing onto the Navajo. Now the Tribe itself, influenced by some acculturated leaders who have taken over many of our values, has a housing program underway: a prefabricated frame structure painted white, with two or more rooms, a simple sink, and other conveniences. These houses are also being promoted by the United States Public Health Service as being easier to keep clean than the more traditional houses. It remains to be seen if the young and more acculturated people will adopt them.

Political Organization

The Navajo people did not have a sense of political unity until very recently—and even now those who live in remote areas have very little knowledge of the political life on the Tribal level, or of social and economic planning. In fact, there was no Tribal unity in the old days, no overall leadership. The Navajo, like the Apache and many other Western tribes, had leadership only on the local level. There would be a strong elder (always with the gift of oratory) who exerted influence over a group of extended families in a given local area. In the more remote days, he was usually the organizer of raiding parties.

At the turn of the century, under the supervision of one of the government agents, a more formal local government known as the *chapter* was formed. This was developed from the traditional informal organization of the extended families in any one area—those who met in council to decide on matters of common interest— such as a quarrel over land grazing rights, or theft of property, or a government policy. These chapters, with elective officers, met in a structure built for the purpose, usually with the helping hand of the Federal Government. They became functioning units of local government in some regions, and remained ineffectual in others where the traditional councils were considered the only instrument of government necessary for local needs.

There was no overall Tribal government until 1923, when one was set up at Window Rock because it was essential to get the consent of the Navajo people to lease certain lands to oil companies. For many years the Tribal Council was only a puppet government. It was not until after World War II that the 72-man elected Council, plus the Chairman and the Vice chairman, began to take responsibility on its own shoulders. With the wise leadership of a number of outstanding Bureau of Indian Affairs officials, the Council grew in strength until today it runs Tribal affairs very efficiently. Generally speaking, the outsider is impressed with the orderly process of government, and the respect for this Council held by the people—that is, those Navajo who are close enough to Window Rock to keep in touch with its activities.

An additional innovation which has had great repercussion in Tribal Government was the hiring of a Tribal attorney, who represents the tribe in Washington to the Department of Interior and other branches of government. He has built up a legal staff at Window Rock which handles local affairs concerning land leases, contracts with mining and petroleum concerns, and all other matters requiring legal determination and documentation. All of this the Navajo leaders have realized is part of living in the modern world. They know that they can't go back to the early days when Tribal business consisted of verbal agreements.

Today there is also a whole new division of management at Window Rock, their own equivalent of the executive branch of the government. The Tribal Chairman selects, at the outset of each term of office, a Secretary-Treasurer, who in turn is immediately responsible for tribal fiscal affairs and office management. This has been essential with the growth of tribal wealth. Some 700 Navajo are employed today in their own government; this includes 100 in the branch of Law and Order. Community Development, Water Development, Industrial Planning and other functions are carried on by a group of young Navajo administrators who will eventually replace the Federal officials in the administration of the Reservation.

In addition to this Navajo civil service, the Tribal Council is broken up into a committee system. An overall Advisory Committee develops and reviews proposed legislation; Health, Education, Resources, Grazing, and Livestock Committees refer and suggest policy that is formulated into regulations for the action of the whole Tribal Council. Many of these committee heads have become very knowledgable about their areas of specialty with respect to the outside world, and they attend regional and national conferences in the interest of their tribesmen.

This is all an unbelievably different world from the Window Rock of 1940, when it was dominated by hundreds of Federal officials. While the Federal Government is still very much in the picture (many officials have been headquartered at the Area Office in Gallup), there is now a realistic basis for the Navajo to assume responsibility for the governing of their own lands.

Appendix II

Health Visitor Medical form

Name _____ C# _____ Age ____ Sex ___ Date _____
PHYSICAL MEASUREMENT:
T _____ P _____ R _____ BP _____
   Height _____ ft. _____ in. Weight _____ lbs.
   Vision: Without glasses R ___/20 L ___/20 Both ___/20
          With glasses   R ___/20 L ___/20 Both ___/20
Hearing: Gross R _____ L _____ Optometric Done ___ Not Done ___
Complaint (Use patient's own words as much as possible):

HISTORY:
General:
1. Have you ever been treated in a hospital or clinic?
   Where? _____ When? _____ What for: _____
2. What operations have you had?
3. Have you had a bad injury in your life?
HEAD AND EENT:
4. Have you ever been bothered with headaches?
5. Have you ever had anything wrong with your hearing?
6. Have you ever had earaches or running ears?
7. Have you ever had anything wrong with your sight?

8. Have you ever had sore eyes?

9. Do you have a sore throat very often?

CARDIORESPIRATORY:

10. Have you ever had a bad cough?

11. Have you ever coughed up blood?

12. Have you ever had a chest x-ray?
    When?

13. Have you ever had severe chest pains?

14. Have you ever had night sweats?

15. Have you lost any weight lately?

16. Do you get out of breath when you do easy work?

GASTROINTESTINAL:

17. Have you ever had any stomach pains?

18. Does any kind of food make you sick to your stomach?

19. How is your appetite?

20. Have you ever vomited blood?

21. Have you ever had anything wrong with your bowels?

22. Have you ever passed blood in your stools?

GENITOURINARY:

23. Have you ever had any trouble passing your water?

24. Have you ever seen blood in your urine?

25. Have you ever had anything wrong with your womb?

26. Are your menstrual periods normal and regular?

27. When was your last menstrual period?

28. Have you ever had any miscarriages?   Baby born dead?

29. How many babies have you had born in a hospital?   Born at home?

FOR INFANTS:

1. Was your baby born at home or in a hospital? _____ Any trouble? _____

2. Has your baby been sick? ____ Colds? ____ Diarrhea? ____ Rash? ____

3. Has your baby had any immunizations?

4. Does your baby get anything other than breast milk?

5. Does your baby grow and behave as your would expect for his age?

SUMMARY AND REMARKS:

Signed: _____ H.V.

Appendix III

Useful Medical Phrases for Doctor and Nurses

USEFUL PHRASES

Hello.	Yá' át'ééh.
How do you feel?	Haa lá nít'é.
Sit down.	Dah nídaah.
Take off your shirt.	Ni'éé hadiiltsóós.
Open your mouth.	Diich'ééh.
Say, "Ah."	"Ah" diní.
Say, "Ee."	"Ee" diní.
Say, "Naana" repeatedly.	"Nááná" diní. Náá'áłdó'.
Stick out your tongue.	Nitsoo' hanitsééh.
Breathe hard.	Yéego nídídzih.
Lie down.	Níteeh.
Relax.	'Áhodiniiltłóóh.
Turn over on your side.	Naaniigo níteeh.
Don't be afraid.	T'áadoo bee níldzidí.
Does it hurt?	Neezgaiísh?
Thank you.	'Ahéhee' łąą.

NUMERALS

1.	t'ááła'í	30.	tádiin
2.	naaki	40.	dízdiin
3.	táá'	50.	'ashdladiin
4.	dį́į́'	60.	hastádiin
5.	'ashdla'	70.	tsosts'idiin
6.	hastą́ą́h	80.	tseebídiin
7.	tsosts'id	90.	náhást'édiin
8.	tseebíí	100.	neeznádiin
9.	náhást'éí	1000.	mííl
10.	neeznáá		
20.	naadiin		

USEFUL WORDS

big	ntsaa
big (barrel-shape)	ntsxaaz
bitter	dích'íí'
black	diłhił
black, dirty	łizhin
blue (includes green and purple)	dootł'izh
broken	sits'il
burnt	díílid
clean, see pretty	
cold	sik'az
cylindrical	níghiz
dirty, black	łizhin
dried	sigan
filthy	nchxǫǫ'í
firm, solid	niłdzil
good, fine (greeting)	yá'át'ééh
hard (as rock)	ntł'iz
hot (object)	sido
jerky	ditsxiz
light (in weight)	'aszólí
little	'áłts'íísí
no good	t'óó baa'íh
pink	dinilchíí'
pretty	nizhóní
red	łichíí'
rotten	dííłdzid
sharp	deení
slender	'áłts'óózí
soft, pliable	dit'ódí
soft, fluffy	yilzhólí
sour	dík'ǫǫzh
spotted	łikizh
squared, ridged	dik'á
striped	nǫǫdǫǫz
sweet, delicious	łikan
thick, deep	ditá
tingling	sisíí'
tough, sinewy	dits'id
wet	ditłéé'
white	łigai
wide	nteel
yellow (includes orange)	łico

Appendix IV

Publications Emanating from the Project

Adair, J.
    1960   The Indian Health Worker in the Cornell–Navajo Project. Human Organization 19(2):59–63.
    1963   Physicians, Medicine Men and Their Navajo Patients. *In* Man's Image in Medicine and Anthropology. I. Galdston, ed. New York: International Universities Press, Inc.
Adair, J. and K. Deuschle
    1958   Some Problems of the Physicians on the Navajo Reservation. Human Organization 16(40):19–23.
    1970   The People's Health: Anthropology and Medicine in a Navajo Community. New York: Appleton-Century-Crofts.
Adair, J., K. Deuschle and W. McDermott
    1957   Patterns of Health and Disease Among the Navajos. Annals of the American Academy of Political and Social Science 311:80–94.
Cleve, H. and A. Bearn
    1961a   Inherited Variations in Human Serum Proteins: Studies on the Group-Specific Components. Annals of the New York Academy of Sciences 94:218–224.
    1961b   Studies on the Gene Specific Component of Human Serum— Gene Frequencies in Several Populations. American Journal of Human Genetics 13:372–378.
Corcoran, P., D. Rabin, and F. Allen, Jr.
    1962   Blood Groups of 237 Navajo School Children at Pinon Board-

ing School, Pinon, Arizona (1961). American Journal of Physical Anthropology 20(3):389–390.

Deuschle, K.

1959 Tuberculosis Among the Navajo. American Review of Respiratory Diseases 80(2):200–206.

1961 Study Methods for Checking Regularity of Isoniazid Self-Medication in Tuberculosis Patients. Proceedings of the XVIth International Tuberculosis Conference:232–240.

1963a The Training and Use of Medical Auxiliaries in a Primitive Rural Community. Public Health Report 78(6):461–470.

1963b The Training and Use of Medical Auxiliaries in a Primitive Rural Community. Health and Nutrition Science, Technology and Development VI: Washington, D.C.: U.S. Government Printing Office. Paper prepared for the U.N. Conference on the Application of Science and Technology for the Benefit of the Less Developed Areas:182–189.

Deuschle, K. and J. Adair

1960 An Interdisciplinary Approach to Public Health on the Navajo Indian Reservation: Medical and Anthropological Aspects. Annals of the New York Academy of Science 841:887–904.

Deuschle, K., J. Adair, and H. Fulmer

1958 The Navajo–Cornell Field Health Research Project at Many Farms. The Navajo Yearbook VII:43–55.

Deuschle, K., C. Jordahl and G. Hobby

1960 Clinical Usefulness of Riboflavin-tagged Isoniazid for Self-Medication in Tuberculosis Patients. American Review of Respiratory Diseases 82(1):1–10.

Ervin, S. and H. Landar

1963 Navaho Word-Associations. The American Journal of Psychology 76(1):49–57.

French J.

1967 Relationship of Morbidity to the Feeding Patterns of Navajo Children from Birth through Twenty-four Months. Amer. J. Clin. Nutr. 20(3):375–385.

Fulmer, H. and R. Roberts

1963 Coronary Heart Diseases Among the Navajo Indians. Annals of Internal Medicine 59(5):740–764.

Hayslett, J., et al.

1962 Endemic Influenza. 1. Serologic Evidence of Continuing and Subclinical Infection in Disparate Populations in the Post-Pandemic Period. The American Review of Respiratory Diseases 85(1):1–8.

Hobby, G. and K. Deuschle

1959 The Use of Riboflavin as an Indicator of Isoniazid Ingestion in Self-Medicated Patients. The American Review of Respiratory Diseases 80(3):415–423.

Landar, H.

1960 A Note on Accepted and Rejected Arrangements of Navajo

Words. International Journal of American Linguistics 26(4):351–354.

1961a   A Note on the Navajo Word for Coyote. International Journal of American Linguistics 27(1):86–88.

1961b   A Note on Preferred Arrangements of Navaho Words. International Journal of American Linguistics 27(2):175–177.

1961c   Reduplication and Morphology. Language 37(2):239–246.

1962a   Navaho Optatives. International Journal of American Linguistics 28(1):9–13.

1962b   Fluctuations of Forms in Navaho Kinship Terminology. American Anthropologist 4(5):985–1000.

1963a   Laughing Boy and Slim Girl: A Study in Bilingual Acculturation. The Voice: Journal of the California Speech and Hearing Association 12(1):15–22.

1963b   Navajo Syntax. Language, September.

1964   Seven Navajo Verbs of Eating. International Journal of American Linguistics 30(1):94–98.

1967   The Language of Pain in Navaho Culture. In Studies in Southwestern Ethnolinguistics. D. Hymes and W. Bittle, eds. The Hague: Mouton and Co.

Landar, H. and J. Casagrande
1962   Navajo Anatomical Reference. Ethnology 1(1):370–373.

Landar, H., S. Ervin and A. Horowitz
1960   Navajo Color Categories. Language 36:368–382.

Loughlin, B. and K. Dennison
1961   A Report of the Demographical Studies During the Past Five Years. The Navajo Yearbook, No. VIII:113–120, 1951–1961.

Loughlin, B., et al.
1960   A Syllabus for Teachers in Navajo Health. Window Rock, Arizona: The Navajo Tribal Council.

Loughlin, B. and E. Mansell
1959   Training Health Workers on the Navajo Indian Reservation. Nursing Times, January.

Mansell, E. and B. Loughlin
1958   The Navajo Health Visitor. Practical Nursing 8:13–15.

McDermott, W.
1966   Modern Medicine and the Demographic-Disease Pattern of Overly Traditional Societies: A Technologic Misfit. Journal of Medical Education 41:137–162.

McDermott, W., K. Keuschle and J. Adair
1957   The Navajo–Cornell Field Health Project. The Navajo Yearbook VI:39–47.

McDermott, W., K. Deuschle and C. Barnett
1972   Health Care Experiment at Many Farms. Science 175:23–31.

McDermott, W., et al.
1960   Introducing Modern Medicine in a Navajo Community. Science 131:197–205, 280–287.

Moulding, T.
  1961   Preliminary Study of the Pill Calendar as a Method of Improving the Self-Administration of Drugs. American Review of Respiratory Diseases 84(2):284–287.
  1962   Proposal for a Time-Recording Pill Dispenser as a Method for Studying and Supervising the Self-Administration of Drugs. American Review of Respiratory Diseases 85(5):754–757.
Omran, A. and K. Deuschle
  1965   A Controlled Evaluation of a Selective Method of Tuberculosis Case Finding. American Review of Respiratory Diseases 9:214–224.
Parker, W. and A. Bearn
  1961   Haptoglobin and Transferrin Gene Frequencies in a Navajo Population: A New Transferrin Variant. Science 134(3472):106–108.
Rabin, D., et al.
  1965   Untreated Congenital Hip Disease. American Journal of Public Health 55, Supplement Part II.
Richards, C.
  1960   Cooperation Between Anthropologist and Medical Personnel. Human Organization 19(2):64–67.
  1963   Modern Residence Patterns Among the Navajo. El Palacio, Spring–Summer:25–33.
Roberts, R. and K. Deuschle
  1959   Comparative Study of Urine Tests for the Detection of Isoniazid. American Review of Respiratory Disease 80(6):904–908.
Sasaki, T.
  1961   Socioeconomic Survey of the Many Farms and Rough Rock Navajos. The Navajo Yearbook VIII 1951–1961:103–113.
Sasaki, T. and H. Basehart
  1961   Sources of Income Among Many Farms–Rough Rock Navajo and Jicarilla Apache: Some Comparisons and Comments. Human Organization 20(4):187–190.
Wauneka, A.
  1962   Helping a People to Understand. American Journal of Nursing 62:88–89.

References Cited

Aberle, D.
   1982   The Future of Navajo Religion. *In* Brugge, D. and C.J. Frisbie, eds, Navajo Religion and Culture: Selected Views. Santa Fe: Museum of New Mexico Press:219–231.
Adair, J.
   1960   The Indian Health Worker in the Cornell–Navajo Project. Human Organization 19(2):59–63.
   1963   Physicians, Medicine Men and Their Navajo Patients. *In* Man's Image in Medicine and Anthropology. I. Galdston, ed. New York: International Universities Press, Inc.
Adair, J. and K. Deuschle
   1958   Some Problems of the Physicians on the Navajo Reservation. Human Organization 16(4):19–23.
   1970   The People's Health: Anthropology and Medicine in a Navajo Community. New York:Appleton-Century-Crofts.
Adair, J., K. Deuschle and W. McDermott
   1957   Patterns of Health and Disease Among the Navajos. The Annals of the American Academy of Political and Social Science 311:80–94.
Apodaca, A.
   1952   Corn and Custom. *In* Human Problems in Technological Change. E. Spicer, ed. New York: Russell Sage Foundation.
Bailey, F.
   1948   Suggested Techniques for Inducing Navaho Women to Accept

Hospitalization During Childbirth and for Implementing Health Education. American Journal Public Health 38(10):1418–1423.

1950   Some Sex Beliefs and Practices in a Navajo Community. Papers of the Peabody Museum of American Archaeology and Ethnology. XL, 2. Cambridge, Peabody Museum: Harvard University.

Bergman, R.
1973   A School for Medicine Men. American Journal of Psychiatry 130(6): 663–665.
1983   Navajo Health Services and Projects. In Handbook of North American Indians, Volume 10, Southwest. A. Ortiz, ed. Washington. D.C.: Smithsonian Institution, 672–678.

Bliss, W.
1952   In the Wake of the Wheel. In Human Problems in Technological Change. E. Spicer, ed. New York: Russell Sage Foundation.

Cassel, J.
1955   A Comprehensive Health Program Among South African Zulus. In Health, Culture, and Community. B. Paul, ed. New York: Russell Sage Foundation.

Caudill, W.
1953   Applied Anthropology in Medicine. In Anthropology Today. A. Kroeber, ed. Chicago: University of Chicago Press.

Cochran, J., C. Clayson and W. Fletcher
1957   Pulmonary Tuberculosis in a Rural Area in South Scotland: The Annandale Survey. British Medical Journal, 27 July:185–187.

Coriell, L.
1967   Clinical Syndromes in Children Caused by Respiratory Infection. Medical Clinics of North America 51(3):819–829.

Deuschle, K.
1959   Tuberculosis Among the Navajo. American Review of Respiratory Diseases 80(2):200–206.
1963a   The Training and Use of Medical Auxiliaries in a Primitive Rural Community. Public Health Reports 78(6):461–470.
1963b   The Training and Use of Medical Auxiliaries in a Primitive Rural Community. Health and Nutrition Science, Technology and Development VI: Washington, D.C.: U.S. Government Printing Office. Paper prepared for the U.N. Conference on the Application of Science and Technology for the Benefit of the Less Developed Areas. 182–189.

Deuschle, K. and J. Adair
1960   An Interdisciplinary Approach to Public Health on the Navajo Indian Reservation: Medical and Anthropological Aspects. The Annals of the New York Academy of Sciences 841: 887–904.

Deuschle, K., J. Adair, and H. Fulmer
1958   The Navajo–Cornell Field Health Research Project at Many Farms. The Navajo Yearbook VII: 43–55.

Dubos, R.
1959   Mirage of Health. New York: Harper and Brothers.

1962   Man Meets His Environment. Health and Nutrition Science, Technology and Development VI: Washington, D.C.: U.S. Government Printing Office, Paper prepared for the U.N. Conference on the Application of Science and Technology for the Benefit of the Less Developed Areas.

Dubos, R. and J. Dubos
1952   The White Plague: Tuberculosis, Man and Society. Boston: Little, Brown and Co.

Fey, H. and D. McNickle
1959   Indians and Other Americans: Two Ways of Life Meet. New York: Harper and Brothers.

French J.
1967   Relationship of Morbidity to the Feeding Patterns of Navajo Children from Birth Through Twenty-four Months. American Journal of Clinical Nutrition 20(3):375–385.

Fulmer, H. and R. Roberts
1963   Coronary Heart Diseases Among the Navajo Indians. Annals of Internal Medicine 59(5):740–764.

Goldschmidt, W. and R. Edgerton
1961   A Picture Technique for the Study of Values. American Anthropologist 63(1):26–47.

Gordon, J., W. I. Chitkara, and J. Wyon.
1963   Weanling Diarrhea. American Journal of Medical Science 245:345–377.

Hadley, J.
1955   Health Conditions Among the Navajo Indians. Public Health Rep. 70:831–836.

Henderson, E.
1982   Kaibeto Plateau Ceremonialists: 1860–1980. In Brugge, D. and C. Frisbie, C., eds., Santa Fe: Museum of New Mexico Press.

Hrdlicka, A.
1908   Physiological and Medical Observations Among the Indians of Southwestern U.S. and Northern Mexico. Washington, D.C.: Smithsonian Institution.

Hyge, T.
1947   Epidemic of Tuberculosis in State School, with Observation Period of About 3 Years. Acta Tuberculosea Scandinavica 21:1–57.

Institute for Government Research
1928   The Problem of Indian Administration. Baltimore, Maryland: The Johns Hopkins Press. (The Meriam Report)

Kayenta Community Based Cancer Control Project
1978   Unpublished Proceedings of the Second Annual Diné Binahagha' dóó Azee' iil'íní Retreat, October 21–22, 1978 Dennehotso Chapter House.

Kluckhohn, C. and D. Leighton
1946   The Navaho. Cambridge: Harvard University Press.

Kluckhohn, C. and F. Strodtbeck
  1961 Variations in Value Orientations. New York: Row, Peterson &
  Co.
Kunitz, S.
  1983 Disease Change and the Role of Medicine: The Navajo Experience. Berkeley: University of California Press.
Ladd, J.
  1957 The Structure of a Moral Code. Cambridge: Harvard University
  Press.
Landar, H.
  1962b Fluctuations of Forms in Navaho Kinship Terminology. American Anthropologist 4(5):985–1000.
  1963 Navajo Syntax. Language, September.
  1967 The Language of Pain in Navaho Culture. *In* Studies in Southwestern Ethnolinguistics. D. Hymes and W. Bittle, eds. The Hague:
  Mouton and Co.
Landar, H. and J. Casagrande
  1962 Navajo Anatomical Reference. Ethnology 1(3):370–373.
Landar, H., S. Ervin and A. Horowitz
  1960 Navajo Color Categories. Language 36:368–382.
Lantis, M.
  1952 Eskimo Herdsman. *In* Human Problems in Technological Change.
  E. Spicer, ed. New York: Russell Sage Foundation.
Lederer, J. and E. Burdick
  1958 The Ugly American. New York: W.W. Norton and Co., Inc.
Leighton, A. and D. Leighton
  1941 Elements of Psychotherapy in Navaho Religion. Psychiatry
  4:515–523.
  1944 The Navaho Door. Cambridge: Harvard University Press.
  no year Therapeutic Values of the Navajo Indians. Unpublished
  mimeographed.
Leighton, D. and C. Kluckhohn
  1947 The Children of the People: The Navaho Individual and His
  Development. Cambridge: Harvard University Press.
Levy J.
  1962a Community Organization of the Western Navajo. American
  Anthropologist 64:781–802.
  1962b Some Trends in Navajo Health Behavior. Window Rock, Arizona: U.S.P.H.S., Division of Indian Health. Unpublished Mimeographed.
  1962c The Influence of Social Organization on Behavioral Response
  to a Health Activity. Window Rock, Arizona: U.S.P.H.S., Division
  of Indian Health. Unpublished Mimeographed.
  1964 Interpreter Training Program. Window Rock, Arizona: U.S.P.H.S.,
  Division of Indian Health.
Lewis, O.
  1966 The Culture of Poverty. Scientific American 215(4):19–25.

Linton, R.
  1936   The Study of Man. New York: Appleton-Century.
Loughlin, B. and K. Dennison
  1961   A Report of the Demographical Studies During the Past Five Years. The Navajo Yearbook, No. VIII:113–120, 1951–1961.
Loughlin, B., et al.
  1960   A Syllabus for Teachers in Navajo Health. Window Rock, Arizona: The Navajo Tribal Council.
Loughlin, B. and E. Mansell
  1959   Training Health Workers on the Navajo Indian Reservation. Nursing Times, January.
Mansell, E. and B. Loughlin
  1958   The Navajo Health Visitor. Practical Nursing April., 8:13–15.
McDermott, W., K. Deuschle and J. Adair
  1957   The Navajo–Cornell Field Health Project. The Navajo Yearbook VI:39–47.
  1966   Modern Medicine and the Demographic-Disease Pattern of Overly Traditional Societies: A Technologic Misfit. Journal of Medical Education 41:137–162.
McDermott, W., et al.
  1960   Introducing Modern Medicine in a Navajo Community. Science 131:197–205, 280–287.
Mico, P.
  1962   Navajo Perception of Anglo Medicine. Berkeley, University of California: Navajo Health Education Project. Unpublished Mimeographed.
Navajo Tribal Council
  1940   Unpublished CJ-1-40 To Prevent Use of Peyote, June 3, 1940.
  1967   Unpublished Co-65-67 Amending 25 CFR paragraph 11.87 NH, Oct. 11, 1967.
Omran, A. and K. Deuschle
  1965   A Controlled Evaluation of a Selective Method of Tuberculosis Case Finding. American Review of Respiratory Diseases 9:214–224.
Paul, B.
  1963   Anthropological Perspectives in Medicine. The Annals of the American Academy of Political and Social Science March: 36.
Polgar, S.
  1962   Health and Human Behavior: Areas of Interest to the Social and Medical Services. Current Anthropologist 3(2): 159–205.
Portney, G. and I. Hoshiwara
  1969   Analysis of Prevalence of Trachoma. Tucson, Arizona: Health Programs Systems Center.
Rabin, D., et al.
  1965   Untreated Congenital Hip Disease. American Journal of Public Health 55, Supplement Part II.
Record, R. and Edwards, J.
  1958   Environmental Influences Related to the Aetiology of Congen-

ital Dislocation of the Hip. British Journal of Preventive and Social Medicine 12:8–22.

Reichard, G.
1928 Social Life of the Navajo Indians: With Some Attention to Minor Ceremonies. Columbia University Contributions to Anthropology VII: New York: Columbia University Press.
1950 Navajo Religion. New York: Pantheon Books, Inc.

Richards, C.
1960 Cooperation Between Anthropologist and Medical Personnel. Human Organization 19(2):64–67.

Riley, R., C. Mills, W. Nyka, et al.
1959 Aerial Dissemination of Pulmonary Tuberculosis: A Two-Year Study of Contagion in a Tuberculosis Ward. American Journal of Hygiene 70(2):185–196.

Sandner, D.
1978 Navajo Medicine. Human Nature. July:54–62.

Sasaki, T.
1960 Fruitland, New Mexico. A Navaho Community in Transition. Ithaca: Cornell University Press.
1961 Socioeconomic Survey of the Many Farms and Rough Rock Navajos. The Navajo Yearbook VIII 1951–1961:103–113.

Sharp L.
1952 Steel Axes for Stone Age Australians. Human Problems in Technological Change. New York: Russell Sage Foundation.

Shaw, J.
1957a Guarding the Health of Our Indian Citizens. Journal of the American Hospital Association 31(7):38–44.
1957b Indian Health Today. New York, Bulletin of the National Tuberculosis Association June:91–93.

Shepardson, M.
1982 Changing Attitudes Toward Navajo Religion. In Navajo Religion and Culture: Selected Views. Brugge, D. and C. Frisbie, eds. Santa Fe: Museum of New Mexico Press.

Vogt, E.
1951 Navajo Veterans. Papers of the Peabody Museum of Archaeology and Ethnology XLI, 1: Cambridge: Harvard University Press.
1961 Navaho. In Perspectives in American Indian Culture Change. E. Spicer, ed. Chicago: University of Chicago Press.

Vogt, E. and C. Kluckhohn
1951 Navajo Means People. Cambridge: Harvard University Press.

Wauneka, A.
1962 Helping a People to Understand. American Journal of Nursing 62:88–90.

Wilken, R.
1955 Anselm Weber, O.F.M., Missionary to the Navajo 1898–1921. Milwaukee: The Bruce Publishing Co.

Wyman, L.
  1950 Religion of the Navaho Indians. *In* Forgotten Religions. V.
  Ferm, ed. New York: Philosophical Library, Inc.
Young, R. (ed.)
  1961 The Navajo Yearbook, No. VIII, 1951–1961. Window Rock,
  Arizona.

Index

Acute cholelithiasis: treating, 169
Adair, John, xix, xxii; input from,
  49–50; photo of, 76
Administrative Visits, 153–54
Advisory Committee (NTC), 36, 41,
  42, 43, 48, 49, 60, 87, 256
'Agaan: meaning of, 133
'Agaan ta' i: meaning of, 133
"Agency Indian": stigma of, 89
Aid to Dependent Children, 120
'Ajaad: meaning of, 133
'Ajaad bita' sitan igii: meaning of,
  133
'Ajaad bita sitan i: meaning of, 133
Akeah, Sam, 58; quote from, 44
Albuquerque, 24, 56, 111, 217, 220
Aliases. *See* Nicknames
American Medical Association, 15
Anatomical charts, 136–38;
  preparing, 134
Anderson, Ruth, 90, 92–93, 96–97;
  photo of, 74; quote from, 92–93,
  96–97
Anemia, 157
Angina pectoris, 135
'Ánii': meaning of, 125

'Anii': meaning of, 125
Animal husbandry: changes in, 250.
  See also Sheep husbandry
Animals: divine aspects of, 6, 8
Anthropologists, 113–14, 208–9,
  216, 228, 229, 245n.3; culture
  barriers and, 235; culture shock
  and, 232; dilemma for, 234–35;
  methodology of, 227;
  recordkeeping by, 112; selecting,
  225–26; work of, 109, 201, 202–
  4, 210–11, 225, 227–28
Anthropology, 227; public health
  and, xxi–xxii
Antibiotics, 19, 22, 29, 193, 194
Apachean languages, 125
Apache Reservation, 45
Apaches, 11, 204, 255
Apache Windway, 91
Appendicitis, 169, 171
Arthritis, 183, 205, 207; translation
  of, 134
Ascending number system:
  bookkeeping by, 111
'Asdzaatsoh: meaning of, 116

Association of American Indian
    Affairs, 15
Athabascan languages: Northern,
    125; sound system of, 125–26;
    Southern, 125; verb system of,
    126–27

Baada-ani: meaning of, 116
Badoni, Charlie: case of, 102
Bahadzid: meaning of, 7
Barnett, Clifford, xviii, xix
Barr, David, 244n.8
Barter system, 251
Beauty Way ceremony, 13, 57
Begay, 116
Begay, Atsidi, 53, 54
Begay, Bah, 3
Begay, Lucie: case of, 102
Begay, Manuelito: photo of, 63;
    quote from, 27, 40–41, 41–42
Begay, Selth, 50, 52, 53, 56, 57, 61
Begay, Tracy, 11, 12; case of, 3–4, 5,
    7
Begay, Tsinajinnie, 107
Begay, Yazzie, 57
Benally, Deswood, 56; photo of, 78
Benally, Rena: case of, 101–2
Benedict, Ruth, 247n.3
Bicenti, Billie, 58; quote from, 42
Bidaghagai bitsi: meaning of, 116
"Bigtwist," 134
Bilingualism, 95, 109
Bima: meaning of, 116
Birth practices, 199, 205–7, 210;
    clans and, 209
Birth rates, 16, 157, 183, 191, 197
Births: chart of, 158, 190; physician-
    attended, 158; records of, 17, 114,
    119–20, 157–58
Bita': meaning of, 133
Bita sitan igii: meaning of, 133
Bitter Water clan, 252
Biye', 116
Black Mesa, 105
Black Mountain, 51, 148, 149, 165
Blessing Way ceremony, 8, 32, 164,
    167
Blessing Way singers, 164, 165
Blue girls, 86, 92, 219
Body painting, 163
Bradley, Frank: quote from, 43–44
Branch of Health (BIA), 22, 24
Brooks, Gyla, xix

Brown, Esther Lucille, xviii
Buckingham, Al, 244n.4
Bureau of Indian Affairs, xiii, xiv,
    xix, 15, 22, 23, 24, 25, 29, 36, 39,
    52, 110, 111, 124, 126, 244n.4,
    256
Bureau of Indian Affairs Boarding
    School, xi
Burkhardt, Fred, xix

Camp file record system, 117, 121,
    203, 217
Camps: isolation of, 117
Canyon de Chelly National
    Monument, 51
Caudill, William: work of, 201
Censuses, 16, 17, 102, 144, 184,
    189–90
Ceremonies, 91; attacks on, 174;
    chart of, 164; clinic visits and,
    169; curing, 13; learning, 163–64,
    175; short form, 164, 167, 177;
    specializing in, 175; types of, 8,
    164, 167–68, 177
Ceremony: Beauty Way, 13, 57;
    Blessing Way, 32, 164, 167;
    Chiracahua Wind Way, 164;
    Enemy way, 167; Flint Way, 171;
    Ghost Way, 164; Mountaintop
    Way, 167; Shooting Way, 164,
    170; Wind Chant, 41
Ch'osh: meaning of, 133
Chants, 163; description of, 8
Chapter: function of, 255
Chapter House: meetings at, 145
Chemotherapy. *See* Drug therapy
Chilchinbeto, 149
Chinle, 3, 24, 50, 51, 110, 145, 149,
    165
Chinle Clinic, 110
Chinle Valley, 52, 57
Chinle Wash, 51
Chiracahua Wind Way ceremony, 164
Christianity: conversion to, 176;
    Navajo religion and, 13–14, 165.
    See also Native American Church
Chronic Voluntary Visit, 153, 156;
    description of, 154
Church of Jesus Christ of Latter-day
    Saints, 176
Circulatory system: drawing of, 138
Civilian Conservation Corps, 90
Civil Service, 23, 88, 124, 215

Clans: birth practices and, 209; congenital hip disease and, 209; importance of, 105–6, 117–19; marriage and, 209, 210, 252; matrilineal, 117, 252; matrilocal, 252; membership in, 89, 117, 203; number of, 245n.2; patrilineal, 118; relations in, 89, 120; responsibilities to, 252–53

Clinical physician system, 112, 184, 198, 199

Clinic population: age of, 147; representativeness of, 153; sex of, 147–48

Clinic usage, 112, 148, 152; chart of, 148; figures for, 143; at Many Farms, 168–69; Navajo medicine and, 161; rates of, 144

Clinic visits: categories of, 153–55; ceremonies and, 169; chart of, 146, 152, 155; cultural barriers to, 159; data on, 144–59; diagnosticians and, 167; medicine men and, 167; nature of, 153–59; pattern of, 147–52, 158; pregnancy and, 154, 157

Co-existence. See Medical co-existence

Collier, John, Jr., ix, 23, 64, 68, 69, 70, 71, 72, 73, 74, 76, 77, 78, 79, 80, 81, 82

Colorado Plateau, 249, 250

Committee of Appropriations: reports to, 15–16

Communications, 238; cultural, xxiii; doctor-patient, 86; horizontal, 226; medical, 229; problems with, 85–88, 228–31; vertical, 223, 229

Conceptual transfer, 59, 127; importance of, 124; problems in, 128–34; training for, 132–34

Congenital hip disease, 21, 180, 185–86, 201, 205–6; clans and, 209; consequences of, 206; cradle boards and, 210; environment and, 210; genetics and, 201, 209, 210; incidence of, 204, 207–8; study of, 210–11; therapy for, 202, 204–8, 210

Congenital malformations, 97

Congestive heart failure. See Heart disease

Conjunctivitis, 18, 21, 243n.3

Contagious diseases: translation of, 129

Cornell-Navajo Field Health Research Program, ix, xix, xxv, xxvi, 2, 222, 246n.7; failures of, 239; successes of, 238–39

Cornell group, 36, 48, 144, 238; evaluation by, 121–22

Cornell University, 42, 214, 215, 216, 217, 220, 221, 229

Cornell University–New York Hospital, xxvi; pilot project of, xiii–xiv

Cornell University–New York Hospital School of Nursing, xix, xxiii, xxviii; contribution of, xxv

Cornell University Medical College, ix, xi, xiv, xvii, xviii, xxii, 45, 50, 180, 238–39, 244n.8; attitudes of, 35; Navajo Tribal Government and, xiii; report from, 36–37; USPHS contract with, 47, 213–14

Coronary heart disease. See Heart disease

Coronary occlusion: translation of, 128–29

Coronary thrombosis: translation of, 128–29

Cottrell, Leonard, xviii

Cradle boards, 207; chronic hip disease and, 210; use of, 206, 208

Cross-indexing, 116

Crown Point, 24, 26, 27, 33, 34, 43, 63, 244n.4

Crown Point Hospital, 34

Crude death rates: hospitals and, 192; reduction of, 191

Crystal gazing: description of, 162

Cultural approach: value of, 122

Cultural barriers, xii, 22, 171; anthropologists and, 235; clinic visits and, 159; overcoming, 47, 123, 152, 233, 235. See also Language barriers

Cultural change: incorporative model of, 11

Cultural determinism: medical relevance and, 4–5

Cultural dynamics: medical records and, 120–22; treatment and, 5

Cultural relevance, 114–17

Cultural transference, 232

"Culture of poverty," 183

Culture shock: dealing with, 231–34; impact of, 221–22
Curers: age of, 173; chart of, 163, 173; numbers of, 164; training of, 163–64; wage work for, 174
Curing ceremonies, 13, 161; medical insurance and, 177

Dancing: ritualized, 8
Death: Navajo concept of, 6
Death houses, 22
Death rates, 16, 187–89, 192
Death records, 17, 114, 119–20, 184
Deaths, 190; chart of, 188; infant. See Infant mortality
Demographers, 226
Demographic profile, 93, 184, 190
Dennison, Kenneth, 53, 132; photo of, 67, 69; quote from, 55; work of, 96, 115
Department of Health, Education and Welfare, xviii, 22, 215; contract with, 213; Indian health and, 180
Department of Medicine (Cornell), 36
Department of Public Health and Preventive Medicine (Cornell), i, xi, 246n.7; work of, xii
Department of Public Health Education (North Carolina), 45
Department of the Interior, 21, 22, 256
Deuschle, Kurt W., xxii, xxiii; photo of, 65, 67
Diabetes, 21
Diagnosis: Navajo methods of, 7–8, 162
Diagnosticians, 165, 245n.1; age of, 173; chart of, 163, 173; clinic visits and, 167; Hopi, 161; numbers of, 162–63; training of, 176; using, 166
Diarrhea, 3, 20–21, 147, 184–85; caring for, 12; infant, 20, 98; nutrition and, 194
Digestive system: drawing of, 98, 137
Diniih: meaning of, 135
Diptheria-pertussis-tetanus immunizations, 157
Disease: behavior and, 14; combatting, xxi–xxii; enteric, 183; gall bladder, 21, 183; helmithic,

197; home environment and, 195–96; infant, 180, 199; infectious, 4–5, 16, 18, 21, 30, 118, 156; at isolated camps, 117, 118; Navajo concept of, 5, 6, 7, 29, 31, 48, 169, 180, 202, 204, 206–7, 209; poverty and, 192; prevention of, 5, 20, 156, 193–94; recording of, 121; translation of, 129–30; understanding, 93–94; water and, 182
Disease patterns, 86, 144, 183, 184, 186, 188, 197, 199, 227
Division of General Medical Sciences, i, 246n.7
Division of Indian Health, i, xii, 17, 22, 32, 213, 217, 246n.2, 246n.7
Division of Indian Health Services, 241
Divorce: records of, 114; regulation of, 119–20
Dobyns, Cara Richards, i, 204
Doctor-dentist draft, xiii, 25, 26, 29, 30, 34, 123, 222
Doctors: medicine men and, 12–13, 27, 30, 34, 40–41; role of, 202–3, 210–11, 222; selecting, 222–24
Dodge, Chee, xiii
Dravidian language, 125
Drug therapy, xxii, 11, 18, 19, 29, 30, 35, 40, 41, 43, 62, 90, 111, 193, 194, 216; benefit from, 37, 38; introduction of, xiv; limits to, 37–38; Navajo religion and, 8, 9
Dry farming, 182
Dubos, René, 31, 48, 244n.8
Dysentery, xii

Ear infections, 21
Earth surface people, 6
Economists, 226
Education Committee (NTC), 256
Education Office (BIA), 110
Enemy way ceremony, 167
Enteric diseases, 183
Environment: genetics and, 210; Navajo culture and, 243n.2, 249–57
Epidemics, 18, 118, 145; studies of, 122, 227; tuberculosis, 19
Ethnolinguistics: studies in, 180
Evil: driving out, 6–8
Evil Way, 91

Explanatory relative expressions: selecting, 133
Extended family: geographic stability of, 117; importance of, 118; matrilineal, 117; matrilocal, 117

Family: composition of, 109; extended. *See* Extended family; relations, 89; structure of, 105–6, 114, 117–22, 253
Far East Mesa, 148, 149
Farley, Eugene, xix; photo of, 79
Farley, Linda, xix
Farmington, 252
Far West Mesa, 149
Febrile illness, 193
Federal agents: suspicion of, 22
Federal Government. *See* United States Government
Fertility rates. *See* Birth rates
Fetishes, 11
Fey, Harold E.: quote from, 23
Field health services, 214, 235; development of, 45
Field work, xix, 101; elements of, 87; by health visitors, 101–8
Fire dance, 3
Max C. Fleischmann Foundation, i, 246n.7
Flint Way ceremony, 171
Fort Defiance, 36, 41, 43, 44, 47, 48, 50, 53, 56, 57, 59, 61, 62, 85, 92, 158, 165, 210, 215, 230; sawmill at, 55, 250
Fort Defiance Hospital, 24, 33, 85, 94, 157
Fort Defiance Sanitorium, 31, 43, 48, 49, 52, 53, 91, 93, 133, 214; photo of, 67
Foster, George, xix
Frejka apron, 208, 209, 210; use of, 205
French, Jean, xix
Fulmer, Hugh, xix

Gall bladder disease, 21, 183
Gallup, 24, 90, 96, 257; USPHS Hospital in, 157
Ganado, 24, 32, 38, 107, 157, 158, 165
Ganado Hospital, 4, 110, 171
Gastroenteritis, 170, 172
Geneticists, 204

Genetics: environment and, 210; studies in, 203
George, Frank Ben, 90–93, 244n.1; photo of, 82, 83; quote from, 91, 97, 107; training of, 97
Germ theory, 4–5, 13–14, 169
Gestalt, 30, 61–62
Ghosts, 6–7
Ghost Way ceremony, 164
Goldschmidt, Walter, xix
Grazing Committee (NTC), 256
Green, Eileen, xx

Hadley, J. Nixon: quote from, 17
Hand tremblers, 162, 170; description of, 13; numbers of, 163
Hand trembling: description of, 162
Harper, Allan, 244n.7
Fred Harvey Company, 92
Health: behavior and, 14; improvement of, xiv; Indian, 15–17; Navajo concept of, 15–21, 48, 169; patterns of, 86, 198; understanding, 17, 93–94
Health care system, 22–24, 179, 192, 196, 199, 238; cross-cultural, ix; effectiveness of, 189–90
Health Committee (NTC), xiii, xiv, 32, 45, 49, 50, 64, 256
Health Division (BIA), 29, 36
Health education, 45, 102, 169, 214, 241; cultural approach to, 122
Health, Education and Welfare Department. *See* Department of Health, Education and Welfare
Health Service, xii
Health statistics: development of, 17–18; need for, 16. *See also* Statistics; Vital statistics
Health Visitor Medical form: sample of, 259–60
Health visitor program, 69, 220, 221; mediation through, 238; resistance to, 216–21; study of, 102–3
Health visitors, 25, 115, 123, 129, 134, 153, 154, 156, 157, 203, 207–8, 213, 218, 229–30, 244n.1, 245n.3; communication with, 230–31; field work of, 101–8; kinship and, 105–6; perceptions of, 104; role of, xxv–xxvi, 87, 93–94, 103–4, 166, 216; selecting, 88–97, 215;

training of, 87–97, 99–108, 128, 132, 166, 180, 220, 246n.2
Heart attack: translation of, 129, 130
Heart disease, 180, 183, 186, 245n.2; immunity to, 21
Helminthic diseases, 197
Herbal infusions, 8, 163
Hindi language, 125
Hitzrot, James, xix
Hogans: description of, 254–55. *See also* Housing
Holy people, 9; definition of, 6
Home environment, 220; cleaning, 193–94, 196; disease and, 195–96; infants and, 195
Home visits, xxvi, 118, 218
Hookworm, 197
Hopi Indian Reservation, 24
Hopi Indians: curing by, 165, 166
Hopi language, 125
Hospital for Special Surgery (New York), 204
"Hospitalism" syndrome, 171
Hospital records, 112, 184
Hospitals, 22, 24, 30, 192
"Hospital without walls," 48, 217
House Blessing Songs, 57
House of Representatives, 15
Housing: description of, 254–55; photo of, 71; religious significance of, 10. *See also* Hogans
Hyland Laboratories, xviii
Hypertension, 21

I: meaning of, 133
Identification system: development of, 144
Igii: meaning of, 133
Illness. *See* Disease
Immunizations, 111, 154, 183–84, 224; diptheria-pertussis-tetanus, 157; level of, 156–57; polio, 157; school, 110; smallpox, 184
Impetigo, 19, 20, 21, 170, 172, 184–85
Incorporative model, 11
Indian Bureau, 250
Indian Division (USPHS), 57, 110, 222
Indian Health Program, xiii
Indian Service, 17, 23, 26, 255

Indigenous curing system, 161–62, 166–67, 183, 217
Infant mortality, 16, 158, 183, 187, 196; decline in, xiv, 191, 197, 198
Infectious diseases, 4–5, 16, 18, 21, 30, 118, 156
Influenza, 246n.5
Innovations, 237; opposition to, 216–21; receptiveness to, 30
Interior Department. *See* Department of the Interior
Interpretation: grammatical factors in, 139–41; problems with, 126–27, 129–34; standards for, 124. *See also* Translation
Interpreters: importance of, 141; training of, 130–31
Isolation: effects of, 233–34
Isoniazid, 41, 43, 154

Jones, Paul, 33–34, 88

Keams Canyon, 24, 91
Kessner, David, 246n.6
King, Martha Ann, xix
Kinship, 89, 117, 253; marriage and, 210; terms of, 105–6, 114, 117–22
Kluckhohn, Clyde, 9; quote from, 126

Laboratory of Anthropology (Santa Fe), 247n.3
Laboratory services, 111, 112
Landar, Herbert, i, 245n.1; quote from, 133; work of, 134–35, 139–40
Land leases, 256
Language barriers, 22, 35, 52, 85–88, 100, 123, 171; overcoming, 43, 47, 95, 127–28; technology and, 59–61. *See also* Cultural barriers
Lateral sanctions, 95
Leighton, Alexander, 9, 31, 34
Leighton, Dorothea, 9, 31, 34
Lesser, Al, 247n.3
Levy, Jerrold, 246n.2
Lewis, Oscar, 182
Life: Navajo concept of, 6
Linton, Ralph, 12, 171–72, 247n.3; quote from, 11
Livestock Committee (NTC), 256
Livestock reduction, 58, 250
Lizard illness, 12

Loughlin, Bernice, 56, 244n.2; photo of, 69
Lovelace Clinic, 56
Low Mountain, 91
Lukachukai, 3, 53, 110

McCabe, Maurice, 44
McDermott, Walsh, xiv, xix, xxii, 244n.8; photo of, 67
McKinley, Pauline, 57, 132; quote from, 85–86, 95; training by, 94–96
McNickle, D'Arcy, 244n.4; quote from, 23
McVey, Frances, xix
Malaria, 20, 197
Mansell, Ellen, xix; photo of, 77
Many Farms, xiv, xv, xviii, xix, xxv, xxvi, xxvii, 2, 35, 45, 47, 51, 52, 56, 57, 59, 60, 86, 88, 89, 91, 95, 102, 110–11, 143, 145, 148, 149, 158, 162, 163, 164, 165, 168, 170, 176, 178, 183, 185, 186, 187, 188, 191, 193, 194, 195, 196, 197, 198, 199, 200, 201, 210, 216, 220, 221, 222, 223, 228, 229, 230, 231, 245n.1, 246n.2; birth rate at, 191; clinic usage at, 168–69; death rate at, 189; demographic profile of, 190; economy of, 182; growth rate of, 190; housing at, 192; medical co-existence at, 169, 171–72; medical records at, 113–14; medicine men at, 175; meeting at, 52–56; selection of, 50, 181; training at, 105; weather at, 182
Many Farms Clinic, xi–xii, xv, xix, 4, 51–52, 96, 144, 149, 153, 156, 157, 158, 161, 167, 168, 171, 204, 208, 238, 241, 243n.1; attendance at, 143, 145; non-attendance at, 152; photo of, 70, 72
Many Farms Project, 203; evaluation of, 121–22
Marriage: clan and, 209, 210, 252; records of, 114; regulation of, 118, 119–20
Masks, 11
Matrilineal clans, 252
Matrilineal extended family, 117
Matrilineal rule, 252
Matrilineal social organization, 109
Matrilocal clans, 252

Matrilocal extended family, 117
Measles, 147, 184–85; epidemic of, 145
Medical care systems, 181; changes in, 10–13; modification of, 143; selecting, 179–80
Medical co-existence, 166–71; benefits from, 178; competitive, 177–78; maintaining, 171–78; at Many Farms, 169, 171–72; Navajo view of, 170, 172; non-competitive, 177–78
Medical insurance: curing ceremonies and, 177
Medical interpreters: training of, 124
Medical phrases, 132, 245n.1; Navajo, 261–62
Medical programs: cross-cultural, 140–41
Medical records: changes in, 120–22; cultural factors in, 120–22; organizing, 109; problems with, 109, 113–14. See also Recordkeeping
Medical relevance: cultural determinism and, 4–5
Medication. See Drug therapy
Medicine men, 4, 9, 32, 91, 107, 144, 168, 170, 171, 177, 187, 243n.4; clinic visits and, 167; curing system and, 115, 183; decline of, 174; doctors and, 12–13, 27, 30, 34, 40–41; educational meetings for, 42; at Many Farms, 175; performances by, 167; powers of, 13; pupils of, 173–74; ridiculing, 26; role of, 7, 166, 169, 172–73; training of, 8, 163–64, 175, 176; wage work for, 174
Meningitis, 184, 246n.4
Meriam report, 17, 18
Mescaline, 165
Methodology: medical, 227–28; training in, 247n.3
Microbial disease, 188
Middle ear disease, 18
Mineral rights, 250, 256
Missionaries: attacks by, 174, 176
Mitchell, Frank: quote from, 175
Modern medicine. See Western medicine
Morbidity, 17, 25, 122, 147; reports on, 214; statistics for, 156

Morbidity rate, 18, 144–45
Morgan, William, xviii; work of, 129, 135, 139
Mormons, 176
Mortality rate, 17, 18, 144–45, 187–88; chart of, 186. *See also* Infant mortality
Moulding, Thomas, xix
Mountaintop Way ceremony, 167
Myocardial infarction, 130; translation of, 128–29

Naa: meaning of, 126
Naash'anh lak'ee: meaning of, 126
Naashne' lak'ee: meaning of, 126
Naming practices: confusion caused by, 115–16. *See also* Nicknames; Surnames
Nammacher, Mark, 149
Nasalization, 125–26
National Academy of Sciences Institute of Medicine, 246n.6
National Health Survey. *See* United States National Health Survey
National Institute of Mental Health, 175
National Institutes of Health, i, 246n.7
National Science Foundation, 247n.3
National Tuberculosis Association, 15
National Tuberculosis Foundation, 244n.8
Native American Church, 11; ceremonies of, 161, 165; curing by, 165; membership in, 165–66. *See also* Christianity
Native curing system. *See* Indigenous curing system
Navajo-Cornell Field Health Research Project, ix, 2, 246n.7; organization of, xvii, 181
Navajo camp: photo of, 68
Navajo Community College, 241
Navajo culture: environment and, 249–57; fluctuations in, 10–11
Navajo curing system. *See* Indigenous curing system
The Navajo Door, 9, 31
Navajo Fair: tuberculosis exhibit at, 27
Navajo language: orthography for, 245n.3; sound system of, 125–26;

syntax, 134–35; translation of, 124–27; verb system of, 126–27
Navajo Medical Center, 24
Navajo medicine, 32; attitudes toward, 30–31, 238; clinic usage and, 161–62; psychotherapeutic benefits of, 171; religion and, 9; understanding, 34–35; Western medicine and, 168, 170–72
Navajo religion, 6–7, 31; Christianity and, 13–14, 165; medicine and, 5–9; respect for, 237; ridiculing of, 26, 119, 174, 176
Navajo Reservation, xii, 4, 10, 15, 19, 24, 29, 35, 56, 57, 100, 112, 131, 181, 218, 221; census for, 17; clinics on, 48; description of, 249–50; economy of, 250–51; health education program on, 45, 214; health workers on, 25–26; hospitals near, 24; livestock reduction on, 250; logistics of, 86; map of, 2, 151; population of, 26; research on, xxii; working on, xxvi
Navajo Sawmill, 55, 250
Navajo Service, 36
Navajo Tribal Council, xiv, 27, 33, 35, 41, 42, 43, 44, 48, 50, 52, 58, 60, 85, 87, 88, 136, 137, 138, 144, 175, 176, 241, 244n.2, 256; cooperation with, 39–40, 41; meetings of, 244n.7; members of, 256; peyote and, 165; photo of, 66, 67; report to, 36–39
Navajo Tribal Government, xiv, xv; concerns of, 256; Cornell University College of Medicine and, xiii; establishment of, 255–56; politics and, 251; tuberculosis and, xii–xiii; United States Government and, 250
Navajo Tribe, xviii, 42, 180, 189; Christianization of, 6; dysentery and, xii; feedback from, 39; health care for, ix; medical education for, xxiii; political life of, 255–57; studying, xxiv; support from 246n.7; suspicions of, 22; transition for, 10; tuberculosis and, xii; wealth of, 50–51; Western medicine and, 10, 58; value system of, 238

Navajo Tuberculosis Control
Program, xii–xiii
Neezgai: meaning of, 135
Neonatal care. *See* Prenatal
examinations
New Deal, 23
New York City, i, 45, 57, 204, 224,
229
New York Hospital, 36, 38, 44, 58
New York Hospital–Cornell group.
See Cornell group
New York Hospital–Cornell
University Medical Center, i, 42,
246n.7; staff of, 228
Nicknames: multiplicity of, 116;
recording, 121. *See also* Naming
practices; Surnames
Nurse aides, 219, 221
Nurses: work of, 203; Navajo, 87–
88; training of, xxvi, 100. *See also*
Public health nurses
Nutrition, 194
Nydegger, William, xviii; research by,
245n.1

Olberg, Kalervo: quote from, 232
Omran, Abdul, xix
Organizational differences: conflicts
from, 228–31
Orthopedists, 204
Osteoarthritis, 205
Otitis media, 145, 147, 188, 192,
246n.6; cases of, 184–85; cause of,
193; preventing, 193–94;
reduction of, 191, 198
Outpost community, 231–34
Overholtzer, Marjorie, xix

Pain: investigation of, 139; language
of, 134–35, 139; stoicism and, 135
Paintings, 11. *See also* Body painting;
Sandpaintings
Patients: age of, 147; identification
of, 114–17; location of, 120–21;
sex of, 147–48; transportation
problem for, 148–52
Patient visits: chart of, 146. *See also*
Clinic usage
Paul, Benjamin, 201
Peace Corps, xxvi
Penicillin, 200
The People's Health, ix, xxvii;
revision of, 241; writing of, xxvi

Periosteum, 43
Peyote, 165
Peyote Way, 11, 91
Charles Pfizer and Company, xviii
Pfrommer, Viola, 244n.4
Phoenix, 24, 251
Phonology, 125–26
Physicians. *See* Doctors
Pilot project, xiii–xiv, 45, 213, 216;
acceptance of, 59–62; failures of,
239; objectives of, 47; purpose of,
xiv, xvii; sight selection for, 48–51;
successes of, 238–39
Pine Springs, 12, 13, 27
Piñon, 90, 91, 102, 149
Pipe lines, 250
Pneumonia, 20, 145, 147, 170, 172,
200, 244n.1, 246n.4; cases of,
184–85; treating, 169
Pneumonia-diarrhea complex, 187;
persistence of, 191; reduction of,
194
Polgar, Steven: work of, 201
Polio immunizations, 157
Poliomyelitis: translation of, 134
Postpartum examinations, 154, 157
Post hoc, ergo propter hoc: principle
of, 54
Poverty: disease and, 192
Practical nursing program, 220
Prayers, 8, 163
Prayer sticks: making, 163
Prenatal examinations, 100, 154, 157
Pregnancy, 148, 186, 191, 198; clinic
visits and, 154, 157
Presenting Symptoms Visit, 156
Preston, Scott, 32, 87, 88, 103; quote
from, 33, 85
Prevention, xxii, 156, 193–94, 229,
241
Preventive care, 229; delivery of,
156–57
Preventive Visit, 153, 156, 157;
description of, 154
Priestcraft, 8
Primary health care system, xxvi,
179, 181–82, 184, 193, 195, 197,
246n.2; improvement of, 198
Protozoan diseases, 197
Psychologists, 226
Public health nurses, 96, 102, 105,
110, 113, 114, 118, 156, 229,
230–31; assisting, 93; opposition

by, 217–21; recordkeeping by, 112;
selecting, 224–25; training by, 87–
97, 101, 104; training of, 86;
working with, 222; work of, xxv–
xxvi, 183–84, 224. *See also* Nurses
Public Health Nursing (Cornell):
contribution of, xxv
Public health nursing, 218; threats to,
219
Public health programs, xxi–xxii,
241; cross-cultural, 239; training
for, 140
Public Health Service. *See* United
States Public Health Service
Public health work, 214; cultural
approach to, 122; education for,
230
Pueblo Indians, 9, 11; tuberculosis
and, 214
Pueblo Reservation, 45
Pyrazinamide, 43

Rabin, David, xix
Radiotelephone: using, 100
Ramadwar, Dr., 80; photo of, 75, 76
Ramah, 9, 44
Recordkeeping: cultural approach to,
122; problems in, 109–22. *See also*
Medical records
Red House clan, 252
Rehoboth Reform Church Hospital,
24
Religion. *See* Navajo religion
Research design, 202; cross-cultural,
109, 201
Residence: chart of, 152; clinic visits
and, 148–52; location of, 114–15;
patterns of, 109; zones of, 148–49
Resources Committee (NTC), 256
Respiratory disease, 21
Respiratory system: drawing of, 98
Rheumatic fever, 154
Rheumatoid arthritis: translation of,
131
Rieder, Donald, i, 245n.1; photo of,
77, 82, 83; work of, 115
Rio Grande Valley, 214
Rituals: learning, 8;
psychotherapeutic value of, 9
Rockefeller, Mary, xx
Rockefeller Research Center, xii
Rock Point, 149, 157
Rock Point Clinic, 158

Role conflict: resolution of, 119
Rough Rock, 2, 47, 51, 53, 88, 105,
110, 156, 183, 186, 187, 188, 189,
191, 195; demographic profile of,
190; selection of, 50, 181
Rough Rock Demonstration School,
175, 176
Round Rock, 53
Russell Sage Foundation, i, xxiv,
246n.7
Rynbergen, Hendrika, xix

Sage Memorial Presbyterian Hospital,
24, 157
Saint Michaels, 26
San Carlos Apaches: congenital hip
disease and, 204
Sandoval, Albert, xviii
Sandpaintings, 8, 162, 163;
memorizing, 9
Sanitation, 27; disease and, 20, 193–
94
Santa Fe Railroad, xviii, 247n.3, 251
Sasaki, Tom T., xviii, 147, 169
School health programs, 102, 110,
224
School of Public Health (California),
45
School of Public Health (North
Carolina), 45
Schwartz, Doris, xix
Science, ix
Secretary-Treasurer (NTC): function
of, 256
Sha'esdzaan: meaning of, 116
Shadi: meaning of, 116
Shaman, 8
Shame sanctions: definition of, 95–
96
Shaw, James R., 32; quote from, 213
Sheep: digestive system of, 98;
dissection of, 97–99
Sheep husbandry, 182, 250, 251. *See
also* Animal husbandry
Shigella, 20
Shima: meaning of, 115
Shiprock, 24, 34, 45, 50, 250
Shooting Chant, 91
Shooting Way ceremony, 164, 170
Short form ceremonies, 167, 177
Shoshone language, 125
Simpson, John Lee, 41
Singers, 7, 12, 27, 91, 165, 168, 169,

170, 245n.1; age of, 173; Blessing Way, 164, 165; chart of, 163, 173; decline of, 174; description of, 8; numbers of, 164; performances by, 167–68; pupils of, 173; status of, 9; training of, 9, 163–64, 175–76; using, 166
Sings, 4, 5, 6, 11, 13, 32, 33, 91, 92; attitudes toward, 30
Sitan: meaning of, 133
Skeletal system: drawing of, 136
Skin disorders, 183
Slivers, Wilfred: work of, 115
Snow, Milton, 63, 65, 66, 67
Social organization, 252
Social psychologists, 226
Social scientists, 230, 239; role of, 225; selecting, 225–26
Social stigma, 206–7
Sociologists, 226
Sociology, 227
Soil conservation movement, 58, 250
Southern Pacific Railway, 251
Southern Ute Reservation, 45
South Valley, 149
Spatial propinquity: principle of, 54
Spicer, Edward, xix
Squaw Dance, 91
E. R. Squibb Division of Olin Mathieson, xviii
Stanford University Medical College, 247n.4
Star gazers, 16, 163
Star gazing: description of, 162
State Welfare Office, 120
Statistics, 16–18, 114, 119–20, 122, 196; collecting, 102; reports on, 214. See also Health statistics; Vital statistics
Stigma. See Social stigma
Stoicism: pain and, 135
Structural differences: conflicts from, 228–31
Sulfa therapy. See Drug therapy
Supernatural powers, 6–7
Surgeon General: report from, 16
Surnames: cross-indexing, 116; multiple spellings of, 116. See also Nicknames; Naming practices
Sway, Albert, xx
Syncytial virus, 200

T'aadoo hooyani hajei d'ishjool baah dahoo'a: meaning of, 129
Taboos, 3, 4, 5; types of, 7
Technical terms: paraphrasing, 132
Technology: Navajos and, 5, 59–61
Telugu language, 125
Tetanus, 139, 187
Thoracoplasty, 43
Time: Navajo concept of, 140
Tohatchi, 24
Trachoma, 18, 20, 21, 183, 185; cause of, 193; description of, 243n.3; persistence of, 191; preventing, 193–94; reduction of, 19, 194
Translation: concept, 127; grammatical factors in, 139–41; problems with, 129–34. See also Interpretation
Translators: importance of, 141
Transportation, 148–52, 181; problems in, 152
Treatment: choice of, 169; cultural dynamics and, 5; by medicine men, 169; Navajo religion and, 5–9. See also Medical co-existence
Tribal Chairman (NTC): function of, 256
Tribal Council. See Navajo Tribal Council
Tso, Nakai, 3
Tuba City, 24, 34, 35, 36, 37, 38, 40, 50; boarding school at, xi
Tuba City Hospital, 33, 157
Tubercle bacilli, 193; reduction of, 191; transmission of, 183, 186, 192–93, 198
Tuberculin skin tests: administering, 100, 184
Tuberculosis, xiv, xxii, 15, 21, 33, 52, 87, 97, 107, 110, 130, 180, 185–86, 192, 193, 214, 215, 216, 244n.6; drug therapy for, 37–38, 41, 43, 59; educational meetings on, 42; epidemic of, 19; fair exhibit on, 27; military service and, 58; Navajo Tribal Government and, xii–xiii; preventing, xxi–xxiii, 62, 193–94; statistics on, 19–20; translation of, 134; treatment for, xii–xiv, 24, 38–39, 42, 169, 238; types of, 19–20, 37; understanding, 89–90, 92–93

Tuchin, Bess, 93; photo of, 72, 73, 75

United States Army, 90
United States Government, 22, 241, 255, 257; Navajo Tribal Government and, 250
United States National Health Survey, 156
United States Public Health Service, 15, 17, 22, 23, 24, 26, 29, 32, 45, 57, 62, 110, 123, 144, 145, 176, 180, 208, 214, 216, 222, 246n.2, 246n.7, 255; contract with, 47, 213–14; Indian program of, 191
United States Public Health Service Hospital, 157
University of California, 45, 219, 244n.4; health education program by, 214
University of Kentucky Medical College, 247n.4
University of North Carolina, 45
University of Pennsylvania: tuberculosis survey by, 214
Usage. See Clinic usage
Ute language, 125

Valley Store, 51, 53; selection of, 50
Vertical communication, 223, 229
Visits. See Clinic visits
Visit with Presenting Symptoms: description of, 153–54
Vital statistics, 114, 119–20, 122, 196; charts on, 214. See also Health statistics; Statistics
Vogt, Evan, 11

Wage work, 174, 177, 251, 253
War Department, 22
War industries, 11, 251
War name, 115
Washing: prevention and, 194
Water: disease and, 182

Watkins, Senator: quote from, 23
Wauneka, Annie, 32, 33, 45, 49, 50, 53, 54, 60–61, 88; photo of, 64, 65; quote from, 52–53; work of, xiii, 55
Way chants, 163
Weber, Anselm, 26
Well-child clinics, 156, 224
Western medicine, 13, 14, 31, 62, 161, 165, 167; attitudes toward, 11–12; education in, 166; exposure to, 10–11; impact of, 12; Navajo medicine and, 168, 170–72; Navajo Tribe and, 10, 58
White, Leslie, 247n.3
The White Plague, 31
Whiting, Marjorie Grant, xx
Wind Chant ceremony, 41
Window Rock, 36, 51, 52, 57, 89, 118, 244n.2, 244n.4, 246n.2, 255, 256, 257
Wind Way ceremony, 11, 91
Winslow, 24, 36, 38, 92
Witchcraft, 6–7, 104
World Health Organization, i, 140
World Health Program, xii
World War II, 15, 23, 29; impact of, 10–11
Wyman, Leland, 8

X-rays, 13, 52, 55, 56, 86, 91, 92, 110, 111, 112, 203, 204, 205, 208; appeal of, 54; for congenital hip disease, 207; star gazing and, 162

Yazzie, Dan, 57; opinions of, 55
Yazzie, Sam: quote from, 12–13, 27
Yei (gods), 8
Yellowman, Mr., 41, 91
Young, Donald, xviii, xxiv
Young, Robert, 39, 40, 43, 89, 127, 129, 244n.7; consultation by, 124; quote from, 126, 128–29, 131–32